TAMERLANE

Edward D. Sokol

CORONADO PRESS   **1977**

ISBN 0–87291–094–6

Set in 10 on twelve point Press Roman
Published in the United States of America
by Coronado Press
   Box 3232
   Lawrence, Kansas, 66044

950.2092
So 6

CONTENTS

Preface 9
Chronology 11

I   The Mongol Background. 15
II   The First Rung of the Ladder 27
III   Master of Transociana, 1370-1380 49
III   Master of.Transoxiana, 1370-1380:49

III   Master of Transoxiana, 1370-1380 49
IV   Iran – First Foray 65
V   The Rupture with Toktamish. 83
VI   The Five Years War–I
      Persia and Mesopotamia (1392-1394) 93
VII   The Five Years War–II
      The Golden Horde (1394-1396) 107
VIII Descent into India. 119
IX   Timur against Bayazid I Yildirim 133
X   The Campaign into Syria. 147
XI   The Battle of Ankara 165
XII   A Diplomatic Interlude. 189
XIII "The Napoleon of Asia". 195
XIV   Samarkand. 205
XV   The Last Campaign 217
XVI   The Timurid Legacy. 227

Footnotes 241
Bibliographical Essay 257
Index 267

57263

TAMERLANE

PREFACE

"The Riddle we can guess
We speedily despise."
– *Emily Dickinson*

Tamerlane, Tamburlaine or, as we shall more properly call him, Timur, since the first two names are Western corruptions of his real name "Timur-i lenk" (Timur the Lame), is a well known historical figure. Surprisingly few biographies of him, however, have appeared in recent decades. This despite the unabated flow of biographies coming off the press dealing with other great conquerors such as Alexander the Great, Chingis Khan and Napoleon. This neglect has not, fortunately, prevented the publication in recent years of numerous monographs on various aspects of Timur's career based on the study of the written sources, ongoing archeological excavations and the material remains of his period. These cast new light on this fascinating and at the same time malign and repellent figure.

Timur's conquests and relations involved a very large number of places and peoples (Mongol, Turkish, Persian, Arabic, Chinese, Russian and others). The rendering of names in these languages in the text may at times seem to be idiosyncratic, cumbrous or ungainly. It should be remembered, however, that there is no commonly agreed upon system of transliteration for these languages into the Roman alphabet. True, the Turkish government in 1928 officially adopted the Roman alphabet, but even this presents difficulties. Many of the sources cited pre-date 1928, nor do authors even today always follow officially sanctioned Turkish spellings, involving as they do diacritical marks, dotted and undotted "i"s and the use of a "c" where the English would use a "j." Though owlish pedants will doubtless wince, the author will employ what seems to him to be the most commonsensible and comprehensible rendering of names. As regards place names, those given in *Webster's Geographical Dictionary* will usually be used. The spelling in the text and in some of the quotations will at times differ but the general reader should have no difficulty in recognizing the variants which is, after all, the main essential. There are some thirty-six variants of the Prophet Muhammad's name (Mahomet, Mehmed, Ahmet, etc.), one of the most common first names in the world and one frequently encountered in the text. The rendering of this name will, accordingly, vary with the individual. "Iran" and "Persia" will be used interchangeably. Iran became the official name of this country in 1935. Yet since 1957 the Iranian government has permitted foreigners to use the old name while it itself, to undercut Iraqi claims to the Persian Gulf area, continues to use that name. And Iranians still call their language Persian.

The numbers cited in the text, especially where military forces are concerned, should be viewed with scepticism. These are based on the sources for the period and are often grossly inflated. Usually, however, there is no way of establishing the true numbers. The adjective "large" may be substituted in the reader's mind for an army stated to number 80,000 men or over, "medium-sized" for forces in the 20-30,000 range and "small" for those below.

There is much in Timur's life that is puzzling, contradictory, obscure or spectral. Some phases of his long career, on the other hand, have been recorded in such luxuriant detail that a problem of selection arises. Space requirements and the desire to avoid a data-bank or laundry-list type of biography have impelled the present author, though not always successfully, to concentrate on the main essentials.

CHRONOLOGY

1336	Timur born at Kesh (Shakhrisyabz), south of Samarkand.
1346	Power of Chagatai khans in Transoxiana destroyed. Emir Kazagan takes over.
1358	Assassination of Kazagan. A power vacuum ensues.
1360	Mongols conquer Transoxiana.
1361	Timur appointed adviser to Mogol viceroy of Transoxiana but soon flees. Joins Emir Hussein whose sister he marries.
1362	Timur and Hussein on the run. Timur grievously wounded and crippled.
1363	Transoxiana cleared of Mogols. Hussein becomes senior emir with Timur as his right-hand man.
1365	Hussein and Timur defeated by the Mogols in the "Battle of the Mud." Serbedars in Samarkand successfully repel Mogol attack.
1366	Hussein and Timur regain Samarkand by trickery. The two then try to eliminate one another.
1369	Timur triumps over Hussein. Death of the latter.
1370	Timur proclaimed ruler of Transoxiana. Makes Samarkand his capital. Rules through puppet khan Suyurghatmish.
1370-1379	Consolidation of power in Transoxiana. Conquest of Khorezm after several campaigns. Flight of Toktamish of the White Horde to Timur's camp. Timur supports Toktamish in his bid to become khan of the White Horde. Campaigns by Timur into Mogolistan to contain the threat from that quarter.
1380	Timur makes plans to invade Iran. Prince Dmitri Ivanovich of Muscovy defeats Emir Mamai of the Golden Horde at Kulikovo. Toktamish reunites the White and Golden Hordes.

1381	Conquest of Khurasan and the end of the Kart dynasty. Takeover of Serbedar state.
1382	Further campaigning in eastern Iran.
1383	Suppression of the Sebzevar revolt. Sistan subdued. Massacres in Afghanistan.
1384	Conquest of eastern tip of Mazanderan. Sultaniya seized in first blow to Jelairid state.
1385	"Three Years Campaign" into western Iran and its dependencies. Toktamish's descent on Tabriz and growing rift with Timur. Conquest of Azerbaijan by Timur.
1387	Siege of Alinjak begins. Invasion of Georgia. Shirvan becomes a tributary state. Gilan annexed. Invasion of the Muzaffarid kingdom and the massacre at Isfahan. Seizure of Shiraz.
1388	Invasion of Transoxiana by Toktamish. Return home of Timur and the withdrawal of Toktamish. Destruction of Urgench. Mahmud succeeds father as nominal head of Timur's empire (1388-1402). Fresh incursion of Toktamish into Transoxiana.
1389	Timur repels Toktamish. Campaign into Mogolistan to secure flank. Dispatch of embassy to China.
1390	Preparations for an expedition against Toktamish.
1391	Invasion of the Kipchak steppe. Defeat of Toktamish at Kunduzcha.
1392-1396	"The Five Years War."
1392	Mazanderan conquered.
1393	Defeat of Shah Mansur near Shiraz. Massacre of the Muzaffarid dynasty. Descent into Iraq and the capture of Baghdad.
1394	Mamluke Sultan Barkuk seeks war with Timur but the latter backs off. Invasion of Georgia. Preparations for a new campaign against Toktamish.
1395-1396	Defeat of Toktamish in the battle of the Terek. Second great invasion of his state, this time via the Caucasus. Timur stops drive short of Moscow. Destruction of the Volga Bulgar kingdom and of Sarai, Astrakhan and Tana. Golden Horde in a parlous state. Circassians harried. In spring of 1396 Timur returns home via the Caucasus and northern Iran. Arrival of Chinese embassy in Samarkand.
1396-1397	Further rebuilding of Samarkand.

1398-1399	Invasion of India. Taking of Bhatnir, Loni, Delhi and Meerut. Campaigning along the Jumna and the Ganges. Return home to Samarkand.
1399	Work begun on Cathedral Mosque in Samarkand. Launching of the "Seven Years War." Order restored in western Iran. Invasion of Georgia.
1400	Sivas seized from the Ottomans. Invasion of Syria and the fall of Aleppo.
1401	Capture and destruction of Damascus. Timur meets Ibn Khaldun. Recapture and destruction of Baghdad.
1401/1402	Winter at Karabagh during which Timur charges Nizam ad-Din with the writing of his biography.
1402	Timur moves west into Anatolia. Muhammad-Sultan arrives with fresh troops from Samarkand. Review of forces at Sivas. Battle of Ankara and the capture of Bayazid. Letter written to King Charles VI of France. Smyrna stormed and pillaged. Death of Mahmud Khan.
1403	Withdrawal from Anatolia. Bayazid dies in captivity. Death of Muhammad-Sultan, Timur's heir presumptive, in Afyon Karahisar. Recapture of Baghdad by the forces of Abu-Bakr. Last campaign against the Georgians.
1403/1404	Winter at Karabagh.
1404	Return home via northern Iran. Castilian envoy Clavijo arrives in Samarkand. Timur sets off to invade China.
1405	Otrar reached. Timur falls ill and dies (Feb. 18).

CHAPTER I
The Mongol Background

No biography of Timur would be intelligible without some prior reference to the Mongol conquests of Chingis Khan and his successors and what followed in their train. The invasion of Central Asia* and points west arose in a curious, haphazard way. In 1218 Chingis Khan's troops, while pursuing an old enemy, overran and occupied Eastern (or Chinese) Turkistan (the western and central parts of the modern province of Sinkiang, China's westernmost territory) and Semirechie (southeastern Soviet Kazakhstan). These conquests gave the Mongol state a common frontier with the great Muslim state of Khorezm to the west. Its ruler, called the Khorezmshah, controlled an area even larger than did Chingis Khan (Iran, Afghanistan and Central Asia). Chingis Khan, who was involved in the conquest of northern China and with other enemies nearer home, seems to have had no aggressive designs upon Khorezm, at least at this time. The Khorezmshah, whose curiosity had been piqued by reports of Chingis Khan's astonishing rise to power, had sent embassies to the latter to gather further intelligence regarding the Mongols. Chingis accorded the envoys a most gracious reception. Though his official letter, which one of the embassies brought back, referred to the Khorezmsha as "son," i.e., "vassal" in oriental diplomatic usage, he nonetheless proposed the establishment of peace between the "ruler of the West" and himself. Chingis also proposed placing commercial relations upon a regular basis between the two states. To these ends in 1218 he sent an embassy accompanied by a caravan of Muslim merchants to Urgench, capital of Khorezm, located south of the Sea of Aral. When

---

*Central Asia may be defined for purposes of this book as the region occupied by the present-day Soviet republics or Uzbekistan, Tadjikistan, Turkmenistan, Kirghizia and southern Kazakhstan, i.e., the area between the Caspian Sea and the present Sino-Soviet frontier to the east. Central Asia can also be understood to include a much larger area. Cf. Gavin Hambly, *Central Asia,* London and New York, 1969, p. xi.

they reached Otrar, not far from Tashkent, the Khorezmshah's govern-or there had the envoys and the merchants put to death on the charge that they were spies. Since the person of an envoy is semi-sacrosanct in Mongol tribal law, this was a very grave offense indeed. When Chingis, who sent a fresh embassy to obtain satisfaction, was unable to get it — indeed, the Khorezmshah had one of the envoys killed and sent the other two back with their beards shaved—Chingis felt that he had no choice but to interrupt his activities in China and turn to Central Asia.

What followed was the terrible Mongol invasion not only of Central Asia, Iran, Afghanistan and northern India but the dispatching of a re-connaissance force into the Caucasus and southern and northeastern Russia. The intelligence gathered by this force would help prepare the way after Chingis Khan's death for the invasion of northeastern and southern Russia and of Eastern Europe. This second invasion in the years 1236-1242 was led by Batu, son of Chingis Khan's oldest son Juchi.

Chingis, in 1224, three years before his death, in accordance with Mongol usage with regard to clan property, divided his possessions among his four sons by his first wife Börte according to the principle that the older the son, the farther away his *ulus* or appanage would be from the Mongolian homeland. The appanage of Juchi, the oldest son, included all land to the west "as far as the Mongol hoofbeats reached," i.e., territories still to be conquered. By the middle of the thirteenth century the Ulus of Juchi, now ruled by his heirs, included the old Vol-ga Bulgar kingdom near the junction of the Volga and Kama rivers, the vast steppe region to the north of the Black Sea extending from the Dniester river in the west into western Siberia in the east, part of the Crimea with its commercial cities, the north Caucasus as far south as Derbent, northern Khorezm with Urgench and the lower course of the Syr Darya.* Though the Russian principalities retained their princes and were not part of the Ulus of Juchi, they had to pay tribute and to fulfill certain political obligations. The Ulus of Juchi was known to the Russian chroniclers as the Golden Horde. Its capital—first Old Sarai and then New Sarai—was located in the lower Volga region. This area had for a long time been settled by Turkic peoples such as the Polovtsy (Kipchaks) and Kangly. Since the Mongols were fewer in number and at

---

*During this period this was known as the Desht-i-Kipchak or Kipchak steppes. It occupied the territory of present Kazakhstan and the South Russian steppes.

a lower cultural level, by the first half of the fourteenth century they began to speak Turkic.

To Chagatai, Chingis Khan's second oldest son, went Maverannahr* or, to use a less cumbrous name, Transoxiana, the region in present Soviet Central Asia between the Amu Darya, upper Syr Darya and the present Chinese border. Chagatai also received Semirechie and East Turkistan. Chagatai's headquarters were first located in the basin of the Ili river, which flows into Lake Balkhash, but in time they were gradually moved westward.

Ugedai, the third son, received lands lying between the uluses of his other brothers, namely western Mongolia and Tarbagatai, with headquarters near the present city of Chuguchak in northern Sinkiang.

In accordance with Mongol custom, when Chingis died in 1277 his youngest son Tului received the core of his father's possessions, i.e., Central Mongolia, to which was later added northern China, as well as Chingis Khan's personal possessions.

It was Ugedai, known for his geniality and good cheer, whom Chingis designated as great khan in his room. Even so, a sharp struggle irrupted among his heirs for his mantle of leadership. Finally, in September 1227 a kurultai of Mongol notables held near the Kerulen river in eastern Mongolia elected Ogedai as great khan, Tului having acted as *locum tenens* or caretaker in the meantime. The election was celebrated with a great feast in the course of which forty beautiful maidens selected from Mongol aristocratic families were sacrificed to the "soul" of Chingis Khan.

During Ugedai's reign (1227-1241) Karakorum in central Mongolia, founded by Chingis in 1220 as the Mongol capital, was reconstructed. A great palace was built for the khan and the city was surrounded by a fortified wall. Other cities are known to have existed in Mongolia at this time. Under Ugedai steps were taken to regularize the collection of taxes and the fulfillment of duties by subjects as well as to determine which taxes from a given area were to be retained by the local ruler and which were to go to the great khan.

————————

*Maverannahr, Arabic meaning literally "that which is beyond the river," i.e., the Amu Darya. Transoxiana means the area beyond the Oxus, as the Amu Darya was known to the ancients who referred to the Syr Darya as the Jaxartes. Darya is the local word for "river" and will be frequently met in our narrative. The Amu and Syr Darya, which flow into the sea of Aral, are the two largest rivers in Central Asia.

Ugedai, upon his death in 1241, was succeeded by his son Guyuk with his mother Turakina acting as regent for about five years. During the regency other Chingisids, or descendants of Chingis Khan, sought to win the great khanship for themselves, Batu, the ruler of the Golden Horde, refused to accept Guyuk's authority even with the end of the regency. Guyuk purposed to bring Batu to heel by force, but died in 1248 while en route with his army. In the struggle that followed Juchids and Tuluids were paired off against the descendants of Ugedai and Chagatai. In 1251 Batu, a Juchid, engineered the election of Munke, son of Tului, thus taking the imperial succession away from the line of Ugedai.

In 1256-58 Hulagu Khan, brother of Munke, founded the Hulagid (or Il-Khanid)* state comprising the territories of Iran, Azerbaijan, Armenia and Georgia. The latter three areas were allowed to retain their local dynasties but had to pay tribute and to furnish troops when ordered to do so.

Munke Khan himself, followed by Kubilai (the famous Kublai Khan of Marco Polo), his brother and successor as great Khan, carried out the definitive conquest of northern China and then of southern China and Korea. In 1271 Kubilai moved the capital of the Mongol empire from Karakorum to Peking or, as the Mongols called it, Khanbalic or "khanial city." Conquests were continued beyond China. In 1257 Annam (North Vietnam) was subdued; in 1287 Burma. In 1292 the Mongols even penetrated the island of Java, forcing the ruler there to pay tribute. Only the conquest of Japan was a failure despite two attempts.

Chingis Khan's internal measures must be briefly mentioned; without them his empire would not have endured. We will refer to many of them in dealing with Timur's career. To help him in his work Chingis enrolled into his administration elements from the more civilized tribes living in Mongolia. Pride of place here goes to the Turkic Uighurs whom he patronized and whose culture retained many steppe customs and traditions despite exposure to more advanced societies. Chingis adopted the Uighur script in a modified form for writing the Mongol language. His officials were entrusted with the assessment and collection of new taxes. They also may have been responsible for the organization of the famous postal system which he used to keep in touch with the various parts of his empire. Chingis was also very anxious to stimulate trade. The safety and security which the post-roads afforded to merchants

––––––––––

*Il-Khans = subordinate khans.

did much to expand trade. The Mongol empire was to carry on trade relations with twenty countries.

With Chingis is associated the Great Yasa* or collection of laws, to be referred to repeatedly in the discussion of Timur's administration. The Yasa unfortunately has come down to us only in fragments or in condensed form. It is thought to be not a codification of customary Mongol tribal law but new legal norms designed to cope with problems of imperial legislation, a juridical superstructure over and above tribal law. Chingis envisaged the Yasa as eternal and believed that disaster would overtake his heirs if they violated it. Each new khan, who could only be elected from his seed by a special kurultai of Chingisids and members of the Mongol aristocracy, was to begin his rule by affirming the principles of the Yasa. While subsequent legislation was not precluded, this could only supplement or amplify the principles of the Yasa. The headings of the Yasa give some indication of its scope: international law, criminal law, commercial law, judicial procedure, amendment procedure. The Yasa, together with the *biliks* or pronouncements of Chingis on a multiplicity of subjects, provided the indispensable framework for the consolidation of Mongol rule and the structuring of world empire.

With the death of Munke in 1259 separatist tendencies within the Mongol empire became so strong that the great khan at Karakorum exercised factual power only in Mongolia and in China, the conquest of which was still far from being effected. Lacking among Chingis Khan's heirs was a successor with the same rare combination of military and administrative acumen, the same manipulative ability as regards the men serving under him. Nor did they have the same drive and will power, the same fire in the belly. Sordid intrigue and factional infighting demeaned the elections of great khans. Since Chingis did not leave instructions concerning the precise delimitations of frontiers between the appanages, this was a fertile source of discord and strife. Drunkenness, a plague to Mongol life down to the present day, carried more than one great khan off to an early grave despite Chingis' call for temperance. Since no limit was placed on the number of wives and concubines a ruler might have, overindulgence in sex was another debilitating factor. The continuation of conquests of non-Mongol areas—that bloody cement Chingis used to keep his people united—was abandoned after a time, the heirs of Chingis now using their martial energies to fight one

---

*Yasa in Turkish and Persian, Yasak in Mongol.

another. Only Kubilai Khan, in the period after 1260, successfully continued the takeover of new areas in his capacity of Chinese emperor and founder of the Yüan dynasty, but this was no longer a pan-Mongol venture. The Chingisids in other uluses were too interested in their own affairs to help Kubilai. The latter, for his part, did not involve himself in their broils. The nature of the Mongol empire itself made unity difficult to maintain: a large number of states and peoples speaking a medley of languages and at vastly differing stages of culture and economic life separated by enormous distances.

The Chagatai realm was the least centralized of the Chingisid uluses. It consisted, as we have noted, of Transoxiana, southern Khorezm and Mogolistan (Semirechie and Eastern Turkistan) where the khans initially resided. In Mogolistan the Mongols, or Mogols as these peoples called themselves, kept to their old nomadic ways, so much so that tilled fields were converted into grazing lands and many cities and towns declined or vanished. Chagatai, the first khan, supported by a large part of the Mogol military-aristocratic elite, also despised Islam and had the nomad's contempt, based on military prowess, for the culture of sedentary peoples. Despite this enmity which harmed sedentary civilization in Transoxiana as well as in Mogolistan the oasis cities of the former were, by the end of the thirteenth century, beginning to recover economically and to develop their culture. This in turn was to exercise a fatal attraction on later Chagatai khans who were no longer content to govern from afar through intermediaries but wanted to move closer to the honey pot. They also began to be attracted to cities, to sedentary life and to Muslim culture. And since many of their followers in Mogolistan did not share their sentiments, the unity of the Chagatai realm would thenceforward be more and more difficult to maintain.

The death of Algu Khan in 1266 brought fundamental changes. Both of his successors, first Mubarak Shah and then Borak Khan, became converts to Islam. Mubarak, moreover, caused himself to be invested as khan in 1266, not in the Ili river valley but in that of the Angren river in Transoxiana. Mubarak, in this transferral of the seat of his power, was accompanied by certain Mongol clans, most notably the Jelairs and the Barlas, the clan of Timur. The heads of these clans bore the titles of emirs in the Arabic, noyons in Mongol, and beks or begs in Turkic. The Jelairs picked as their grazing lands the district of Khodzhent and the Angren river valley, the Barlas the lush Kashka Darya valley near Karshi and Kesh. Already partly Turkified before they left Semirechie, this process would be speeded up in the new location. By Timur's time they would no longer speak Mongol but a Central Asian Turkic language known as Chagatai or Old Uzbek. The clan elite began to acquire large tracts of arable land or immovable property in the cities.

The settlers in Transoxiana also included the numerous authentically Turkic tribes who accompanied Chingis Khan in his western conquests. These reinforced the already substantial indigenous Turkic element, giving the country a Turkic cast, though a minority of Iranian-speaking Tadjiks would continue to remain. As a result the historical works of the time refer to these settlers more and more as "Turks" and less and less as "Mughals" (Mongols). The majority of pure Mongols remained in Semirechie and Eastern Turkistan which, in the fourteenth to the sixteenth centuries, became known as Mogolistan. Differences between the two parts of the Chagatai realm, one predominantly sedentary, the other predominantly nomadic, hardened to such an extent that no lasting reunification could be imposed, not even by Timur. The situation was complicated by the fact that the nomad aristocracy of Transoxiana fought to retain undefiled the old nomad ways and opposed the gravitation of the central authority towards the oasis cities of Transoxiana and towards a sedentary life.

The reign of Kebek (1318-1326) as khan was of major importance in this factional struggle. Selecting a site some eight miles from the city of Nesef in the Kashka Darya valley in the present south Uzbek SSR, he built his palace or *karshi* (Mongol for "fortified palace"). This gave rise to the new city of Karshi whose growth was achieved by sucking the life out of the nearby city of Nesef. Karshi was later to become one of Timur's places of residence. Though Kebek remained true to Mongol shamanism, the Muslim faith fared well under his rule. Kebek as khan looked to the Barlas clan, from which Timur was to spring, for support.

Kebek's rule is also significant for long overdue monetary and administrative reforms. The lack of a solid and uniform coinage had hobbled economic life in Central Asia even in pre-Mongol days. In 1321 Kebek, determined to bring his coinage into line with that of the Golden Horde and the Il-Khanid state, ordered the minting of new silver and gold coins. He also called upon his experts to devise a standardized system of weights and measures, though whether his order was implemented we do not know. Finally, Kebek abolished tax farming, to the great relief of the urban and rural populations.

An administrative overhaul of the country was also put in hand. Two administrations coexisted in Transoxiana. Nomadic tribes or clans had their emirs or beks. In the cities local dynasties, consisting in some cities of members of the Muslim establishment and in others of lay persons, ruled as they had before the Mongol conquest. At the same time general overall authority was exercised by the tax farmer aided by Mongold *darugas* (governors), *baskaki* (tribute collectors) and military detachments. These arrangements had led to many abuses.

Kebek sought to bring the administration of Transoxiana more directly under his control. Leaving the existing local governmental arrangements intact, he overlaid them with a new military-administrative unit — the *tuman* — borrowed from Mongol usage. The tuman was supposedly able to muster ten thousand troops (which it was seldom able to do) or to provide the wherewithal to do the same. The heads of the tumans, into which the country was now divided, were appointed by Kebek and were directly responsible to him. Though because of the resistance of the local power structure the new tuman administration did not fully live up to Kebek's expectations, it was a positive step forward. His reforms brought some improvement in the country's economic life and a curbing of the power of the nomad aristocracy.

If Kebek's policies were generally pleasing to the sedentary peoples of Transoxiana, they displeased the nomad aristocracy. The latter was aided in this opposition by some of the local rulers in the cities who felt that the khan had become too powerful. The nomad aristocracy bided its time until Kebek's death in 1326 and his replacement as khan by his brother Tarmashirin. The new khan, a convert to Islam, was an avid protagonist of his predecessor's policies. He declared Islam the state religion* and made Bukhara his capital. In the fighting that irrupted between the khan and the nomad aristocracy operating from the east the khan was killed (1334). A series of khans succeeded one another in quick succession. Their policies, by and large, favored the nomad aristocracy. The khanial headquarters was even for a time transferred back to Semirechie.

The ascension of Kazan, a Chingisid prince of the Chagatai sprig, to the Khanial throne in 1343 brought a few years of peace to the sorely afflicted settled peoples of Transoxiana as the pendulum once more swung back in their direction. Kazan represented the interests of the sedentary feudal lords, the merchants and the Muslim establishment; under his energizing rule the country began to recover its self-possession and prosperity. The new khan constructed a fortified palace named

---

*The Golden Horde and the Il-Khans of Persia had adopted Islam somewhat earlier.

Zindger-sarai near Karshi, a town not far from the center of Transoxiana, which he made his headquarters. Concurrently, he did all he could to strengthen the central authority. These policies met with the sharp opposition of the nomad aristocracy who found their paladin in one of their own number, a bek by the name of Kazagan. Though Kazan riposted with a campaign of terror, a conspiracy was formed and in the end he was killed in a battle.

Since Kazagan was not a Chingisid he could not be elected khan. He therefore became a kingmaker rather than a king. He ultimately installed Kuli-aglen as khan. Kazagan, the de facto ruler from 1346 to 1358, was able to impose his writ only over Transoxiana. Mogolistan went its separate way.[1] Kazagan diverted the martial energies of his nomadic supporters by making razzias (forays) into neighboring states, especially the Kart kingdom to the south.

Meanwhile, analogous developments were taking place in Mogolistan. After a period of anarchy, unity was restored by three brothers who belonged to the powerful Dughlat clan of Mogols. Since they were not Chingisids, they sought to legitimize their rule by installing Tugluk-Timur, putatively a descendant of Chagatai, as khan.

Tugluk-Timur, however, soon turned the tables on the Dughlat brothers; he had no intention of serving as their docile instrument. Adroit, able and energetic, he soon established his ascendancy in Mogolistan. Though in his policies he was careful to retain the fealty of the nomad aristocracy, he became a Muslim convert with a large number of his followers following suit. This act was not without political calculation. It was part of his grand design to extend his authority westward into Muslim Transoxiana and thus to reunite the Chagatai ulus. The Mongol-Turkic elite of Transoxiana, who were by this time called Chagatais, began calling the Mogols *Jats* or brigands; the latter repaid the compliment by referring to the Turkified and only semi-nomadic Chagatais as mongrels or half-breeds.

Despite their adoption of Islam, the Chagatais retained the Chingisid military organization and in external appearance continued to look like Mongol warriors right down to the wearing of tresses of hair or pigtails. Also, the Yasa enjoyed greater authority than did the Shariat or Muslim law code. Later Muslims in the west would consider neither Timur nor his followers proper Muslims. In Mogolistan Islam rested even more lightly on the brows of the Mogols.

The time for a reunification of the two parts of the old Chagatai realm seemed opportune. In 1358 Kazagan was assassinated by someone bearing a personal grudge. His son Mirza Abdullah attempted to succeed his father as factual ruler but his actions soon antagonized his followers. He transferred the seat of power to Samarkand despite their objections. He then became infatuated with the khan's wife. The inconvenient husband was killed and Timur-Shah-Oglan, another Chingisid, was installed in his place as khan.

The aristocracy, headed by Bayan Selduz, were deeply incensed by this infamous and wanton deed and rose up in revolt. When Bayan Selduz passed through Kesh, the Barlas clan seat, on his way to Samarkand he was joined by Hadji Barlas, head of that clan. The two, together with their troops, defeated Abdullah who fled to Badakhshan, a mountainous region in northeastern Afghanistan, where he ended his days. The straw khan Timur-Shah-Oglan was killed. Control of the country now passed to the two leaders of the revolt, but not for long. Neither was astute enough politically to maintain power; indeed, Bayan Selduz' brain was becoming increasingly addled by chronic alcoholism. The unhappy country relapsed into anarchy and hopeless political dismemberment. The twelve to fifteen independent statelets which emerged were at odds with one another save for periods of transient, unstable alliances. The heads of these petty states, even those with only a small military force at their back, swaggered about in a proud and insolent manner. The common people groaned in their misery. Trade, handicrafts and agriculture declined and with the general decay of authority an economic stasis developed which deepened with every passing year.

The parlous state of affairs was well known beyond the borders of the country. In March 1360 Tugluk-Timur, judging the moment propitious, invaded Transoxiana to plunder and annex it. No serious resistance was encountered, since no single ruler was strong enough to do battle with the invader. Nor were any of the local rulers willing to suspend their petty squabbles long enough to band together and make a common stand. Bayazid Jelair, the ruler of Khodzhent and its environs, even joined the invaders. Other princelings either made their submission or fled.

Reaching Tashkent, Tugluk-Timur drove straight towards Kesh, the nest of Hadji Barlas. The latter dallied momentarily with the idea of offering resistance but his brave resolve soon evaporated and he fled

across the Amu Darya into Khurasan.* It was at this juncture that
Timur, barely 24 years old and with his father but recently laid to
rest, comes into our story.

---

*Khurasan today is just a province in northeastern Iran, but in medieval
times it included the area around Merv in the present Soviet Turkmen
republic, Balkh and Herat in Afghanistan as well as Nishapur, its chief
Persian city. In other words, it included parts of what are now the
Turkmen SSR, Afghanistan and Iran.

CHAPTER II
The First Rung of the Ladder

In dealing with remote historical figures it is seldom that we know much about their formative years. This certainly holds true for Timur who enters the full light of history at the age of only 23 or 24, that is, around 1359-1360. He was born on April 9, 1336 in the village of Khodzha Ulgar near the city of Kesh (today Shakhrisyabz), some thirty-six miles south of Samarkand. The Castilian envoy Clavijo, who visited Kesh in the summer of 1404 while en route to Samarkand, described it as a great city standing in the middle of a plain and girded by a rampart of earth and a very deep ditch. Access to the city was by gates. Kesh had many fine houses and mosques, while its environs, studded with well-populated villages, struck Clavijo as "most beautiful."[1] Agriculture based on irrigation flourished; cereal grains, grapes and cotton were the principal crops.

Timur's father Taragai belonged to the Turkified Mongol clan of Barlas who were settled in the Kashka Darya Valley. Kesh and and Nesef (Karshi) were the chief cities. Though he was of noble birth, Taragai's pretensions, ambitions and wealth were small. Like his father Burkul, he preferred the placid, sedate life of a country squire to the hurly-burly, excitement and intrigue of court life. One of his ancestors had been vizier to Chagatai, son of Chingis Khan, who had received Transoxiana as his patrimony. The Barlas clan head was not Taragai but rather a man called Hadji Barlas. Taragai was a pious Muslim—putatively the first convert in his clan—and was partial to the company of religious divines, scholars and dervishes. Historian-panegyrists writing after Timur's death assigned him descent from Chingis Khan himself and drew up appropriate genealogies, one of which appears on Timur's epitaph. The late Bashkir scholar Zeki Velidi Togan claimed to have found a common ancestor in a certain Buzanchar. Finally Ibn Arabshah in his very hostile biography of Timur asserts that he was descended from Chingis through females, those "snares of Satan." Serious doubts arise nonetheless. Timur did not claim descent or kinship during his lifetime, though if he could have done so with some show of plausibility this would have been of inestimable political advantage to him.

Timur's mother, Takina Khatun, remains something of an enigma, Muslim reticence about their womenfolk notwithstanding. Our main sources (Sharaf ad-Din, Clavijo, Ibn Arabshah, etc.) pass over her in silence. Our sources also tell us that Taragai had a second wife named Oadak-Khatun (d. 1389).

The sources are similarly unforthcoming about Timur's first wives. We know that in 1360 he had two wives, each of whom presented him with a son. Who was the mother of Timur's oldest son Jehangir is a mystery. We know the name of the mother of his second son Omar-Shaykh, but nothing more. Though scattered hints and references in the sources indicate that family connections played an important role in Timur's ascent, we do not have the details. Since Timur apparently in his youth led a gang which robbed merchant caravans, the official historians hurriedly pass over the embarrassing beginnings of their subject.

Timur's formal education was nil. He could neither read nor write. Ibn Arabshah states that "Timur did not know Arabic, but of Persian, Turkish, and the Moghul [Mongol] language he understood enough but no more," that is, only a little. Some doubt exists as to whether he knew Mongol.[2] Even more questionable is the statement made by many authors that he was a Mongol. True, his ancestors were Mongol but during their long sojourn in Central Asia[3] they had become Turkish in spirit as well as in language "as much as the Normans established in England were to become 'English'" (Léon Cahun). "It would be the same error," the same author adds, "to take Timur for a Mongol as it would be to take the Black Prince for a Frenchman."[4] Timur's father's name Taragai, "The Lark," is Turkish, while the name Timur itself is Turkish for iron, a metal used in the forging of weapons and as such venerated in old Turkish religious cults. Babur, the founder of the Moghul (Mongol) empire in India and a descendant of Timur, despised the Mongols. One scholar, on the basis of an examination of the words used by Timur in conversation and in his choice of the Persian motto "rasti rusti," that is, "truth is safety," hazards the opinion that he preferred Persian as his language.[5]

Timur's early training followed forms appropriate to his period and station in life: riding, hunting, archery and other martial or semi-martial exercises. Learning to read and write would have been considered a frippery of no practical application in the pursuit of a military career. His knowledge of horseflesh was such that he could tell the quality of an animal at a glance. One of our sources, indeed, declares that he was a hippiatric expert or horse doctor and that this skill helped facilitate his rise,[6] a not implausible assertion in days when swift-moving cavalry was the "Queen of Battles." A successful commander had to look after his mounts for a campaign could go desperately awry if horses sickened and died.

Despite this emphasis on practical skills, Timur was no rough barbarian; in fact, he had the appearance of an educated man. He enjoyed the company of savants and theologians, a predilection which he perhaps owed to his father, and even had these men accompany him on his military campaigns. He could follow the thrust of an intricate theological debate and when abroad loved to bait local theologians with difficult and dangerous questions. He also interested himself in dervish sorcerers. He had a powerful and tenacious memory — one needed to tell Timur something but once. He later created the post of "court reader" and listened to readings from the chronicles and annals by the hour, correcting the reading if a slip were made. This prompted Iban Arabshah, who was extremely hostile to Timur, to comment spitefully that "Repetition even makes an ass wise." His knowledge of history (chiefly Arabic, Persian and Turkish) made a profound impression on Ibn Khaldun, himself "the greatest historian of the Arabs and perhaps the greatest historical thinker of the Middle Ages,"[7] who conversed with Timur in 1401. He characterized Timur as one who "is highly intelligent and very perspicacious, addicted to debate and argumentation about what he knows and also about what he does not know."[8]

Timur used his historical knowledge when stimulating his troops, recalling in this way Napoleon. He also drew upon his considerable knowledge of Muslim law and theology to find pretexts for his conquests and to animate his followers. Timur patronized poetry and literature, but he probably did this because it was the done thing for a sovereign of his time. He preferred useful knowledge set down in a simple, unadorned manner — the perfumed rhetorical style favored by Oriental writers of his day finding no sympathetic response. Soothsayers and physicians were also admitted into his intimate circle. He appreciated workmanship of artisans and craftsmen when it was of the highest order. He took an ardent interest in architecture.

Timur had a passion for chess which he played with consummate skill. He, indeed, made it more complicated by adding extra squares and pieces so that the "greater game," as Ibn Arahshah called it, consisted of 110 squares instead of 64 and such chess piece oddities as camels and giraffes. Chess even inspired the name of his fourth and youngest son. He had just made the classic move in chess of exchanging the king (shah) for the rook (rukh) when he was informed of the birth of a son. He promptly named him Shahrukh.

Timur knew not only the life of the nomad but also that of the sedentary commercial and agricultural community with which the Muslim establishment was closely tied. In his youth he would often visit Kesh where Muslim divines, especially the dervish shaykh Shams al-Din Kular, enjoyed much influence. Timur, like his father Taragai, was much attracted to this dervish whom he considered his first religious preceptor.

Even at this early age Timur had a General Douglas MacArthur-like feeling that he was a man of destiny. Ibn Arabshah relates how in these youthful days of scruffy poverty and dour prospects he would tell his companions that he "aimed at royal rank and would attack the kings of this world with fatal onset," — predictions which were received with derision and scoffing.

Brave and impetuous, Timur could later be seen in the hottest part of the fray, fighting at times as a common soldier. Ordinarily he was, as military commander, ever the prober, showing great boldness in his strategic and tactical dispositions. At other times he would back and fill, displaying infinite patience as he waited for the right time to strike. Crafty, treacherous and devious, he was a past master at cloaking his true intentions, at lulling his opponents into a false sense of security. He might float rumors that his forces were weak and badly disorganized. Or he might achieve the same effect by an exaggerated show of caution. Though illiterate himself, Timur knew well the use of "flattery and the harlotry of language" (Ibn Arabshah) in his correspondence.

No authenticated pictorial representation of Timur has come down to us, though there are numerous Persian and Indian miniatures. These miniatures, which are exceptionally dissimilar in their depiction of Timur, were painted considerably after his death and are completely at variance with descriptions of him in the written sources. Nor do the latter provide, as it were, a pen portraiture. Observers have left us a few partial descriptions. The most quoted and relied upon is that of Ibn Arabshah who could not have been more than fourteen when he saw the conqueror, but eked out his youthful memories with the recollections of others. According to him,

Timur was tall and of lofty stature as though he belonged to the remnants of the Amalekites, big in brow and head, mighty in strength and courage, wonderful in nature, white in colour, mixed with red, but not dark, stout of limb, with broad shoulders, thick fingers, long legs, perfect build, long beard, dry hands, lame on the right side, with eyes like candles, without brilliance.[9]

Timur's voice was stentorian, the same source adds. And though he died in his seventieth year the onset of old age brought no dimming of his mental powers.

Another eyewitness account which has come down to us is that of the Spanish envoy Ruy Gonzales de Clavijo, who was with Timur in Samarkand in 1404, i.e., just before his death. In describing his first audience with Timur, he says that the latter was dressed in a plain, unembroidered cloak of silk and wore "a tall white hat on the crown of which was displayed a balas ruby, the same being further ornamented with pearls and precious stones."[10] Timur had Clavijo and his colleagues come closer so that he could see them better, as his eyesight was by this time so poor that "his eyelids were falling over his eyes and he could barely raise them to see."[11] Though Clavijo saw Timur several times after, the only details that he thought of sufficient moment to record were that Timus was lame in the right leg and right hand from which latter he had lost the little finger and the one next to it, and was by now so infirm of body that he could not sit a horse but had to be carried from place to place in a litter. Ibn Khaldun, who saw Timur three years earlier, wrote: "Then he was carried away from before us, because of the trouble with his knee, and was placed upon his horse; grasping the reins, he sat upright in his saddle."[12]

It has been the wont of Soviet archeologists to open up the tombs of famous historical figures to see if the remains tally with or shed further light on what is known of them from written sources. In May–June 1941 a special archeological commission sent to Samarkand carried out exhumations in the Gur–Emir mausoleum. Timur's coffin was opened on June 17 despite the warnings of the local inhabitants that violating the tomb of such a great conquerer would surely bring disaster. Five days later the Nazis invaded the USSR. Twenty million Soviet citizens perished in the ensuing conflict.

Timur's generally well-preserved remains were subjected to a rigorous and minute examination by the archeologist-sculptor M. M. Gerasimov, who was a member of this team and who fabricated a bust

of Timur based on his skull and the scraps of hair, skin and other remains. The methods used to assure authenticity and the results of this
exhaustive enquiry have been published, along with a reconstruction of
Timur's skull.[13] Gerasimov's findings indicate that the remains found in
Timur's putative tomb tally closely with information about him in our
most reliable sources. The skeleton belonged to a strong individual who,
though possessing typically Mongolian features, was five feet seven
inches in stature — relatively tall for someone of Mongol stock. Examination shows that some bones of the right arm had actually grown
together at the elbow joint in a somewhat half-twisted way. Yet, in
Gerasimov's opinion, Timur did not lose mobility of this arm in the
shoulder joint. Indeed, it not only functioned but was exceptionally
strong, though its stiffness may have been the basis for the legend that
Timur had but one arm.

Timur's lameness is also amply substantiated. The kneecap had
coalesced with the thighbone in such a way that the leg could not be
straightened. Though the bones of the right and left legs differ little in
length, their nature is quite different. Those of the left leg are massive
and strong; those of the right considerably weaker.

Apparently Timur's right leg was affected throughout by the process
of tuberculosis. Gerasimov believes that this caused him much physical
suffering. This well may be a clue to Timur's unusual cruelty. As one
writer observes, "suffering generally brings hardness of the heart rather
than compassion."[14] Examination also indicates that the entire torso
was awry so that the left shoulder was considerably higher than the
right. Yet this did not affect the proud setting of the head.

Timur, after receiving his grievous wounds, could walk only short
distances without experiencing difficulty. In later years he more and
more took to a litter. Ibn Khaldun asserts that "when he would go long
distances men carried him with their hands." Riding, apparently, caused
him no physical suffering and his stamina rivalled that of his lustiest
warriors. Here he could temporarily forget his physical inadequacies
and maintain an imperial presence.

Timur no doubt suspected that his shattered, crippled body inspired
contempt for him in others. This need continually to prove his qualities
may well have acted as a goad pushing him on to ever greater exploits.
As Francis Bacon wrote many centuries before the appearance of
psychohistory: "Whoever hath anything fixed in his person that doth
induce contempt, hath also a spur in himself to rescue and deliver himself from scorn."

Timur was a septuagenarian at the time of his death. Yet his skeleton exhibits remarkably few traces of senility. According to Gerasimov, it shows the biological growth of a man of fifty. His extraordinarily firm constitution is indicated by the massiveness of the healthy left leg, the wide shoulders, the size of the chest and the rather high stature. His body also had a well-developed muscular structure, However, he was not fat. Indeed, there is indication of a certain emaciation which Gerasimov thinks is quite natural in view of the long hours spent in the saddle and the rigors of almost ceaseless campaigning. Examination of Timur's skull reveals that his large face was strong and muscular, but not fat. The forehead was short and wide, the eyebrows short and thick as befits someone of Mongol provenience. His eyes were large and round. His mouth was wide with thick but firm and well-penciled lips. Timur lost many teeth long before death and those that remained were much worn out, with traces of caries.

Timur s hair, specimens of which are preserved, was thick, straight and reddish-gray in color. He wore a long moustache which, unlike orthodox followers of Islam, he left unclipped over the lips; the ends hung loosely from the corners of the lips. His beard, though thick, was not long and was cut in a wedge shape. The hairs of the beard were stiff, almost straight and of reddish color intermixed with many gray hairs. The color was natural—Gerasimov could find no evidence that henna had been applied.

Ordinarily serious and saturnine, Timur did not like jesting or cajolery; during the mammoth festivities which he would organize from time to time, however, he did participate in the stupendous amount of drinking which accompanied these, and would on such occasions make merry. Truth, however troublesome and inconvenient, pleased Timur, who hated to be told lies, flattering though they might be. Biographers of Timur have pointed out the sharp contrast with Alexander the Great in this regard; how the latter killed Cleitus, his friend and companion, with his own sword for telling him an unpleasant truth and ordered the execution of the philosopher Antisthenes for the same reason. Timur, though despising lies in others, would, in taking a city or executing an enemy whose life he had promised to spare, break his word directly or through some logical legerdemain or casuistry. Excellent in judgment, he could see his way through a problem beset with labyrinthian difficulties. At times he would test scholars by feigning ignorance of a subject and asking them to explain something with which he was thoroughly familiar.

Timur was neither downcast in adversity nor exultant in prosperity. Despite his cruelty and love of war he "did not allow talk of bloodshed or captivity, rapine or plunder" in his company, nor obscene talk nor tales about violation of the harem, although Ibn Arabshah, on whom most of this is based, adds later that Timur, in his old age, "was wont to deflower virgins."[15] He had eight wives together with countless courtesans and concubines. He married his last wife at the age of seventy, the Koranic injunction limiting believers to a total of four wives at a time notwithstanding. Like Caesar, Timur required his wife to be above suspicion. He had one of his wives – a famed beauty – killed, even though the allegations made against her proved baseless, on the ground that "Whether it is true or false, it is a fault that she is suspected" (Ibn Arabshah).

As we have previously noted, when the Mogols in 1360 invaded Transoxiana the local rulers either made their peace with the conquerors or fled. The young Timur, for his part, decided to submit. Tugluk-Timur, the Mogol khan, rewarded Timur for his timely capitulation by assigning him a tuman or district which included Kesh and Karshi. The historian Sharaf ad-Din skates over Timur's quisling-like collaboration with the enemy by claiming that he made this sacrifice to avert an even greater calamity for his people.

But the agreeable task of ruling over this small but rich tuman was not his for long. Dissension in the Mogol camp caused Tugluk-Timur to depart with his troops for home. The Chagatai feudatories immediately resumed their old quarrels. Indeed, the infighting had continued even during the Mogol invasion in unoccupied sections of the country. Timur took part in the tumult in alliance with a local lord by the name of Hussein. But now Hadji Barlas, the head of the clan to which Timur belonged, who had fled abroad during the Mogol invasion, returned fresh and full of fight. He defeated Timur in battle and resumed his position as clan head. Timur's troops lost faith in their leader and abandoned him. At this point his luck had played out; he abased himself and asked for a pardon. This Hadji Barlas graciously granted and Timur became his client. The young man thereupon hired himself out as a *condottiero* to various petty lords, recognizing no higher loyalty than the furtherance of his own personal advantage and career.

In 1361 Tugluk-Timur and his Mogols again irrupted into Transoxiana; this time he would complete the conquest of this rich country. As before, some of the local lords capitulated, others fled the country. The former included three of the most prominent lords: Bayan Selduz,

Mir Bayazid, emir of Khodzhent, and Hadji Barlas himself. Tugluk-Timur, however, was determined to teach the turbulent and fractious local nobility a lesson. Mir Bayazid was executed without apparent cause *pour décourager les autres*. With this Hadji Barlas took fright and fled into Khurasan where he perished at the hands of brigands. Timur, at the head of a punitive force, made a great show of avenging his death by tracking down and killing Hadji Barlas' assassins. The plain fact was, however, that Timur was now rid of his chief rival. He had hurried to make his submission during the second Mogol invasion; now he moved in to claim the mantle of Hadji Barlas. It happened that one of the khan's great favorites at court was a friend of Timur. He spoke up in the latter's behalf, asking that Timur be given the same authority and possessions as Hadji Barlas. The khan acquiesced. Timur was summoned and invested with a tuman and given all the territories formerly belonging to Hadji Barlas, plus the rich village of Corache.

Tugluk-Timur spent the winter of 1361-62 making war against Hussein, a war which went badly for the latter. At the beginning of autumn in 1362 the khan returned to Samarkand. Bayan Selduz was put to death along with other men suspected of planning to revolt. This act testifies that the slaying of Mir Bayazid earlier had not been effective as a salutary warning. An oath of fidelity was now extracted from the other lords, and the khan made preparations to return to his own country after having subdued all of Transoxiana. He left behind his son Ilyas Khodja as his viceroy. Bikidgek, a Mogol lord, was appointed his viceroy's aide and given seniority over all the other princes at Ilyas' court. The khan, impressed with Timur's sagacity, assigned him to his son Ilyas Khodja as an advisor. This done, the khan departed for Mogolistan.

Timur's fortunes were but briefly in the ascendant. He soon broke with his Mogol overlords and fled to Hussein. The cause of this rupture and defection is not made clear by the sources. As usual, Sharaf ad-Din tries to put a good face on the matter. He asserts that Timur, seeing that Bikidgek was flouting the khan's orders, "foresaw the great disorders this contempt of the [khan's] orders would cause in the kingdom" and "deemed it prudent to leave." More probably, Timur was piqued at not being chosen Ilyas' senior assistant; he seems to have privily made contact with Hussein before betraying his patron.

After some difficulty Timur found Hussein at Khiva where he had fled after losing all his troops and possessions in his struggle with the Mogols. The next years, 1361-1365, though a time of adversity for the two emirs, also marked the period of their greatest intimacy. The ties between the two were strengthened when Timur married Uldja-Turkan-agha, Hussein's sister, for whom he apparently felt a real affection. The two young men occupied their time with organizing plundering raids; these had no loftier motives than self-enrichment. Successes were inter-mixed with failures. During 1362, while carrying on operations in the area south of the Sea of Aral they were captured by the Turkoman Ali-Bek of Makhan near present-day Mary, who kept them imprisoned in a foul cell for sixty-two days. Then Timur hid out for forty-eight days in Samarkand in the home of his sister, Kutluk-Turkan-agha, until he was forced to flee when he learned that his enemies had discovered his whereabouts. Timur and Hussein some time later surfaced in Sistan in southeastern Persia. Here, at the head of a thousand well-armed men, they fought as mercenaries for the ruler of Sistan against some of his subjects in revolt. The revolt put down, Timur and Hussein were in turn treacherously attacked by their employer. He had no intention of honoring the promises of handsome rewards he had made them; indeed, he now feared Timur and Hussein as much as he had the rebels. A sharp clash ensued during which—if one discounts the stories about Timur re-ceiving his injuries while stealing sheep—he was badly wounded in the right arm and leg and permanently lamed.

Transoxiana, meanwhile, was growing restive under the Mogol yoke. Volunteers, including some princes, began to gravitate to Timur and Hussein. Successes against the Mogols alternated with reverses. One night the enemy slipped past the guards and caught Timur and his men asleep in camp. A skillful covering action fought by Timur with some of his men allowed the remainder to make an orderly withdrawal. On another occasion, after the desertion of six thousand men, Timur and Hussein faced an enemy force with only two thousand warriors. A bat-tle took place near Pul-i-Sangin, some twenty-four miles from Garm. Neither side could prevail. Timur then resorted to guile. At night he had many small bonfires lit on the surrounding hills. Then, with a small force, he attacked the enemy's rear. The Mogols, thinking themselves surrounded by a large force, fled. Thereupon Timur, with a small caval-ry force, left posthaste for Kesh. He had some of his men drag small trees with leafy branches behind their horses. When the Mogols in Kesh saw the thick dust cloud they believed that a huge army was approach-ing and abandoned the city. "Thus fortune, which was always favorable to Timur, caused him to triumph over an army by fire, and to conquer a city by dust,"[17] wrote Sharaf ad-Din.

In the spring of 1363 Ilyas and his Mogols, thirsting for revenge, again invaded Transoxiana. Timur and Hussein met the enemy at Kibi-mutan, near Kesh. Timur, on the eve of battle, had an encouraging dream which he told to Hussein, then to the army. Everyone was inspir-ited. Timur and Hussein's army was far outnumbered by that of the enemy. The battle began when Timur, who was commanding the left wing, had his men discharge a great cloud of arrows. The arrows cut down most of the forward ranks of the enemy. Then he and his men, swords in hand, attacked the enemy before they could release an answering shower of arrows. They advanced so quickly that the first rank of the enemy was driven back on the second. Timur's men then pursued those who fled with lances.

Meanwhile Hussein, who led the right wing, was heavily involved in the fighting on that side. Timur came to his aid and attacked Bikidgek's rear so that the latter was assailed on both sides. A number of promi-nent men were killed on the Mogol side. Ilyas Khodja, Bikidgek and others were taken prisoners but "owing to the natural generosity of the Turks" (Sharaf ad-Din) they were then released by some of Timur's men without his knowledge. Timur and Hussein pursued Ilyas beyond Khodzhent and finally stopped at Tashkent. Then Timur engaged in mopping-up operations while two of his aides were sent by him to Samar-kand to take over the city. This they did without any difficulty. Timur and Hussein then entered Samarkand in triumph; they were greeted cordially by the people "who expected from these princes a milder government than they had enjoyed under the Getes [Jats or Mogols]."[18]

Though Transoxiana and Turkistan were now cleared of the enemy, peace was still to be achieved. The turbulent local nobility—especially any who had had any sort of hand in defeating the Mogols—made themselves sovereign in their territories. To solve this problem, Timur and Hussein convened a kurultai of the nobility. They presented two arguments in favor of electing a new khan: that it would better preserve the unity of the country in the event of a renewed threat from the Mogols; and that it would prevent continual war and ruin as each lord tried to get the better of his neighbor. There were other considerations. Neither they nor any of the other local nobility thought that they could get along without a legitimate Chagatai sovereign—so tenacious was the Chingisid tradition. Having their own authentic khan would, moreover, cut the ground out from under the claims of Ilyas Khodja who, in the meantime, had succeeded his father as khan in Mogolistan. The two emirs, while preserving the outward forms, intended to exercise the real power from behind the scenes. Timur, at this point, was junior partner to Hussein.

Their choice for puppet khan settled on Kabul-Shah-Aglen—a most reluctant candidate. To avoid the vicissitudes of princes living in such troublous times, he had donned the robes of a dervish and was living a cloistral and contemplative monk's life. Brushing aside his protestations, Timur and Hussein had him stripped of his monk's habit and accoutered in the magnificent raiment of a Chingisid khan. Then amidst public rejoicings and feasts in Samarkand, Kabul-Shah ascended the throne and was presented with a golden goblet; this was the Turkic manner of crowning a sovereign. Then the clan heads, each in turn, made nine ritual bows before the khan. This mock obeisance over, the new khan was thenceforth neglected and ignored.

During this period differences arose between the two brothers-in-law over some Mogol POWs—a presentiment of future trouble. One of the prisoners whom Timur wished to liberate was Emir Hamid, a leading general, "whose father had always been [Timur's] friend."[19] When Timur learned of Emir Hamid's death at the hands of Hussein he dissembled his anger but he did not forget.

Relations between Timur and Hussein were, however, outwardly amicable as each administered his respective territories. Though their affairs were in good order, this situation did not last long. In the spring of 1365 Ilyas Khodja Khan raised another army and again made an incursion into Transoxiana. Timur and Hussein combined their forces and rode out to do battle with the enemy in the area north of the Syr Darya between Tashkent and Chinaz. Their troops were cocky and self-confident. They had previously defeated far larger Mogol forces; now they were joining battle with a Mogol army measurably inferior numerically to their own.

The encounter, which historians dubbed the "battle of the mud," took place on May 5, 1365. A lashing rainstorm began at the moment the troops went into action. Horses were caught in the slippery, adhesive slime and lost their balance, tumbling their riders to the ground. Bolts of lightning and the crack of thunder unnerved even the most fearless. The Mogols were prepared for such a contingency. They had covered their camp, horses and persons with felts and had dug canals to carry off the water. Mounted on fresh horses, the Mogols met the advance of their drenched and dispirited opponents. At one point in the battle Timur went to the rescue of Hussein who was hard pressed by the enemy. After routing them he then sent word to Hussein asking that he reform his troops and join the counterattack which seemed to have a good chance of success. Hussein not only refused but abused and manhandled each of the three different messengers sent by his partner. Furious at the missed opportunity, Timur called off his own attack; the battle, thanks to the discord between the two emirs, ended with a rout of Timur's and Hussein's troops. Together they lost over 10,000 men, killed either on the battlefield or in the subsequent pursuit by the enemy.

Timur and Hussein, with the pitiful remnants of their forces, beat a retreat as far as the Amu Darya, separating on the way. Hussein headed for Balkh and Timur for Sali-sarai, north of Kunduz. Transoxiana, abandoned to its fate, lay prostrate at the feet of Ilyas Khodja Khan. He directed an immediate advance on the great prize—Samarkand— where he expected to gain much booty. Nothing, it seemed, could save the city. Its walls and citadel, demolished by Chingis Khan during his invasion of the country in the early thirteenth century, lay dismantled. The defending garrison had fled. The population of the city, left to fend for itself, expected the worst.

To the defense of the city there rallied the lower orders, especially the artisans, among whom Serbedarism was widespread. This curious populist movement has been poorly elucidated by historians owing to the exiguous and blatantly hostile nature of our sources.[20] The Serbedars were especially strong in Transoxiana and Khurasan in northeast Persia. In medieval times Khurasan also took in the Merv area of present-day Soviet Turkmenistan and the Balkh and Herat districts of Afghanistan. In 1337 the Serbedars founded in Khurasan a republic of brigands with Sebzevar as its capital.[21] The movement had a religious tincture in that Shiite dervishes played a leading role.

In the 1365 crisis the Serbedar successes in Khurasan provided a powerful example to elements among the Samarkand population bitten with Serbedarism. The leaders of the movement there were Maulana-zada Samarkandi, a young student, Maulana Khurdek Bukhari, a cotton scutcher, and Abu-Bakr Kelevi who is described as "a good shot with a bow."

As the Mogols approached the city, a crowd of about ten thousand persons gathered in the cathedral mosque. Counsels were hopelessly divided as to what should be done. It was at this point that Maulana-zada Samarkandi, known for his bravery, stepped forward. Girt with a sword, he slowly mounted the *mimbar* or pulpit. In an impassioned speech he declared that a numerically superior force of infidels had come to plunder the homes of Muslims. And though the ruler [i.e., Hussein] had illegally collected a poll tax from the Muslims, he had deserted them upon the approach of the enemy. Neither the payment of a ransom or gifts could save the city's inhabitants. Maulana-zada ended his peroration by asking who would assume responsibility for the defense of the city. The aristocracy, the natural leaders, made no response. Turning to the townspeople, Maulana-zada then asked whether they would help him if he himself took on this charge. All present agreed. Ten thousand youths of parts swore an oath to support the new leader. Before dismissing this newly fledged scratch force, Maulana-zada again exhorted his hearers to heroic action against the Mogols.[22]

With the aid of his associates the new leader began an able and energetic organization of the city's defenses. For three days and nights he went without sleep as he elaborated his plans. A list of all adult males, married or single, native or foreign, was compiled and brought to him. Guards were posted over the city gates. Patrols were positioned at the approaches to the city, to warn of the enemy advance. Only the wide street which formed the entrance into the city was left open; the side streets leading off it were barricaded and cubicles with embrasures for shooting were constructed over the barricades. Archers lay in ambush on both sides of the main street. Maulana-zada himself, with a picked corps of bowmen, awaited the Mogols at the end of the main street. Individual action against the Mogols either within the city or without was prohibited; all would await the signal for a co-ordinated attack. Each man was to remain at his post day and night, not leaving it even to go to the aid of his comrades. They swore to this on the Koran; they vowed to divorce their wives if they were untrue to their oaths.

The unsuspecting Mogol force of 10,000 troopers, knowing of the flight of the city's garrison, advanced nonchalantly and incautiously. Passing by the ambushes on the main street, they presently reached Maulana-zada and his men. He personally sounded the attack signal with a blow on a drum. The archers plied their bows dexterously. Others let fly stones with slings and with their hands; still others threw sticks. The astonished Mogols were pressed from the front and from both sides. According to one source, the Mogol losses in dead and wounded were about two thousand, with one hundred of their number being taken prisoner, before they could effect a withdrawal. The next day the attack was renewed by the Mogols, moving along the same thoroughfare. This time they were more cautious and used the standard nomad tactics of simulated flight and sudden counter-attack, but all to no purpose. Finally, in a change of tactics, they decided to lay siege to the city in form. The sources do not tell us how long this lasted, but we are told that the inhabitants were at length reduced to desperate straits and were on the point of surrendering the city. Providentially, an epidemic broke out among the horses of the Mogols. Soon, according to Sharaf ad-Din, only a quarter of the horses remained alive. The Mogols, "gnashing their teeth in rage," were forced to lift their siege and retreat, confining themselves to pillaging the city's environs. Then they evacuated Transoxiana completely.

The Serbedars now controlled Samarkand for about a year. What transpired in the city during this time can only be surmised from the scanty documentation. Sharaf ad-Din states that the Serbedars believed it was they who had saved the city from the Mogols, rather than Allah who, in his compassion, afflicted the Mogol horses with disease, thereby saving the city. "Moreover," he adds, "they [the Serbedar leaders] would have respect paid 'em, and claimed a sort of superiority over the rest; they at length formed great parties, spilt the people's blood, and caused strange disorders in the city, to maintain themselves in their usurpation."[23] Quite possibly this anti-Serbedar violence was originally prompted by the aristocracy. It is plausible to assume that they would not be content with leaving the city government in the hands of students, artisans and other lower-class elements now that the external danger had passed, but would attempt to take over power themselves. At any rate, it appears that Maulana-zada and his associates were forced to broaden the leadership base to include others. The Serbedars did manage to effect a series of measures directed against the feudal aristocracy, including a certain redistribution of wealth. Presumably they also repealed the *jizya* or poll tax.

Timur quickly learned of the Mogol rout at the hands of the Serbedars and of subsequent developments in the city. He sent word of this to Hussein. A conference was held at which their ties of friendship and alliance were refurbished; measures were concerted for seizing control of Samarkand. They agreed to meet again in the spring of 1366, since they were still too compromised by their craven flight in the face of the Mogol advance to attempt an immediate recoup of power. Hussein spent the winter of 1365/66 at Sali-sarai. Timur wintered at Karshi. He used this time in erecting fortified walls and constructing a firm base for the subsequent struggle with Hussein, for which he was already revolving schemes in his mind.

With the coming of spring the two emirs joined forces and advanced upon Samarkand. An open assault on the city was ruled out; Timur and Hussein had too healthy a respect for the demonstrated abilities of the Serbedars in organizing a successful defense. Rather, it was decided to gain their objectives with guile and trickery. The first steps to that end had been taken soon after the 1365 conference of the two emirs. Emissaries were dispatched to Samarkand bearing honorary gowns, belts, swords and diplomas for the city's rulers. Decrees were also sent, sanctified by solemn oaths, in which the Serbedars were promised immunity from prosecution for any usurpation of power. The Serbedar leaders, easily gulled by these reassurances and flattering marks of attention, responded with an embassy of their own bearing gifts to Timur in Karshi. This action showed that they favored him more than Hussein. One author (Musevi) even states that Timur was informed of the victory over the Mogols by Maulana-zada himself.

In the early spring of 1366, before joining with Timur in the advance upon the city, Hussein sent envoys to the Serbedar leaders. They were flattered and lulled into dropping their guard by Hussein's honeyed assurances that he had "full confidence" in them, indeed, that they were worthier than any of his own emirs. The envoys then proposed a meeting in the meadow of Kan-i-gul to the northeast of the city as soon as he arrived there. As soon as Hussein, together with Timur, encamped at the appointed spot, the Serbedar delegation appeared trustingly with gifts in hand. Hussein played the role of gracious host to the hilt, allowing the delegates to depart once the audience was over. Any last lingering suspicions were now removed. On the next day the leaders came again with still more gifts. This time they were ordered seized and, after a drumhead trial, condemned to death. Timur's personal intercession won a pardon for Maulana-zada, further indicating the ties between Timur and the Serbedars and his desire to win the sympathy and passive support of the townspeople by his pose as Hussein's reluctant associate in the guileful and cruel treatment of the Serbedars.[24] This calculated demagogic gesture — for Timur had no real sympathy for the Serbedars — indicates that he was casting about for future allies in the inevitable power struggle with Hussein. An unknown number of Serbedars were executed following the act of treachery. As the historian Abd-ar-Razzak put it: "They caught the jackal to whom they had given the name of young lion, in a trap by means of the call: 'young lion!'"[25]

After a triumphal entry into Samarkand in late spring, the two emirs imposed a duumvirate over Transoxiana. Hussein, however, soon sought

to regain his paramountcy over his brother-in-law. He had three important advantages: (1) possession of important holdings outside of Transoxiana (the cities of Balkh, Herat, Khulm and Kunduz); (2) a more distinguished lineage—he was Kazagan's grandson; (3) Timur had once
served him as a junior associate.

But Hussein had serious failings. He was miserly, avaricious and
grasping. He began levying very heavy taxes upon his followers though
they had not recovered financially from the "battle of the mud." Not
even Timur's entourage was spared these exactions. Timur further enhanced his reputation for unstinting generosity by using his own wealth
to help others meet Hussein's demands. This even included the jewelry
of his wife, Hussein's sister. Though Hussein recognized the bracelets
and earrings, he took them regardless. He then demanded additional
sums. Since nomad leaders were included in these levies, his popularity
began to suffer in the very group which constituted his chief support.
Nomads expect of their leaders not only just distribution of booty but
frequent gifts. Stinginess, like lack of bravery, is to them blameworthy
and not the mark of a real leader.

Timur's territories of Kesh and Karshi, while not as extensive as
those of Hussein, lay at the very gates of Samarkand, the cynosure of
Transoxiana. Moreover, he understood much better the needs of the
time. Unification, internal tranquility and good order were urgently
desired not only by the merchants, artisans and Muslim clergy but by
the mass of the population engaged in agriculture. Hussein little appreciated or understood these needs. Though Samarkand was ostensibly
the capital, Hussein was customarily to be found at Sali-sarai on the
banks of the Amu Darya, absorbed in campaigning against the Mogols
and against refractory local followers.

In 1366 Hussein learned that Timur was preparing an armed revolt
against him. Though Timurid historians brand this intelligence as false,
there is good reason to think otherwise. The death at this time of Hussein's sister, Timur's wife, sundered the last bond between the two.
Timurid historians depict Timur as a knight *sans peur et sans reproche*.
Sharaf ad-Din descants on how Timur was the long-suffering, aggrieved
party who tried to keep on good terms with Hussein despite the latter's
sundry plots and acts of treachery; Timur at length consented to head
a conspiracy against Hussein only as an act of self-preservation. These
protestations have a hollow ring, for however antithetical in personal
traits, in their morality they were like two peas in a pod. Each was determined, now that their common enemies were gone, to get rid of his

rival by any means that came to hand. Sharaf ad-Din is nearer the mark
when he observes that "But as the sun never shews itself till the stars
disappear, Timur could not arrive at that pitch of greatness destined for
him, without the ruin of Hussein."[26]

In any event, it was Timur who began open hostilities after trying
secretly to recruit allies for himself among Hussein's principal captains
and vassals. He did win over Keikosrau, a sworn enemy of Hussein ever
since the latter ejected him from Khuttalyan and killed his brother
Keikubad in 1360. Keikosrau was the scion of an old Iranian family;
thus Timur strengthened his ties with the Iranian feudatories of Transoxiana. He further cemented his alliance by arranging the marriage of
Jehangir, his oldest son, with Keikosrau's daughter.

At first Hussein had the upper hand in the struggle. Timur's attempt
to capture Samarkand went awry. Hussein at one point even captured
seized Bukhara, the second most important city in Transoxiana. Next
Hussein advanced with an army superior in number. Thinking himself
outmatched, Timur fled to Khurasan, leaving subordinates to defend
Bukhara and Karshi. When both these cities fell to the enemy, Hussein
became the master of almost all of Transoxiana.

During this period, Timur had adopted polities indicating his growing appreciation of the economic factors which could be of use to him
in his ascent to supreme power. During his brief tenure of authority in
Karshi he gave succor to poor families ruined by war, and fostered economic revival. He instructed his deputy in Bukhara to do the same.
Timur divined more accurately than Hussein that the nurturing and
stimulation of economic life increased his treasury and, at the same
time, attracted the sedentary population to his cause. This man, who
earlier had pillaged merchant caravans, now cultivated a new public
image. When he learned that his men had attacked some merchants
whom they mistook for the enemy, he ordered the full restitution of
the seized goods. Henceforward merchants would find in him a stead-
fast friend and defender. The poacher had now become the game
warden.

For the moment, however, the future seemed bleak for Timur. In his
extremity he did not scruple at making an alliance with the Mogols
against Hussein, knowing full well the misery their advent would bring
to the people of Transoxiana. This rapprochement was facilitated by
the fact that Keikosrau, whose daughter had married Timur's son, was
related by marriage to the Mogol princely family. Though Timur had

once defected from the Mogols and had fought them, this mattered little since they were primarily interested in using the rivalry of the two emirs as an opportunity to plunder the country.

This alliance and the projected invasion of Transoxiana by Timur with a force of half-pagan Mogols struck fear into the heart of Hussein. He approached the shaykhs and the Ulema of Tashkent and persuaded them to intercede with Timur, knowing that he reverenced holy men. The latter reminded Timur of the ruin to the country attending his struggle with Hussein, and of the even worse calamities that would ensue if the infidel Mogols came to bathe their hands in the blood of Muslims.

Timur affected to be moved by these pious considerations. He knew that the thoughts voiced by the holy men mirrored those of the sedentary feudatories who sought surcease from turmoil. Also his struggle with Hussein, with its many alternations of fortune and misfortune, seemed to be barren of result. A change of tactics seemed appropriate, and this was sanctioned by a dream that conveniently came to him. Timur broke with the Mogols and came to an accord with Hussein in which he regained possession of Kesh. In 1368 and 1369 he even aided Hussein militarily against certain of the latter's vassals who had taken advantage of his involvement with Timur to assert their independence.

Despite this refreshment of their old alliance the two emirs still eyed one another warily, each regarding this as but a tactical maneuver. As Grousset aptly puts it: "What follows is a marvellous comedy of oriental hypocrisy, with protestations of friendship, embraces of reconciliation, pious Koranic maxims uttered at every turn, then betrayals, *coups de main* and summary executions in the Turkish manner."[27]

Transoxiana, during this period, came more and more under the control of Timur as many of the feudal lords transferred their fealty to him. Hussein, seeing this, concentrated his attentions increasingly on his possessions in Afghanistan. Realizing the importance of a large city with a citadel and supporting agricultural districts as a strategic base in his struggle with Timur, he transferred his treasury and armory to Balkh and rebuilt its citadel Khinduvan, once famed for the cyclopean masonry of its towers and walls and for the depth of its moat. The population of Balkh was moved to the citadel and the old city abandoned. Timur, apprehending that this move was directed against him, tried to dissuade Hussein, citing as a cautionary tale how Mirza Abdalla, Hussein's uncle, had encompassed his own ruin by insisting on residing in Samarkand in defiance of his emirs' advice.

A new showdown between the two emirs was postponed when Timur, at Hussein's pleading, led a force against the Mogols who had again invaded Transoxiana. He successfully repelled this new incursion.

Timur then declared open war against Hussein, and departed with his army from Kesh in the direction of Balkh. Again, his actions are glossed over by the Timurid court historians; they declare it was Hussein who brought matters to this impasse by his renewed treacheries. Three leagues outside Termez Timur was met by Sayyid* Bereke, a putative descendant of the Prophet Muhammad and a native of the holy city of Mecca who had acquired a great reputation for learning and piety. He presented Timur with a drum and a standard, the symbols of kingly sovereignty, and predicted Timur's future greatness. Timur welcomed Sayyid Bereke warmly. The latter thereupon decided to attach himself to Timur's entourage and to follow him for the rest of his life. Timur, on his part, "order'd that after his death they shou'd both be laid in the same tomb, and that his face shou'd be turned sideways, that at the day of judgment, when every one shou'd lift up their hands to heaven to implore assistance of some intercessor, he might lay hold on the robe of this child of the prophet Mahomet."[28]

The support of Sayyid Bereke was of great advantage to Timur. The sayyids of Termez had for a long time enjoyed much influence among both the Muslim leaders and the population of Transoxiana. Their adhesion to Timur's side at this point has been interpreted as an expression of the mood of the sedentary population of Transoxiana.

Crossing the Amu Darya at Termez, Timur was joined by all the princes and emirs, anxious to get on the bandwagon now that the outcome was no longer in suspense. Though Hussein was still ensconced at Balkh, Timur already considered himself the victor. He drove this point home by a political act: halting in the vicinity of Orpuz near Balkh, he caused a Chingisid—Suyurghatmish Oglan—to be proclaimed khan. The kurultai, according to Mongol custom, went through the motions of electing the khan, but all of this was *pro forma*. And, again following old Mongol custom, this elevation of a khan was celebrated by many days of feasting.

Though the final bearding of Hussein in his lair at Balkh was anticlimactic, the taking of Balkh was no military promenade. Hussein's forces, upon the approach of Timur's prodigiously numerous army, sallied forth. A savage battle ensued which lasted until nightfall and in which Timur's son, Omar-Shaykh, a lad of fifteen, was wounded in the foot. The next day the struggle was resumed in all its furious

---

*Sayyid, a descendant of the Prophet Muhammad, more particularly through his grandson Hussein, son of Ali.

intensity. In the picturesque language of the Timurid historian Nizam
ad-Din Shami, "torrents of blood flowed on the field of battle and famous heads fell like balls into the net during a game of polo."[29] At length
Hussein, looking down at the fell game of battle from his citadel of
Khinduvan, panicked and ordered the citadel to be secured. Timur
thereupon sent a messenger to tell Hussein that he must surrender if he
hoped to save his life. Hussein, realizing the hopelessness of his situation, replied that he would cease resistance if he were given safe passage
out of the citadel so that he could go on the pilgrimage to Mecca, as enjoined by the Koran.

Timur acquiesced and Hussein promised to emerge the next day.
Despite Timur's safe conduct pledge, Hussein remained mistrustful. He
was mindful not only of Timur's past treacheries but perhaps also of
what he himself would have done in a reversal of roles. That night he
slipped out of the citadel undetected. On reaching the old city, Hussein
lost his way and decided to hide at the top of a minaret in the first
mosque he encountered. By chance one of Timur's soldiers had lost his
horse; to spot it the more quickly, he climbed the minaret. There he
discovered Hussein, whom he recognized. Hussein who, in the plenitude
of his power "did not give one dinar to a warrior or a crust of bread to
a knight,"[30] now gave him a handful of pearls to keep mum and promised him even greater riches if he would help him escape. But the
soldier, as soon as he had descended, ran immediately to Timur to tell
all. Hussein, who was discovered hiding in a hole, was brought with
hands bound before Timur. The latter, recalling former intimacy, even
melted into tears. When Keikosrau, whose brother had been killed by
Hussein, asked that he be allowed to exact vengeance, Timur adjured
him to let time and fortune take their retribution. Hussein was allowed
to leave for Mecca as Timur had promised, but he was overtaken on the
way and slain by Keikosrau and Emir Muiad, the husband of one of
Timur's sisters. Sharaf ad-Din, in extenuating this violation of a solemn
promise, explains that this was done according to the law of vendetta as
sanctioned by the Shariat, the Muslim code of laws. Since, he continues,
the Shariat was the supreme law, Timur's protection availed Hussein
naught.

No mercy was shown to the family of Hussein. Two of his sons were
burned alive and their ashes cast into the air. The two other sons escaped to India, but soon perished. The puppet khan raised up by Hussein was also executed. Timur added Hussein's four wives to his own
seraglio. That these included Sarai-Mulk-Khanum, Kazan-khan's own

daughter, was of utmost importance to Timur from the point of view of prestige and titulature. This marriage gave him the right to the title "gurgan," that is, "son-in-law" [of the khan] and as such related him to the Chagatai dynasty. This is a title which Timur would use with pride for the remainder of his life.

Hussein's other wives, together with his daughters, were distributed among Timur's followers. Condign punishment was meted out to the inhabitants of Balkh for having supported Hussein. Some were bound with chains, others were beheaded; their wives, children and treasure were parcelled out among Timur's officers. The inhabitants' houses were destroyed and the countryside laid waste. Timur made a lavish distribution of the riches amassed by Hussein among his own governors, emirs and other notables. At the same time, they received promotions and other enlargements of their perquisites. As for the citadel, it was rased. The inhabitants who had escaped the holocaust were moved back into the city to rebuild it.

Though Timur's name became a byword for cruelty so that clammy terror would seize the populations of towns and cities lying athwart his line of advance, he had given no indication of this penchant for bestiality prior to his seizure of Balkh. Indeed, he is pictured as a man of moderation.[31] When in the later 1360s, during his struggle with Hussein, he was informed that some of his followers were conspiring to desert him, he turned down suggestions that the leaders of the plot be seized, saying that such harsh action would alienate others. One may surmise that this deep vein of cruelty was perhaps latent in his character and was certainly stimulated by the intense suffering he felt from the grievous wounds sustained in Sistan. However, he had not dared to give vent to it until his own position was unassailable. With Hussein's demise he could now bare his fangs; the princelings of Transoxiana had no one else to turn to.

CHAPTER III
Master of Transoxiana, 1370-1380

Timur's victory over Hussein marked the great watershed in his life. His rise up to now had been painfully slow and laborious, attended by many defeats, desertions by followers and other setbacks. Unlike Alexander the Great, the son of a king, he did not inherit a kingdom with a well-trained army but had to raise himself up from a relatively modest background by dint of a murderous elimination bout with the feudal lords of his own country, in which his rival Hussein seemed at first to have the upper hand. It was in this crucible of hard, daunting struggle that he gradually elaborated those military skills which were to give him the habit of victory, so that the roster of his further campaigns is but a monotonous recital of almost uninterrupted successes. No less important was the appreciation he developed for political, administrative and economic factors as potent adjuncts of the military side of his activities; the scanting of these would have gravely prejudiced his rise to power. He had to be, in a general sense, an administrator, general manager, politician and diplomatist as well as a general.

On April 11, 1370, while still at Balkh, Timur, now 34 years of age, convened a kurultai for the purpose of having himself recognized as master of his new domains. The assembly was attended by the leading notables of Transoxiana, including the emirs, princes and generals of his army and leaders of the Ulema, or Muslim establishment, headed by Sayyid Bereke. The convening of kurultais, to which the top lay and spiritual leaders of the realm were invited, was to be a standard feature of Timur's mode of governing; they were called whenever there were pressing problems, economic, political and military, to be discussed and resolved. During the Balkh kurultai Timur was given the title of Saheb Caran, or "emperor of the age and conqueror of the world."[1]

Timur had already acquired the title of Gurgan by marrying Hussein's widow. He never claimed the title of khan since he stood in awe of Chingisid legitimacy to the end of his life. Suyurghatmish continued on as khan. Though he was nominally superior to Timur, this was but a polite fiction.

Before returning home Timur named a member of his own Barlas clan governor in Balkh and regulated the internal government of his new state. He appointed the leaders of the *tumans, hazaras,* districts and subdistricts. These were obliged to mobilize ten thousand, a thousand, a hundred and ten warriors respectively on call. Timur also appointed lieutenant generals who were to serve him as his principal assistants. Finally, he set up a *divan* or council which would assist him in governing. Emir Davud became head of the divan and *daruga* or governor of Samarkand which was officially designated as the capital. It was to this city that Timur now repaired.

Timur marked his arrival in Samarkand by initiating a feverish, ever-intensifying pace of constructional activity which would go on until his death and which would leave a mark on the city which still has not been effaced. Involved in this urban redevelopment which began in 1371/72 were the citadel (*kala*) located in the western part of the city, the fortified center (*hisar*) of the city located to the east of the citadel, the city suburbs and, at the outer rim of the perimeter, a ring of villages.

The walls encircling the fortified part of the city were apparently constructed in the main on the foundations of the walls of the pre-Mongol period. These were surrounded by a deep moat full of water. Unfortunately, unlike Bukhara, no remnant of the walls has been preserved, the walls and gates having been pulled down by the Russians after their conquest in 1868 of the emirate of Bukhara, to which Samarkand then belonged. We can, however, obtain some notion of them from extant sixteenth-century miniatures. They were high and were constructed of brick. Saw-toothed in appearance on top, their rhythm of towers and embrasures gave them a grim and severe aspect. The walls varied in thickness and height according to defensive requirements. Since the enemy, in attacking, favored the northern and eastern sides, the walls here were thick enough to allow a man to ride on top of them on horseback. The walls were pierced in six places by great gates —two each on the northern and southern sides and one each for the east and west, the latter abutting the southern side of the citadel. A sixteenth-century miniature depicts one of the two northern gates. The dark, massive gates proper were apparently fashioned out of cast iron and fitted into a high lancet arch frame flanked by towers, saw-toothed parapet and embrasures. The frame was faced with blue tiles. The oblong panel over the arch bore an inscription glorifying Allah: "O, opening all doors!"

The citadel, covering an area of up to 86 acres, contained the main governmental offices, workshops for making weapons and armor, a mint, a prison and two palaces—the Kok-Sarai and the Bustan-Sarai. The Kok-Sarai, the main governmental palace, was a three-story affair and took its name ("Blue Palace") from the abundance of blue tile with which it was faced. It probably dominated the city, since it was built on an eminence. Despite its elegant facade, it acquired a grisly reputation as the place where Timur's political opponents were tortured and secretly murdered. It contained the state coffers and the thronal stone called Koktash or "blue stone" onto which khans were raised on a large piece of white felt during their coronations. The Koktash is all that remains today of the palace or its furnishings and may be seen in the Gur-Emir mausoleum. It is a large parallel epiped of grey marble. Its sides are covered with richly carved ornaments and it is flanked on the corners by figured columns.[2]

Timur gave the merchants and artisans better facilities in which to display their wares and do their work. He adorned the city with palaces and gardens. This was the first reconstruction of the city since the Mongol invasion. Various measures were also taken to attract more people to the city, causing "so vast a number of people to settle there, that even Grand Cairo and Bagdad envy's its prosperity and glory" (Sharaf ad-Din)

Timus apparently vacillated a long time in choosing Samarkand as his capital over Kesh, the city of his youth, where the bones of his ancestors lay buried. Some authors say that he picked Samarkand because it was from here that the famed Afrasiyab had ruled Turan, "the land of the Turks," in ancient times. More probably, what appealed most to Timur's practical, matter-of-fact mind was the central position of the city in Transoxiana and its climate and natural surroundings. It had access to a plentiful supply of water. Enclosed on three sides by hills, it felt the interplay of three currents of air: from the hills, from the river and also from the fields, forests and meadows. The environs contained large reserves of construction materials which could be tapped as well as non-ferrous and rare metal ore which even the technology of that day could refine and put to the use of the state.[3]

Timur s firm hand was felt not only in Transoxiana but also in the adjacent Ferghana and Tashkent areas. Indocile or troublesome chieftains, especially those of the semi-nomadic Jelair, Barlas and Selduz clans, were brought to heel with punitive expeditions and executions. Timur's efforts to bring law and order and to increase the power of the central authority received strong support from the urban population, the Muslim establishment and the peasants. However, a policy simply of basing himself on the sedentary population while curbing the nomadic elements would have been foredoomed to failure, as rulers who preceded Timur learned. Timur was astute enough to avoid a rupture with the nomadic feudatories with whom he had ties reaching back into his youth. Though he knew that his work of unifying the State was not popular with the nomads, he sought to keep them loyal by organizing expeditions into neighboring territories where they could indulge their penchant for pillaging and looting. These campaigns also served another purpose. As one scholar observes: "State revenues for the upkeep of the army did not exist, and these campaigns of conquest were the sole means for the maintenance of his numerous army."[4]

In the 1370s Timur conducted a series of campaigns against the kingdom of Khorezm. This state, which lay astride the lower reaches of the Amu Darya and included the delta formed by that river at the point of discharge into the Sea of Aral,[5] played a significant if ephemeral role in the history of Central Asia in the period around 1200. In 1224 Chingis Khan assigned North Khorezm and the North Caucasus to the appanage of Juchi, his oldest son. Around 1242 Juchi's son Batu, after further conquests, formed what Russian sources called the Golden Horde and eastern sources the Ulus of Juchi. It included the northern Caucasus, northern Khorezm, the Volga Bulgar state, the Kipchak steppe, the Crimea and Western Siberia. The Russian principalities located north of the Kipchak steppe became tribute paying vassals. Southern Khorezm formed part of the Ulus of Chagatai.

Soon, however, Khorezm became the apple of discord between the Juchids and the Chagatais. In the early 1260s all of Khorezm came under Chagatai rule. This situation was not inappropriate since in pre-Mongol times it had been linked with Transoxiana culturally, economically and politically. The conquest was not destined to endure; soon afterward the Golden Horde regained northern Khorezm, including Urgench. Southern Khorezm, with Kyat and Khiva, was retained by the Chagatais. Then around 1360, Hussein Sufi, a Turkic chieftain of the Kungrat clan and a Juchid through the female line, took advantage of the serious internal strife in the Golden Horde to carve out an independent state for himself in Khorezm comprising the northern or Juchid part. Then he similarly used the distracted condition of Transoxiana to seize Kyat and Khiva, thereby reuniting the north and south. Timur, once he became master of Transoxiana and claimant to the Chagatai patrimony, demanded restitution.

Hussein Sufi's refusal in 1371 to accede to this peremptory demand precipitated a protracted struggle which ultimately led to his demise. Hussein Sufi imprisoned Timur's envoy, his ambassadorial status notwithstanding. Timur, who had expected this provocative response, followed behind with his army. Kyat, the first enemy stronghold in his path, barricaded itself against a siege. Though Timur had no engineers with him, he had his soldiers fill up the trench surrounding Kyat with faggots and other material. This done, a general assault was ordered which succeeded despite a valorous defense. Most of the adult males were slain and their women and children enslaved. On the next day, in an excess of magnanimity, Timur freed the captives.

Timur pressed on relentlessly into the land, ordering his troops to make inroads on all sides. At length Hussein Sufi, who in despair had shut himself up in Urgench, decided to ask for pardon and quarter. At this time Timur's old ally Keikosrau, who now was jealous of the former's swift rise to power, persuaded Hussein Sufi to continue his resistance, promising to desert Timur at an opportune time and to aid Hussein with his (Keikosrau's) troops. Hussein, who foolishly believed the promises of the wily Keikosrau, ranged his army for battle two leagues from his capital. His forces were quickly overrun by the impetuous assault of Timur's troops; Keikosrau defaulted on his promise of assistance to Hussein Sufi, who retired to his capital with the tattered remnants of his forces and soon died.

Hussein's brother, Yusuf Sufi, succeeded as ruler and sued for peace. Timur agreed, on condition that Yusuf's niece Sevin Bey, or Khan-zada, who was a great beauty, be given in marriage to his son Jehangir. This proposal was accepted, and Timur withdrew, leaving the northern part of Khorezm to Yusuf Sufi, while annexing the southern portion for himself. On arriving home Timur ordered that Keikosrau be arrested and tried. The court, primed for a conviction, bound the hapless schemer over to Emir Hussein's former officers to be executed. Thus Timur could now plume himself on having punished, though belatedly, one of the men who had killed Emir Hussein despite his safe-conduct guarantee.

That winter Timur learned that Yusuf Sufi had laid waste Kyat and its environs in southern Khorezm. The approach of Timur's punitive expedition quickly caused Yusuf to mend his conduct and to fulfill all the terms of the peace treaty, including the delivery of the lovely Khanzada to Timur's court. In the spring of 1373 the maiden was brought to Samarkand where she and Jehangir were united in marriage.

During the two years that followed Timur was preoccupied with military campaigns on other fronts. In 1375 Yusuf Sufi profited from this distraction to reoccupy southern Khorezm. Later that spring Timur again moved against the rump Khorezmian state, only to cut the campaign short upon news of a revolt back home by two of his lieutenants. Early in 1379 while Timur was away making war against the White Horde, Yusuf Sufi led a force into Transoxiana and ravaged the countryside around Samarkand. Timur decided to put an end to this dangerous neighbor. Accordingly, that same spring he assembled an army and invested the city of Urgench. His men prepared elaborate entrenchments; meanwhile other elements of his army were allowed carte blanche in the countryside round about, where they "ravished the handsomest virgins of the country" (Sharaf ad-Din), and carried off many slaves and animals.

From his besieged capital Yusuf Sufi had the audacity to write a mocking letter to his opponent. Why, he asked, should so many good Muslims die in further struggle when the two of them could settle the quarrel easily with a duel. "Let the victor," he continued, "be the one whose hands are red with blood dropping from his saber." He concluded by giving the time and place of the proposed combat.

Timur, rejecting his entourage's arguments that this was a trick, accepted the challenge. Putting on his armor, he painfully mounted his horse. Arriving before the great gate of Urgench, he shouted in his stentorian voice to those inside: "Tell your master Yusuf Sufi that I am here!" Timur then waited, an easy target for the numerous enemy archers who were, however, too flabbergasted by this bravado to shoot. His opponent did not appear. The challenger was nothing more than a blowhard! Timur finally returned to his own lines. This gesture, superb and yet foolhardy, illustrates another side of Timur's multifaceted personality—a love of theatricality and grandstand play, a desire to stun and dazzle others by his swank.[7]

Timur now began the siege in earnest. Battering rams and ballistas were unlimbered and soon created such devastation that Yusuf Sufi had to leave his palace for a safer refuge. The investment lasted more than three months. Yusuf died before the city was taken by storm, just as Timur had predicted after the incident of the duel. At once there broke out a struggle between two factions, the one advocating coming to terms with Timur, and the other clamoring for resistance to the bitter end. Although Khadzhi-Lak, leader of the appeasers, lost out and had to flee to Timur for refuge, this schism in the ranks of the ruling circles greatly aided Timur in taking the city.

The capture of Urgench in late October of 1379 was accompanied by the usual excesses. The rich state treasury was seized; so was the wealth of the private citizens. The booty included gold, silver, weapons, textiles, horses and cattle as well as slaves. Many of the city dwellers were put to death. "All the Cheriffs,* doctors and learned men were sent to the city of Kech, as also the tradesmen, together with a number of women and children."[8] Timur's transportation of these people to Kesh rather than to Samarkand demonstrated his ambitious plans for his native city. It had formerly held a reputation as a center of Islamic learning; thus, sending holy men to Kesh was not unusual. Around March of 1380 Timur, "charmed with the beauty of this city, the purity of the air in its plains, the deliciousness of its gardens, and the goodness of the waters made it his ordinary residence in summer, and declar'd it the second seat of his empire."[9] Timur ordered that new walls be raised around the "verdant city." He also built a magnificent palace called Ak Sarai (literally "White Palace") "because the walls of it were exceeding white and very high," so that the green city now had a white palace. The artisans enslaved during the Khorezmian campaign participated in this work. Henceforth the city bore the honorary name of "Dome of knowledge and culture." The portals of the palace of Ak Sarai with their grandiose pylons and the ruins of the mausoleum of Jehangir, Timur's oldest son, may still be seen today.

The definitive annexation of Urgench and of southern Khorezm brought Timur full mastery over Transoxiana.

During the 1370s Timur became increasingly involved in the affairs of the Golden and White Hordes. Since any strong and hostile state to the north posed a threat, he kept abreast of developments in these two states in order to exploit any opportunity that promised to redound to his advantage.

Originally, in the thirteenth century, the Golden Horde and the White Horde (Ak Orda) formed two segments of the Ulus of Juchi. Military organization partly accounted for this division. In wartime the White Horde furnished the troops of the right wing; the Golden Horde, the troops of the left wing. At first the two hordes shared the same khan. Early in the fourteenth century, the White Horde somehow managed to keep itself aloof from the succession struggle which broke out after the death of khan Mangu-Timur (1282) and elected its own khan, named Sasy-Buka (1291-1310). He was descended from Orda, eldest

---

*Cheriffs = Sharifs, descendants of the Prophet Muhammad, more particularly through his grandson Hasan, son of Ali.

son of Juchi. The White Horde, with its capital at Sygnakh near Kyzl Orda, included most of the Syr Darya basin and the steppes to the northeast, an area extending from the Sea of Aral to the Ishim and Sary-su rivers in present-day northern Kazakhstan.

The death of Janibeg, khan of the Golden Horde, in 1357, brought fresh tumult to that state. In the early 1360s Khorezm asserted its independence while Lithuania seized lands in the Dnieper river basin. During both the 1360s and 1370s a tuman leader named Mamai became factual ruler of the western part of the Golden Horde. Since he was not a descendant of Chingis Khan he let puppet khans exercise nominal authority. In Russia he continued the policy of playing off the various Russian princes against each other. Descrying in Muscovy's growing strength his greatest threat, he supported the Lithuanian Grand Prince as well as the Grand Prince of Tver and other Russian opponents of Muscovy. Mamai's possessions comprehended the lands to the west of the lower Volga, including the Crimea and the north Caucasus.

In the eastern section of the Golden Horde to the east of the Volga, a struggle broke out among the descendants of Batu and Orda, Juchi's two sons, which lasted through the 1360s and 1370s. None of the contenders could establish his ascendancy permanently, however, and from 1360 to 1380 twenty-five different khans sat successively on the great throne at New Sarai. Significantly, four of these came from the White Horde.

The growing interposition of the White Horde in the affairs of the Golden Horde went *pari passu* with a waxing of its economic and political might. Major credit for transforming this formerly backward part of the Ulus of Juchi into a state of some consequence belongs to Urus Khan, a descendant of Orda. His vaulting ambitions now included nothing less than the reunification of the entire Ulus of Juchi. This could ultimately threaten Transoxiana. Urus Khan had, moreover, given aid and comfort to Timur's enemies. In 1376/77, for example, the emirs Adil Shah and Sari-Buga took refuge with him after sparking an unsuccessful revolt against Timur.[10] But Timur, remembering that it had taken him four campaigns to gain mastery over Khorezm, preferred subduing Urus Khan by proxy through a client Juchid prince. An opportunity soon presented itself: in 1376 Toktamish, a White Horde princeling, fled from Urus Khan and sought asylum with Timur.

Urus Khan had killed Toktamish's father Tuli-Khodja, ruler of Mangishlak on the eastern coast of the Caspian Sea and an emir of the White Horde, because he had refused to participate in a campaign against the

Golden Horde. According to one source, Urus Khan and Tuli-Khodja were brothers, both descendants of Orda, Juchi's oldest son.[11] In any event, Toktamish was an authentic Juchid prince with a burning desire to avenge himself on Urus Khan. According to one source (Anonymous Iskender), while still a minor Toktamish had "once or twice fled from the Horde and again returned there and, since he still had not attained majority, he was pardoned."[12]

Toktamish, upon his arrival in Samarkand, was warmly received. Timur called him his "son," i.e., vassal, and assigned him Otrar, Syg-nakh, Sauran (Sabran) and other towns on the northern banks of the Syr Darya opposite the White Horde steppe. In Sauran he was proclaimed khan.

Toktamish, however, proved to be a weak reed. Soon after his elevation in Sauran, he was attacked by Kutlugh-Buga, son of Urus Khan. Though Kutlugh-Buga was killed in a battle near Sauran, Toktamish was defeated. He fled to Timur who re-equipped him. But now Tokhta-Kiya, Urus Khan's oldest son, anxious to avenge his brother's death, fielded an army as numerous as "pissmires and grasshoppers" (Sharaf ad-Din)—four times as large as the forces of Toktamish. The latter was again put to flight and entered "into a wood naked and wounded."

Despite Urus Khan's successes, some of his emirs apparently began to sense that Toktamish, who enjoyed Timur's unflinching support, would ultimately prevail. An earnest of this was the defection to Tok-tamish of Edigei, an emir of the Mangit tribe of the White Horde and son of Baltychka, senior emir at the court of Urus Khan. Thus far both Urus and Timur had acted against each other at second remove. The new defector brought news that Urus Khan was making preparations to confront Timur directly. Soon after Timur received an ultimatum from Urus Khan in which the latter complained about his son's death during the first battle with Toktamish and demanded the extradition of Tok-tamish as his son's "murderer" under threat of war. Timur's answer was laconic and to the point: he had given Toktamish asylum and would not surrender him; as for war, he was ready for it.

Hostilities began in the winter of 1377. Timur did not wait for the enemy's attack; with a large army he entered the district of Sauran, where he halted near Urus Khan's camp. Both sides sustained heavy losses of human and animal life in an unexpected snow-and-sleet storm which was followed by severe cold. After a series of desultory and inconclusive scrimmages Timur routed his opponent in an attack. Unfortunately for Timur, his losses, which totaled ten to fifteen thousand horses and the better part of his army, prevented him from pressing his advantage and winning a decisive victory. He returned to Samarkand to regroup his battered forces. A fortnight later he managed to defeat Urus Khan in a surprise attack. Both Urus and his oldest son Tokhta-Kiya died soon afterwards.

Once again Timur established Toktamish as khan in Sygnakh. Before leaving for Samarkand, he presented his protégé with a fine stallion, observing that: "This horse will serve you on several occasions: for you may easily overtake the enemy when you pursue him; and no one will be able to overtake you if you are obliged to fly" (Sharaf ad-Din).

Timur's forehandedness was not misplaced. In 1378/79 Timur-Malek Aglen, another son of Urus, claimed the title of khan and took the field against Toktamish. Once more Toktamish was worsted in battle and, alone among his followers, was able to outdistance his pursuers with Timur's horse. As for Timur-Malek, he soon lost interest in governmental affairs and sank into drunkenness and debauchery, an example followed by his court.

Through his spies, Timur soon heard about this parlous state of affairs. In the winter of 1379 Toktamish again set forth with a large army. He was accompanied by a retinue of Timur's emirs who were under strict orders to re-install him on the throne of Sygnakh. Meanwhile Timur-Malek was loitering at Karatal, to the south of Sygnakh. As the invading army drew nearer, most of his chief emirs defected to Toktamish. Even Timur-Malek's closest relatives advised capitulation. Timur-Malek would have none of this; he executed a senior commander suspected of secret contacts with Toktamish and warned that the same fate awaited defeatists.

Presently Toktamish attacked him near the Karabak river. Despite a stubborn defense Timur-Malek was defeated and captured, together with his chief emir Baltychka, the father of Edigei. Timur-Malek was immediately executed; Baltychka was invited to join Toktamish's service. Faithful unto death, he refused, and so shared his master's fate.

Using Sygnakh as his base of operations, Toktamish now brought all the territory of the White Horde under his sway. Judging by numismatic evidence,[13] Timur at this time also transferred the province of Khorezm to him as a fief. Though Khorezm had suffered catastrophically from Chingis Khan's invasion, it had made a good recovery. Urgench, the chief city, again became a populous trade center. Khorezm played an outstanding role in the extensive international trade between the West and the Orient.

Earlier, as noted, Timur assigned Toktamish various cities in the Syr Darya basin. This area was called Turkistan in the 14th-16th centuries. The Syr Darya cities were of great importance, above all for economic reasons.[14] They served as contact points between the nomads of the north and the sedentary agricultural districts of Central Asia which sent goods in trade. The cities were also production centers in their own right. They exchanged the wool and hides of the nomads for articles made in their own shops (ceramics, metal objects, etc.) and locally grown fruits and vegetables. Quite naturally, both the rulers of the Golden Horde and of Transoxiana sought to gain control of these Syr Darya cities.

Security also figured into Timur's calculations. He sought to convert the Turkistan area into a bastion protecting Transoxiana from the Golden Horde. It is a measure of Timur's confidence in Toktamish that he assigned to him areas of such prime strategic and commercial importance and left their defenses intact. Ordinarily Timur destroyed the defensive installations of his vassals. His confidence that Toktamish would do his bidding proved to be a major blunder; the latter would ultimately turn on his benefactor. Despite his ragged beginnings as a military commander, Toktamish was to prove, by all odds, the deadliest opponent Timur faced in his very long military career. Clavijo (the Spanish envoy) was told while in Samarkand that Timur rated his victory over Toktamish a greater one than the battle of Ankara and that Timur regarded Toktamish as a far more redoubtable foe than that great scourge of Christendom, the Ottoman Sultan Bayazid I Yildirim. Our sources, by the way, characterize Toktamish as a just, vigorous and handsome ruler.

Russia, except for the western areas in the hands of Lithuania, still lay under the Mongol yoke imposed by Chingis Khan's successors. During the decay in authority in the Golden Horde in the 1360s and 1370s, however, the Russian princes had strengthened themselves. In 1371, as an indication of their new feelings of power and independence, the Russian princes had refused to pay tribute to Mamai, ruler of the Golden Horde possessions in the west; thus their subjection to him became a mere formality. In 1376 Russian forces led by Dmitri Ivanovich, Grand Prince of Muscovy, managed to seize and hold for a time the Great Bulgar state in the Volga-Kama region, a vassal state of the Golden Horde of great commercial importance. In 1378 Russian forces even won a victory over the Mongols near the Vozh river, an affluent of the Oka. This achievement, though of only local importance, dealt a hard blow to the mystique that Mongols always won when they fought

Russians. Mamai's response was to form an alliance with Yagailo, grand duke of Lithuania, and to launch a great plundering expedition into Russia in the summer of 1380. The expedition was designed to weaken the country and to force the Russian princes to resume paying tribute. A coalition of Russian princes, led by Dmitri Ivanovich of Moscow, administered a crushing defeat to the forces of Mamai in the famous battle of Kulikovo (1380) [15] on the banks of the Oka near the upper reaches of the Don. Mamai was defeated before Yagailo of Lithuania and Oleg of Riazan could join him with their forces.

Toktamish meanwhile had apparently captured New Sarai, Mamai's capital, in the spring of 1380, since after the battle of Kulikovo Mamai fled to the Crimea rather than to the lower Volga. Here he regrouped the badly shattered remnants of his legions and set out to confront his new opponent Toktamish. This second battle was fought on the Kolmak river, an affluent of the Vorskla.[16] Mamai, again defeated, drew back into the Crimea. Convinced by now that Mamai's bright flame was finally guttering out, the Mongol princes and mirzas who had been supporting him now executed a lemming-like rush over to the side of Toktamish. The hapless Mamai was now left to the tender mercies of the Genoese at Caffa (Feodosiya), who were eager to avenge themselves on him for his seizure of eighteen of their villages back in 1365. After hard bargaining, the Genoese concluded an agreement with Toktamish in the fall of 1380 stipulating: the retrocession of these villages in return for handing over Mamai to Toktamish, a treaty of friendship and alliance with the latter, and a promise by the Genoese to pay taxes "according to former custom." It is almost superfluous to add that Mamai soon met his end at Toktamish's hands.

Toktamish, now ruler of both the White and Golden Hordes, proceeded with the enterprise which Mamai had begun: namely, restoring the Ulus of Juchi to the prestige it had enjoyed during the halcyon days of Uzbek Khan (1312-1342) and of Janibeg (1342-1357), when the Golden Horde was blossoming forth as one of the mightiest states of medieval times. First came the conquest of the Bulgars of the Volga-Kama region; this also took place apparently in the fall of 1380. Then in 1381 Toktamish's envoys appeared at the courts of the various Russian princes, demanding that they present themselves forthwith before the new khan. The matter was put thus: Dmitri and his allies did not defeat the Horde, but rather the *temnik* Mamai, enemy of Toktamish himself, and with the coming to power of the "legal" khan it behooved the Russian princes to appear before him with their arrears in

tribute. Their negative response, especially the refusal of Dmitri Ivanovich of Moscow, spurred Toktamish into making preparations for a
mammoth invasion of Russia. The Mongol feudal aristocracy, shaken by
the defeat at Kulikovo,[17] even decided for a time to subject itself to
Toktamish and to cease the infighting which even Mamai had been unable completely to suppress.

Kulikovo did prefigure eventual unification of Russia under the
leadership of Moscow—and not of Tver, its principal rival for leadership
—and the breaking of the Tatar hold. These future lineaments of history were, however, shrouded from view in the fateful year 1382. By defeating Mamai the Muscovites and their allies helped raise up a far more
dangerous foe—Toktamish. The latter now proceeded to carry out
Mamai's project of reimposing the Mongol or Tatar yoke. Just how he
did this will be alluded to later since it would bear an important influence on the course of Timur's campaign of 1395 into Russia. Suffice it
to say at this point that Moscow and other Russian cities were sacked
in that same year of 1382. The Russian princes, including Dmitri Ivanovich, hastened to make their submission to Toktamish. All northeastern
Russia now lay prostrate at his feet. Southeastern and northwestern
Russia were still controlled by the Grand Duke of Lithuania; however,
he was now paying tribute to Toktamish for those lands where Tatar
tribute collectors had once resided.

Toktamish was now at his meridian power. He was, however, behold-
en to Timur for his successes, as he and his court circle well knew.
Three influential emirs, Urluk-Timur, Ak-Buga and the senior emir Ali-
Bek, originally members of the White Horde and favoring the economic
interests of Central Asia, did what they could to persuade their master
to nurture his friendship with Timur. At first Toktamish took their
advice. Then it happened that Urluk-Timur and Ak-Buga died, and Toktamish brought into the circle of his intimates certain men interested in
a western orientation and in a rupture with Timur. Singled out are the
emir Kazanchia and other "troublemakers" belonging to the Mangit
clan. These unnamed persons were probably Edigei and his older brother Isa-Bek. Edigei, who was married to Toktamish's daughter, was the
leader of the emirs of the army's left wing.[18] Toktamish, whose self-
confidence grew apace, listened more and more to their vehement coun-
sellings and began to revert in his policies to the old traditions of the
Ulus of Juchi which stressed opposition to the Chagatai ulus. These
growing differences between Timur and his ungrateful former protégé
would not lead to an actual break, however, for several more years.

Timur's third great involvement in the 1370s was with the Mogols, his neighbors to the east. The series of campaigns he directed against Mogolistan are not nearly as well documented as those into India, Persia and the Ottoman state. Despite their indeterminate results, they were fully as remarkable as any of the latter and provided perhaps an even greater demonstration of Timur's military talents. In these maneuvers he was operating in a very difficult terrain against an elusive enemy, skilled in enticing the foe ever onwards and then springing from ambush in the many passes that seam this wild, sere and desolate mountainous area. The fighting qualities of the Mogols yielded in nothing to those of Timur's soldiers. They were, indeed, a kindred people.

Around 1366 Qamar ad-Din, a Mogol lord, killed Ilyas Khodja because his father had not appointed him *Ulus-begi,* a high official position. Ilyas Khodja's young brother Khizr Khodja fled from Kashgar to the Pamir region to await better times. Although Qamar ad-Din had killed Timur's enemy, this did not bring him peace. Timur was determined to put an end to the periodic incursions into Transoxiana by the Mogols, whoever their ruler happened to be. In 1370 he mounted the first of a series of campaigns against Qamar ad-Din, now ruler of Mogolistan despite his non-Chingisid pedigree. Timur deputed the conduct of this first campaign to his emirs. After some successes near present-day Alma-Ata they made peace with the enemy and withdrew. Timur, nettled because he thought the peace terms too lenient, disowned the treaty and personally led an army out from Tashkent. Marching in a northeasterly direction to Talas (now Dzhambul) he defeated or put to flight all who barred his way. The slippery Qamar ad-Din, however, managed to elude his grasp.

During the winter of 1374/75 Timur undertook a third campaign against Qamar. At first the cold, the rain and the snow caused so many of his horses to perish that he had to return to Samarkand and wait there until the weather improved. Once more on his way, Timur made straight for his foe, who kept luring him on into more and more inaccessible regions in the mountains to the northwest of Issyk-kul. He crossed three defiles in this forbidding territory and three great rivers. The enemy was pursued and defeated wherever encountered and the countryside was harried. Inhabitants of districts which submitted voluntarily were pardoned; their weapons were collected and sent to Samarkand. In one of the palaces of Qamar ad-Din that he ransacked and razed, Timur had the good fortune to capture the wife and daughter of his enemy. He married the daughter, Dilshad-agha, and added her to his out-sized harem. In revenge, Qamar attacked the Ferghana region in Timur's territory and sacked the city of Andijan. Timur hastened to the relief of Ferghana; the enemy retreated as he approached, enticing him onwards into the mountains of the mid-T'ien Shan range. Here Qamar cunningly prepared another ambush for him. As luck would have it, Timur had only two hundred men with him; he had sent off the main body of his force, five thousand soldiers, to pursue the enemy in another direction. Suddenly he found himself faced with two thousand horsemen. After fierce fighting he managed to extricate his small force from this trap, setting his men an example of personal bravery by plunging into the midst of the enemy ranks "with his lance, war-club, sabre and net" (Sharaf ad-Din).

In the next engagement Timur routed the enemy but again Qamar ad-Din slipped through his fingers. At this point Timur had a premonition that his oldest son Jehangir had died at the age of twenty. When he returned to Samarkand the sad fact was confirmed. Jehangir left two sons born of different wives: Mirza Muhammad-Sultan and Pir-Muhammad, the latter born forty days after the death of his father.

In 1376-77 Timur waged a fifth campaign against Qamar ad-Din. The two forces clashed in a battle to the west of Issyk-kul. Qamar was once more defeated but somehow avoided capture, though pursued for some distance. Timur ravaged the countryside, made the people his subjects, and returned home.

By the year 1383 the tranquillity of Timur's eastern marches was again disturbed by Mogol depredations. Timur's men succeeded in killing and enslaving a number of the enemy, and penetrated as far as Issyk-kul. Further operations would be necessary later on; Timur was presently involved in the conquest of Greater Iran.

CHAPTER IV
Iran — First Foray

Timur's campaigns against Khorezm, his own mutinous emirs, the Golden Horde and the Mogols were occasioned by the need to consolidate his rule over Transoxiana and to secure his borders from attack. These campaigns were against Turco-Mongol peoples. The campaigns into Iran, which then included roughly the area between the Tigris and the Oxus as well as Afghanistan, were pre-eminently against Persian-speaking peoples and were pure campaigns of plunder and conquest. Timurid historians quote the same words attributed earlier to Alexander the Great and to Chingis Khan, namely that it was not fit and proper "that the habitable world should be governed by two kings. . . . As there is but one God, there ought to be but one king." The absence of a strong, unified state in Iran or even of a common peril would facilitate the work of Timur. The country was, moreover, distracted by the constant quarreling and warfare which went on among its diverse rulers whose possessions lacked definite borders.

Plans for invading Iran had been maturing in Timur's mind for several years. He already had some firsthand knowledge of eastern Iran, having, as will be recalled, spent some time there as an adventurer in the early 1360s. He now took steps to obtain more exact knowledge concerning the state of affairs in Iran as a whole. In 1375 Sayf al-Din Barlas, one of his principal emirs, started out on the hadj or pilgrimage to the holy cities of Mecca and Medina. Ostensibly the death of Jehangir, Timur's oldest son, had so dispirited him that he "became averse to all worldly things,"[1] and wanted to spend the rest of his life in these two holiest of Muslim cities. In 1379, however, "hadji" Sayf ad-Din Barlas returned and briefed Timur not about Mecca and Medina but about the "state of the kingdom of Iran. . .the governors of whom acted like absolute sovereigns."[2] The hadj of Sayf ad-Din Barlas, then, cloaked an extensive intelligence mission.

Four large kingdoms and a cluster of bagatelle principalities and statelets had emerged out of the collapse of Mongol Hulagid or Il-

Khanid rule in Iran after the death of Abu Said in 1336. The eastern
part of Iran contained two of the four large kingdoms. One of these was
the Kart state ruled by Ghiyas ad-Din Pir Ali. The Kart dynasty's beginnings may be traced back to 1245. At first the Kart state was a vassal
dependency of the Il-Khanids but with the end of their rule it attained
independence. Muizz ad-Din (1331-70), Ghiyas ad-Din Pir Ali's predecessor, had expanded his possessions up to the Murgab river, so that
they included almost all of eastern Khurasan as well as part of Afghanistan. The Karts ruled their state from Herat, a very ancient Afghan city
located some seventy miles from the present Soviet and Iranian frontiers, and an important commercial center situated on the overland
routes linking the Mediterranean with India and China. Builders of
many mosques and other buildings, the Karts also gave much encourage-
ment to literature and the other arts. They were Afghan Sunnites and
were at daggers drawn with their other principal neighbor in northeast
Iran, the Serbedars, Persian Shiites by and large, with their capital at
Sebzevar. The Serbedar state has been described earlier in connection
with the 1365 popular movement in Samarkand. The Serbedar state
was the weakest of the four major kingdoms in Iran, and the Kart kingdom the second weakest.

Timur, in bringing the Kart state under submission, first resorted to
diplomacy. During the winter of 1379/80 he sent a messenger to Ghiyas
ad-Din Pir Ali, the Kart sovereign, summoning him to a kurultai which
he had scheduled for the spring of 1381. Timur, in effect, was asking
for Ghiyas ad-Din's submission. The latter, however, played for time by
asking that Hadji Sayf ad-din Barlas be sent to him so that the Hadji
might accompany him. Though Timur complied with this request,
Ghiyas ad-Din stalled for more time, ostensibly to prepare himself for
the long journey. Meanwhile, he hurriedly prepared the city for a siege
by storing victuals and other necessaries and by strengthening its fortifications. He supplemented the wall surrounding the old city with
another one two miles in girth. This encompassed the city's suburbs and
gardens. The Hadji, who soon saw through this sham, hurried back to
Samarkand.

Timur lost no time in getting military operations under way. He appointed his fourten year old son Mirza[3] Miranshah governor of Khurasan and ordered him to begin the conquest, for which he gave him an
army and a suite of emirs. By the end of the winter of 1380/1381
Miranshah and his forces had seized Balkh and other towns. Then in the
spring of 1381 Timur followed with an army. On reaching Andkhui he

visited a half-mad holy man or dervish. The latter, "in an enthusiastik fit,"[4] threw a breast of mutton at Timur, which the latter interpreted as an augury of victory, since Khurasan had "always been called the breast or middle of the inhabited world."[5] Muslims take an indulgent view of the insane, believing that Allah has imparted to them a special knowledge of his ways.

Timur then learned that in a town called Khawaf there lived a Muslim holy man whose wisdom, brilliance of discourse and piety were extraordinary. His name was Shaykh Zayn ad-Din Abu Bakr. Timur hastened to his side. Informed that Timur had come to see him to obtain his blessing, the old man made no sign. Even when Timur approached him on foot the holy man remained in meditation on his carpet. When at length Timur reached him the shaykh arose, while Timur bowed. The shaykh thereupon placed his hands on Timur's back. Timur later related: "If the old man had not quickly removed his hand from my back, I should have thought it was broken; and I truly thought that the sky had fallen on the earth, and that I was to be broken between the two with a mighty breaking."[6]

In their subsequent conversation Timur asked the shaykh: "Venerable master! Do you teach nothing to your kings concerning justice and equity and warn them not to turn to violence and in tyranny?" The shaykh replied that he did just this, but that the kings whom he had visited did not allow themselves to be taught, adding "and so we have appointed you Lord over them." Delighted with this blessing, Timur later declared: "I am Lord of the World by the Lord of the Kaaba."[7] The Kaaba, which houses the sacred black rock in Mecca, is the chief objective of the hadj.

The visit with the holy man over, Timur continued on his campaign. The governor of one town who offered his submission had his province spared the ravages of Timur's men. Fushanj, south of Herat, offered Timur his first real obstacle. This was a strongly fortified town protected by a deep ditch full of water. After three days of preparation the attackers crossed the moat on planks and rafts and took the town with the first assault. Timur, to stimulate his men, circulated among them without wearing his armor. Though he was hit by two arrows, the wounds were not serious.

Herat was one of the most massively fortified cities in Khurasan. To help take it, Timur had recourse to psychological warfare. The Kart ruler Ghiyas ad-Din's personal qualities should have brought him loyal and unwavering support from his subjects. Though not very firm in character, he was a brave man who had always attended to their welfare. Timur, however, sapped the will of the Heratis to resist by promising to safeguard their lives and property in return for their neutrality during the siege. After the failure of the first sally led by Ghiyas ad-Din's garrison of rough Afghan tribesmen from the province of Ghor, the populace refused to oppose a second attack, or even to repair the breaches in their defenses made by the attackers.

Timurid historians, depicting Ghiyas ad-Din as a pleasure-sotted monarch, claim that in taking over the city of Herat Timur was only acceding to the wishes of its inhabitants for good government. As one of them put it: "Constantly playing with the perfumed curls of beautiful women, kissing their sweet lips, contemplating the movement of cups filled with wine. . .he did not understand that in the pleasures of the palace of the world there are no roses without thorns and wine without drunkenness." Consequently, "The great people of Herat brought complaint against Ghiyas ad-Din and begged that His Highness throw the shadow of his benevolence over this possession."[8]

Abandoned by his subjects who felt that they could sup with the devil, and supported only by his Afghan tribesmen, Ghiyas ad-Din had no recourse but to submit to Timur. Though he was pardoned and appointed vassal governor, Timur soon revealed the worthlessness of his promises to the inhabitants. They were forced to pay a heavy tribute while the head of the Ulema and two hundred notables were deported to Kesh. Timur also sent the city gates, celebrated for their artistic embellishment, to Kesh where they were installed in the palace of Ak Sarai. The vast state treasure laid up over a period of two centuries was seized. Though the famous citadel of Ikhtiya ad-Din was left standing, both sets of city walls were razed, apparently out of Timur's fear that the heavy tribute imposed upon the badly duped Heratis might incite them to revolt. Two years later (1383) these fears were amply justified when the Heratis, joined by Ghor tribesmen, rose in futile rebellion. Miranshah drowned the rebellion in blood and as an object lesson, erected a high tower with the heads of the slain. Those left alive paid a ransom even more extortionate than the one of 1381. Timur, learning of the revolt, ordered the execution of Ghiyas ad-Din, his brother and his grandson. These had earlier been sent to Samarkand as hostages for the good behavior of the Heratis. The Kart possessions were assigned to Miranshah. In 1389 at a banquet he playfully cut off the head of the last representative of the Kart dynasty, an action which he later put down to an excess of alcohol.

Timur is associated with the construction of towers of human heads. It was Miranshah who introduced him to this grisly custom in suppressing the 1383 Herati rebellion. He, in turn, was inspired by Malek Hussein Kart, an earlier Herati ruler, who in 1340 had raised two minarets of the heads of his slain enemies. Under Timur the erection of such towers enjoyed a great vogue. They were positioned near the approaches to great cities, to certain fortresses and on the grazing lands of seditious nomad tribes. We may gain some idea of their dimensions from those erected at Aleppo later, which measured ten cubits high, twenty in circumference and six in diameter, giving them a squat appearance. The heads, to make them more expressive, were cemented into these constructions in such a way that their faces looked out at passers-by. Their purpose was to serve as a warning of the wrath that would descend on those who contemplated rebellion.[9] These warning beacons served their purpose at night as well as by day, for the decaying organic matter gave off fire.[10]

After taking Herat, Timur pushed on to complete the conquest of eastern Iran and its dependencies, the bulk of which he conquered by the mid-1380s. Almost contemporaneously with the fall of Herat, Timur acquired Sebzevar and the rest of the Serbedar state without any fighting. It so happened that Imam Ali Muayyid, his state weakened by civil war, found himself besieged in his capital by Emir Wali of Mazanderan, who had decided to put an end to the Serbedar state once and for all. In desperate straits after a four months' siege, Ali turned to Timur for aid in a desperate bid to preserve his state. Timur, who planned to annex the Serbedar state himself, seized upon this petition to intervene. At his approach Emir Wali scampered off, while Timur made a triumphal entry into Sebzevar. Ali hastened to greet him and to declare himself his vassal. Ali was notorious as a Shiite. When queried about this, he replied that the ruler of a region determined its religion, i.e., now that Timur was the suzerain, Sunnism would prevail.[11] Timur, seemingly satisfied, acknowledged Ali as sovereign. His troops, however, occupied the Serbedar state, while Ali himself was forced to join Timur's court. In 1386, considering Ali's usefulness to be at an end, Timur had him executed without any provocation on Ali's part.[12]

The cities of Nishapur and Tus also submitted peacefully. Tus is now known as Meshed which means "place of burial," since a list of the illustrious men buried there reads like an Islamic *Who's Who*. Even today Meshed attracts shoals of Muslim pilgrims from afar. The tombs include that of the Abbasid general Abu Muslim who allegedly caused the death of 600,000 persons while overthrowing the Umayyad Caliphate around 750 A.D. Timur visited only his grave, where he prayed that this monster of cruelty might aid him from the grave in his subsequent military operations.

The area's fortresses gave Timur much difficulty and each had to be taken by a siege in form. These included Shaburkan, Kabush "and the one situated between Balkh and Kelat called Kahkaha, meaning 'giggling,' since it repulsed all efforts of its enemies to capture it with laughter and giggling."[13]

Timur, during these operations, gave further proofs of bestiality which would have done Abu Muslim proud. In 1383 he crushed a revolt in Sebzevar. "There were near two thousand slaves taken, who were pil'd alive one upon the other with mortar and brick, so that these miserable wretches might serve as a monument to deter others from revolting."[14] Similar treatment was meted out to the inhabitants of Sistan. At Zarendj, the capital, a general massacre of the population included "both women and children, from persons of a hundred years old, to infants in the cradle."[15] Everything of value was carried away, down to the nails in the doors and walls. The rest was burned. The King of Sistan and his top officials were sent as hostages to Samarkand.

Timur's rage against Sistan, where he had been earlier maimed and crippled for life, was even directed against the land. The canal system and the dam over the Hilmand river were destroyed. In 1936 archeologists discovered only sand dunes.

The rebellions which confronted Timur in Iran in 1383 were much more dangerous than any of his initial opponents. This explains in part the bestial manner with which they were suppressed. With Sistan subdued, Timur moved eastward into Afghanistan where, south of Kandahar, he put to the sword the people who had once owed him allegiance. Then on to Kandahar, where his arrival was attended by fresh atrocities.

The conqueror, after repairing to Samarkand for three months of needed rest from his butcheries, returned to Iran. His objective was Mazanderan, which lies at the southern shore of the Caspian Sea. The dense forests which protect it from the east obliged Timur's men to use axes to cut a passage. The going was toilsome—under two miles a day. Emir Wali, the local ruler, offered stubborn resistance. He even attacked Timur's camp at night. Timur, however, had not only strongly entrenched his camp but had positioned thirty picked companies in ambush. During the ensuing fighting Emir Wali's men were repulsed. In retreating they fell into pits containing embedded stakes which the emir himself had dug in the roads. Astarabad, his capital, was destroyed by Timur's warriors who spared neither "old men, women or children, or even sucking infants."[16] Emir Wali managed to flee westward. Timur annexed the eastern tip of Mazanderan.

Later in the spring of 1384 Timur took his first nibble at the Jelair kingdom when he marched westward and took Sultaniya, one-time capital of the Il-Khans, by surprise. The city was pillaged, though the mausoleum of the Il-Khanid ruler Uldjaitu was spared. The Jelairids, whose kingdom comprehended northwest Iran, some of eastern Anatolia and Syria and much of Iraq, were descendants of the Mongol Jelair clan which had imposed control after the collapse of Il-Khanid rule. Sultan Ahmed Jelair ibn Oweis, the current ruler, had attained his position by dint of a murderous elimination bout with his brothers. He was the only one of the four major rulers of Iran who managed to outlast Timur. Although put to flight repeatedly, he always contrived to return. Cruel, treacherous and brave, he was withal a generous and appreciative patron of the arts and of learning.

Timur, for the nonce, postponed further operations against Sultan Ahmed. His return home along the southern shore of the Caspian Sea took him through Amol and Sari, the rulers of which hurriedly acknowledged his overlordship. Timur was now master of Transoxiana, Khurasan, Sistan, Afghanistan, easternmost Mazanderan and Sultaniya. His compulsive restlessness abated, so that the bulk of 1385 was devoted to distraction and pleasure. The summer was spent at Samarkand "in the pleasures of the season" and the winter of 1385/86 at Zindger-sarai "in the delights of conversation and entertainment" (Sharaf ad-Din). During that winter an event occurred which foreshadowed the impending rupture between Timur and his old protégé Toktamish. Early in 1386 Toktamish led almost 90,000 marauders through the Caucasus by way of Derbent. Devastating Shirvan, he then continued southwards to Tabriz. Upon arrival he found that the inhabitants of this populous city had barricaded all approaches and, arms in hand, were prepared to resist fiercely. For eight days his men probed the city's defense perimeter looking in vain for some weak point. Then Toktamish turned to guile. He promised to lift the siege upon payment of a large ransom. The townspeople remitted a huge sum of gold to him. Toktamish, treacherously breaking his pledged word, suddenly threw his army into the city, catching the population off guard.[17] For ten days his men, who "were for the most part infidels" (Sharaf ad-Din),[18] gave vent to their lust for looting, raping and killing. Nakhichevan, Maraga, Marand, Sultaniya and other nearby cities received similar treatment. According to one contemporary source, 200,000 persons were carried off into slavery. Then, before the winter was out, Toktamish withdrew his army northward.

On learning of this, Timur affected outrage over the barbarous treatment accorded to Muslims by this all but heathen force. The real cause of Timur's anger, however, was that he regarded these cities as lying in the penumbra of his domains and earmarked for future pillage and annexation; Toktamish clearly had poached on Timur's preserve. This depredation allowed Timur to legitimize his conquest of western Iran. According to Sharaf ad-Din, Timur now resolved to conquer the remainder of Iran because of the anarchy there and the need to protect the Muslims of the area from further outrages at the hands of the infidels.

The Three Years' Campaign

"Kiss the hand you cannot bite."
— Saadi

In 1386 Timur issued mobilization orders for a campaign into western Iran and its dependencies which would go down in history as the "Three Years' Campaign." This was the first of his distant campaigns in which he would be operating in unfamiliar territory and which would take him away from Samarkand for several years. Until now he had, except for the winter of 1384/85, which he spent at Rayy (near Teheran), returned to his capital for the winter. After appointing emirs to a four-man council which would run the day-to-day affairs of his empire, he set out with his army in a direction which dissembled his true intentions.[19] He made it appear that he was headed eastward for Khodzhent (now Leninabad) and the steppe, but then wheeled about and marched in a southwesterly direction to Sebzevar. The mountainous province of Lurs on the western border of Iran was his ultimate objective.

Timur's sudden and unexpected line of march caught the Lurs tribesmen, who had pillaged caravans bound for Mecca, off guard. Timur used this caravan raiding as an excuse for a holy war of pillaging and extirpation in Luristan where he was actually attacking a Muslim population. Captives were hurled from mountain tops. He then hurried north to Tabriz to seize Ahmed Jelair but the latter, in his flight, would manage to writhe and wriggle his way clear of his pursuers and to reach Baghdad. Timur himself spent the summer in Tabriz. Its inhabitants were allowed to keep their lives and property upon payment of a heavy contribution, though the ablest masters in the arts and sciences were deported to Samarkand.

The flight of Sultan Ahmed brought northwest Iran under Timur's control except for the fortress of Alinjak near Nakhichevan. This mighty stronghold was built on a mountain overlooking the Alinja river. It was girded by massive walls and towers. The top of the mountain was crowned with a citadel. The walls enclosed vineyards, gardens, cultivated fields and pasture land as well as sources of water. The defenders were determined to hold the fortress at all costs. Finding this too tough a nut to crack, Timur left some troops behind to continue the siege and went his way.[20] The blockade would continue, with interruptions, for fourteen years.

Later in 1386 Timur moved northward to the ancient kingdom of Georgia.* Clavijo thought the Georgians "a very fine race of men, very handsome in face and gallant in bearing." Georgia had suffered grievously from the Mongol invasions, which began in the 1220s. But though the Mongols conquered the eastern and southern parts, they were never able to subdue western Georgia. This was partly a matter of geography. Access to the south and east presented fewer obstacles. The western side was more difficult, for invaders would have rougher terrain to traverse. The eastern shore of the Caucasus area contains a long and narrow sandy stretch adjoining the mountains which leads to the north. The seaport of Derbent, where the mountains come closest to the Caspian Sea, is its most defensible point. This pass acquired the Turkish name of *Temir-kapi* or "Iron Gate." The eastern approach was preferred by a long list of invaders, not excluding Timur.[21] In the period of the Mongol overlordship Derbent became a bone of contention between Il-Khanid Persia and the Golden Horde, a rivalry to be resumed when Toktamish fell out with Timur and invaded Azerbaijan via Derbent. It was the desire to contain Toktamish which now brought Timur to nearby Georgia.

In warring against Christian Georgia Timur posed as a *Ghazi* or Muslim warrior for the Faith. En route to Tiflis (presently Tbilisi, capital of Soviet Georgia), Timur's army engaged in a battue both to replenish its larder and to hone its battle-preparedness. During a battue one needs perfect coordination of movement to hem in the animals in an ever more constricting circle.

---

*Birthplace of Joseph Stalin.

Tiflis, lying in hilly country at the southern terminus of what is now the Georgian Military Highway, has for centuries owed its prosperity to its position as a crossroad for trade routes linking Persia, Turkey and south Russia as well as the Black and Caspian Seas. Despite the strength of its walls and its 1,580-foot high castle hill, Timur's men took it with a sharp assault. King Bagrat V and his queen Anna Comnena were taken captive. Timur then sent detachments which harried Sheki and other locales and planted the flag of the Jihad, or Muslim Holy War, on Mt. Ararat where, according to legend, Noah had landed his Ark.

Returning to Karabagh, Timur had a talk with the king, in the course of which he gave him "a thousand good reasons why he should turn Muslim" (Sharaf ad-Din). Bagrat, to placate Timur, presented him with a coat of mail allegedly forged by the prophet David as well as other antique curiosities. Bagrat won his release by feigning conversion to Islam and abjuring Christianity.

At about this time Emir Shaykh Ibrahim (1382-1417), the ruler of Shirvan, a khanate on the eastern shores of the Caucasus region with Shemakha as its capital appeared before Timur to make his submission. He was a remarkable ruler who was able to maintain a special and lasting relationship with Timur. Until 1382 he was a member of a very distinguished but impoverished family, living as a small landowner in the Sheki district in the small Shirvan state. Discontent among broad segments of the population with the rule of the local dynasty which owed subordination to the Jelairids led to its deposition. The aristocracy, casting about for a successor, fixed their gaze on Ibrahim. According to tradition, he received word that he had been designated the Shirvanshah or King of Shirvan during a hot day while he was resting under a tree after walking behind a plough on his acres.[22]

A skillful diplomat, Ibrahim was determined to preserve his state from the ravages of foreign conquerors and at the same time to secure as much independence as possible. Since his army was too small to resist such mighty rulers as Ahmed Jelair, Toktamish and Timur, he was determined to play one conqueror against the others. Timur's seizure of the southern districts of Azerbaijan presented Ibrahim with a clear and imminent danger. He now hurried to Timur's camp with rich presents of silks, horses, jewels and slaves. In accommodating himself to Mongol custom, he presented his offerings in nine of each kind, including nine female slaves. The male slaves, however, numbered only eight. When taxed about this, Shaykh Ibrahim, who was prepared for this question, answered that *he* was the ninth slave. The apt reply so pleased Timur that he freighted him with presents and favors and confirmed him as ruler over Shirvan, Derbent and its dependencies. In further talks with Timur he skillfully played upon the deep antagonism Timur now felt towards his former protégé Toktamish. In the end Ibrahim succeeded in saving his kingdom from being ravaged by Timur's men and retained control over its internal affairs. Timur, in turn, laid upon him the defense of the Derbent gate from the incursions of the Golden Horde.

At this time Timur also secured the submission of the princes of Gilan, adjoining Mazanderan on the southern Caspian Sea littoral, who until now had confided in the security offered by their mountain redoubts, forests and swamps.

During the winter of 1386/87, having learned through his spies that Toktamish was in revolt against him, Timur sent a reconnaissance force north across the Kura river by way of Derbent. This reconnoitering party was surprised by Toktamish's men and saved from certain annihilation only by the timely arrival of a force led by Miranshah, sent as a precaution by Timur to follow on the heels of the first force. Marvelous to relate, though the number of Toktamish's men captured was large, Timur did not butcher them but harangued them instead in a speech replete with reproaches against their master Toktamish for his ungrateful and treacherous conduct. The prisoners were then released with money, clothes and a guide to take them back to their master.

Timur's next theater of military operations was in the mountainous region straddling the present Turkish-Iranian frontier. Called Greater Armenia in the Middle Ages, its population consisted of a confused welter of peoples.

The Turkomans (or Turcomans) played a dominant role in the region. These nomads had emigrated into the area from Central Asia, some to escape Chingis Khan's Mongol hordes and others later. By Timur's time two great tribal confederations had emerged which took their names from the figures represented on their banners: Black Sheep (Kara Koyunlu) and White Sheep (Ak Koyunlu) Turkomans. The White Sheep encampment was in Diyarbekir in present-day southeastern Turkey. The Black Sheep, on the other hand, had their power center in the area to the north of Lakes Van and Urmia. Both were Muslim, the Black Sheep being Shiites and the White Sheep Sunnites. Deep hostility divided the two, the Black Sheep blocking White Sheep expansion to the east.

The Kurds will also play an important part in our story. A primitive and warlike people, obscure in origins and having a violent and confused history, they belong to the Iranian language group. Even today, however, they are set apart by their pronouncedly different customs, dress and sense of being Kurds. Most are Sunnite Muslims. Moving with their herds from higher elevations in the summer to lower areas in the winter, they are difficult to reach even in winter owing to the deep cover of snow that lies upon the land. A redoubtable foe, organized into tribes headed by chiefs called emirs, begs or beys, they opposed the march of Xenophon and his Ten Thousand. The Turkomans, in their penetration of the area, preferred to stick to the more accessible routes, bypassing the difficult mountain recesses inhabited by the fierce Kurds.

Finally, there were the Armenians, early converts (ca. 300 A.D.) to Christianity. They were nowhere strong enough seriously to resist an invader such as Timur.

The deep enmity between the two great Turkmen confederations would play into Timur's hands. Moreover, Kara Mehmed, the Black Sheep leader, was now at odds with his erstwhile ally Sultan Ahmed Jelair. The two were, indeed, preparing to clash with Tabriz as the prize when Timur loomed on the scene. All this, plus the fact that Greater Armenia was in the hands of many masters, helps explain the rapidity of Timur's conquest. Yet withal Timur never effected more than a transient mastery over the area. Though repeatedly mauled, some Turkomans and Kurds would always escape into the mountains to fight another day.

As for the Armenians, the coming of Timur was the last measure of woe and affliction. Mongols, Turkomans and other herdsmen had already traversed the country for more than three centuries and, in their implacable quest for pasturage, had dislocated the agriculture and forced many of the Armenians into the hills. Timur's advent would bring even greater miseries as chronicled vividly by their historian Thomas de Medzoph.

Timur's operations in 1387 in Greater Armenia may be quickly summarized. He especially sought to impose his control over two important Turkoman emirs: Kara Mehmed, leader of the Black Sheep, and Emir Taharten, prince of Erzinjan and of Erzerum, south of Trebizond. In Kara Mehmed's case Timur had especially good pretexts; he was a Shiite and had dared attack caravans bound for the holy city of Mecca. Using the city of Nakhichevan as his jumping-off point, Timur marched posthaste to Erzerum, taking two strongholds (Bayazid and Avnik) on the way. The conqueror captured Erzerum on the very day of his arrival. He thereupon sent an envoy to Taharten at Erzinjan demanding sub-

mission. Meanwhile, Miranshah was detailed to take three crack squad-
rons and seek out and seize Kara Mehmed. But though Miranshah
ravaged the area around the city of Mush to the east of Lake Van, Kara
Mehmed eluded his grasp in the difficult mountain terrain. A second try
by Timur himself also failed.

The taking of Van Castle, which belonged to Kara Mehmed, would
be the highlight of Timur's operations in the area. This celebrated fortress was perched atop a limestone rock 360 feet above the eastern
shore of Lake Van. The latter is one of the largest lakes in the Middle
East, and one of the highest in the world. Van Castle sat athwart a difficult but practicable trade route linking Anatolia with Persia. Timur's
men, making use of stairways cut into the stone, took the fortress by
storm after a twenty-day siege despite desperate resistance by the defenders. It took a tuman, nominally ten thousand men, an entire day to
demolish the massive rock constructions. Captive defenders were either
despatched on the spot or bound neck and heels with thongs and cast
to their death below; their women and children were taken off into
slavery.

Meanwhile a deputation arrived from Taharten, offering homage to
Timur. The latter's successes, coming like claps of thunder, had apparently convinced the emir of the futility of further resistance. Timur
allowed Taharten to stay on as his vassal upon payment of the haradj, a
special tax exacted by Muslim rulers from Christians and Jews resident
in their domains.

Persia once more became the object of Timur's unwelcome attentions as he finally moved against the Muzaffarid state, the most important of the major kingdoms there. It included Fars, Persian Iraq and
Kirman. Some time before, its ruler, Shah Shuja, had on his deathbed
written a letter to Timur commending Zayn al-Din and his other sons
and brothers to Timur's protection. In the autumn of 1387 Timur
dusted off this implied act of submission and vassalage; he sent an
envoy to Zayn al-Din, who had succeeded his father as ruler, ordering
him to appear before him to acknowledge his overlordship. Zayn al-Din
retorted by imprisoning Timur's envoy. The glove being cast down in
this manner, Timur saw no recourse but to set his warriors in motion.

Timur and his army, taking a southeasterly course, came upon the
city of Isfahan. Though its most illustrious days still lay in the future,
by this time it was already a rich and cultured city. Indeed, from the
tenth century on it was one of the greatest cities of the Near East. Bro-
cades, silk and cotton textiles, silverwork, faience and mosaics were

only the most famous of its products. As to its loveliness, even today Iranians say: "When one has seen Isfahan, one has seen half the beauty of the world."

Though Timur's reputation had preceded him, the Isfahanis, whom Ibn Battuta described as a "brave and generous people," had no presentiment of the tragedy awaiting them, since the first contacts were reassuring. A deputation of the leading citizens hurried through the city gates to Timur, who had drawn up his troops at the battle ready. He promised the Isfahanis clemency, on condition of the payment of a large sum of money. Accompanied by a small escort, Timur then made a triumphal entry into the city, visiting the bazaars, the various quarters and the citadel where he installed a garrison. Then he returned to camp, leaving some emirs and troops to collect the tribute. Eight of the nine gates in the city wall were sealed up with bricks and mortar. This had a double purpose: to prevent the city dwellers from slipping out with their valuables, and to keep the rowdies in Timur's army from coming in and causing trouble. A banal incident—the violation of a woman in the bazaar in the course of the ransom collection—touched off a concatenation of events which led to an eventual bloodbath. During the night of November 17/18, 1387 a young blacksmith by the name of Adi Kutshapa awakened the Isfahanis with blows on his drum as a signal to fall upon the hated intruders. Timur had only a small force in the city to help collect the tribute, though some warriors had managed to insinuate themselves into the city. The rebels soon slaughtered some three thousand Chagatais either in the streets or in their beds. These included most of the emirs sent by Timur into the city. The rebels then rushed to the city gates which they shut, after killing the guards stationed there. Wealthy Isfahanis, however, refrained from participating in what was really a popular rebellion. Some of them, indeed, even protected the Chagatai ransom collectors and officers from mob violence.[23]

Retribution was not long forthcoming. "When," on the next morning, "Timur perceived that evil crime and Satan puffed up his nostrils,"[24] he ordered an exemplary punishment meted out to the hapless citizenry of Isfahan. The defenses of the city were quickly breached and his men re-entered the city on the same day. Timur ordered that each soldier bring a severed head to the roving bureaus headed by commissioners of his divan. Some of his men, too busy with looting or squeamish about killing fellow Muslims in cold blood, purchased their heads, possibly from non-Muslim Chagatai warriors. At first the price was a gold coin but soon the supply so exceeded the demand that merchandise went begging. Even before this happened, however, the supply of males ran out so that soldiers shaved off the heads of women before cutting them off. These heads were then submitted to the bureaus for counting.

Only the quarters inhabited by Muslim savants and the homes of certain illustrious citizens and those who had saved the lives of Chagatai warriors were spared this saturnalia. These were cordoned off and protected by armed guards. During the bloodbath one of the Isfahani Ulema, in compassion, asked one of Timur's senior emirs how his wrath might be appeased. To this the emir replied, "Collect some infants on the hills, and he may be a little softened by the sight of them – as by chance may happen." A company of orphaned children was accordingly placed in Timur's path as he was riding by with a group of horsemen. The same emir tried to engage his sympathy by pointing out their pitiable condition. Timur, making no reply, urged his horse into the multitude of children, bidding his followers to do the same. All perished under the horses' hooves.[25]

Seventy thousand Isfahanis lost their lives at this time, according to Sharaf ad-Din. Other sources with access to the registers put the number much higher – almost 100,000 according to one and nearly 200,000 according to another. Pyramids of heads, averaging 15,000 each, were constructed around the walls of the city as a "lesson," though the city's main buildings were evidently spared. The crops standing in the fields outside the city were also destroyed. Some Isfahanis found refuge in the mountains, only to succumb to famine and the cold.

Timur's final stop on his Persian itinerary was Shiraz, the city of roses, wine and nightingales, lying almost directly south of Isfahan. The city's ruler Zayn al-Din, on news of Timur's approach, fled to his cousin Mansur, governor of Shustar, despite the bad blood between the two. What followed was characteristic, for the Muzaffarids were always tearing at each other's throats. Mansur, after bribing the troops that Zayn al-Din had brought with him, seized his cousin, put him in chains and blinded him. He then turned on the soldiers who had betrayed their master for gold and had them slaughtered.

The citizens of Shiraz, wanting no trouble, quiescently accepted the conqueror. The city owed its pre-eminence partly to its central location in Fars province. A network of roads linked it with Hormuz on the Persian Gulf, Isfahan, Kashan, Sultaniya, Kirman and other important cities. Shiraz abounded with sayyids and other holy men who were mostly Sunnis, as was the bulk of the population.[26]

Timur's entry into Shiraz in December of 1387 was accompanied by the submission of the entire province of Fars and its dependencies to his lieutenants. The Muzaffarid princes, the lords of Kirman and of Yezd and the Atabegs of Luristan hastened to Timur's headquarters to pay their devoirs.

While in Shiraz, Timur had a celebrated encounter with the great lyric poet Hafiz (1320-89), who in his poetry celebrated the beauty of his city, his garden of pleasure and youth. According to a story now considered by many scholars to be true in substance,[27] Timur summoned Hafiz and taxed him severely for having written:

> My Shiraz Turk if she but deign
> To take my heart into her hand,
> I'll barter for her Hindu mole
> Bukhara, yea, and Samarkand.[28]

Timur, with a touch of Oriental hyperbole, heatedly dilated on how he had conquered most of the inhabited world and with the avails had adorned Bukhara and Samarkand. "And you," he concluded, "miserable wretch that you are, would sell them both for the black mole of a Turk of Shiraz!" To which tirade Hafiz, who then was living in penury, replied: "Sire, it is through such prodigality that I have fallen upon such evil days."[29] The apt rejoinder so pleased Timur that he not only forgave Hafiz but gave him presents as well.

Timur might have loitered longer in Shiraz but for disturbing news from back home. In late 1387 Toktamish had invaded Transoxiana by way of Sygnak, and had pillaged the Samarkand area and had even (unsuccessfully) besieged Bukhara. Omar-Shaykh, Timur's second son, tried to blunt this advance with the forces at his disposal but sustained defeat near Otrar and was in fact nearly taken prisoner. He then limited himself to organizing the defenses of Samarkand and of Termez. Toktamish's men penetrated as far as the Amu Darya and the suburbs of Karshi, where they burned Timur's palace of Zindger-sarai. To exacerbate matters, the Mogols struck from the east, executing a razzia into the Ferghana valley. And finally Toktamish, by sending a detachment of troops to Khorezm, induced his secret allies there to come out in open revolt. Timur's two governors in Khorezm, unable to abort these proceedings and fearing the wrath of their master, fled for their lives to Toktamish. Transoxiana, denuded of troops by Timur who had taken the bulk of his forces with him to Iran, clearly was in dire peril.

Timur met the challenge with his usual promptitude and decisiveness. Emir Osman Abbas, one of his most trusted commanders, was dispatched posthaste to Samarkand with thirty thousand of Timur's bravest light cavalry, while Timur himself quickly regulated affairs in Iran prior to his own departure. He singled out three of the Muzaffarid princes for marks of his favor by granting them territories to be held as fiefs. He gave the government of Shiraz to Shah Yahya, nephew of the late Shah Shuja; Kirman to Sultan Ahmed, brother of Shah Shuja; and the province of Sirjan to Sultan Abu Ishac, grandson of Shah Shuja. Simultaneously he ordered the deportation to Samarkand of the illustrious scholar Sharif Gurgani, many of the local notables, and the most adept artisans and craftsmen together with their families.

In 1388 Miranshah, Timur's viceroy in Iran, put down a revolt in Tus with great severity. The males were put to the sword, while his Chagatai warriors "took from the city, by dragging them by the hair, women and girls of whom the sun had never seen the shadow."[30] This incident aside, Iran was to enjoy a four-and-a-half year respite from Timur's attentions while he busied himself elsewhere. It is to this new involvement that we now turn our attention.

CHAPTER V
The Rupture with Toktamish

During his meteoric rise, Toktamish had reunited the White and Golden Hordes and by a brutal *coup de main* had forced Muscovy and other Russian principalities to resume paying the annual tribute. He had obliged Lithuania to pay tribute for the Russian territory it held which had formerly been part of the Golden Horde. An authentic Chingisid, he had no need to raise up and rule through *fainéant* khans, but governed directly as khan himself. His feudatories even bestowed upon him the title of "the great," one which no previous khan—not even Uzbek, Mangu-Timur or Batu himself—had received.[1] One cardinal factor impelling the Golden Horde lords to rally around Toktamish was the humiliation felt after their heavy defeat at the battle of Kulikovo (1380) and their apprehension with regard to the growing power of Muscovy.

Toktamish's achievement seemed all the more impressive when contrasted with the parlous times upon which Mongol rule had fallen elsewhere. Il-Khanid rule in Persia had come to an end in 1336. The Mongol or Yüan dynasty in China had been overthrown by the native Chinese Ming dynasty in 1368.

Toktamish, however, had the mischance of being confronted by an opponent of first-class ability who also posed as a restorer of Chingisid fortunes, though not a Chingisid himself. Toktamish was beholden to Timur for extending invaluable help in climbing up the first rungs of the ladder of success; but gratitude is a highly perishable commodity where ambition is concerned. Toktamish viewed Timur with the lofty disdain of the blue blood for the parvenu. Moreover, Toktamish regarded himself as a more authentic representative of nomad traditions than Timur, whose early associations with town and city life caused Toktamish to regard him with the same contempt that Timur reserved for the sedentary Tadjiks.[2] Timur was for Toktamish but an adventurer whose successes had been the result of freakish luck.

Quickly winding up affairs in Iran, Timur, via a series of forced marches made in February when the rigors of winter still lay upon the land, returned to Transoxiana with such celerity that Toktamish decided to flee rather than to try conclusions with his former mentor. Some of Toktamish's men fled to Khorezm, some to the Kipchak steppe itself. According to Timurid historians, the troops sent after Toktamish pursued his men for a long time and inflicted heavy losses. This seems to be confirmed by certain signs of crisis in the politics of the Golden Horde.[3] It was at this time that Timur-Kutluk and Kunche-oglan, of the house of Urus Khan, and Edigei, leader of the Mangit tribe, fled to Timur's camp, after staging an unsuccessful mutiny against Toktamish.

Timur postponed a further reckoning with Toktamish. By way of reprisal for his devastation of Transoxiana, Timur, in the spring of 1388, mounted his fifth and last campaign against Khorezm. A shepherd informed him that Ilichmich Aglen and Suleiman Sufi, Toktamish's governors, had fled to him and that the city of Urgench was destitute of troops. Timur's men made forays into the country and returned with great booty. Though Urgench opened its gates without a fight, Timur gave his warriors ten days in which to plunder and pillage the rich and beautiful city. Then he ordered the capital to be razed and its land sowed with barley. Only a few of the city's handsome buildings were spared in the savage destruction that followed. The city folk, especially the numerous artisans, were deported to Samarkand. Only in 1391 did Timur allow a partial restoration of the kingdom's prosperity. The countryside was repopulated, the cities of Kath and Kavac had their walls restored and one of the quarters of Urgench was rebuilt. Even so, the kingdom never recovered its former commercial and cultural significance. With the addition of northern Khorezm, Timur ruled all of what is now Soviet Central Asia excepting Semirechie and the lower Syr Darya region.

While Timur was away in 1388 invading Khorezm, Suyurghatmish Khan, the nominal ruler of his empire, died. He was succeeded by his son Mahmud Khan. One of Timur's most trusted generals, Mahmud later died in 1402 while on active service. Timur then left the khanial throne empty, though he continued to mint coins in Mahmud's name.

Timur intended to pass the winter of 1388/89 tranquilly in Samarkand. Ominous developments were, however, occurring in the northwest. Toktamish had recruited a formidable army which included contingents from the Volga Bulgar kingdom, Circassia, Crimea, Azov and the Russian principalities. In late 1388 he directed this huge, polyglot array against Timur. Galvanized into action upon receipt of this hot alert, Timur immediately rallied the troops of Samarkand and Kesh and encamped at a village near his capital. Tavachis—high-ranking couriers on special command—were dispatched in all directions to levy troops and to bring them back posthaste to Timur's encampment. "This winter the cold was so violent that the earth was cover'd with snow, and the men were almost froze[n] to death."[4]

Meanwhile Timur learned that Toktamish's forces, led by Ilichmich Aglen, had crossed the Syr Darya near Khodzhent and had camped at a village nearby. Champing at the bit, Timur decided to attack forthwith with the forces on hand. Rejecting his war council's arguments that military action should be postponed until spring, Timur left in January 1389 with his household troops and plunged into snow so deep that it touched the bellies of the horses. Marching day and night, Timur was soon joined by the troops of Omar-Shaykh. As he approached the enemy encampment, Timur detached a force led by two of his emirs to position itself in the enemy's rear and in that manner to interdict their flight. At dawn the next day, as Timur's troops passed over the scruff of the hill, they came in sight of the enemy. The great cry "Surun!" ("Forward!") was immediately made by Timur's forces and the fell game began. Nothing could be heard above the cacophany of battle, the boom of the kettle drums, the neighing of the horses and the cries of the men. Soon Timur's forces won the upper hand and the shattered remnants of the enemy host sought to effect their escape. Some cast themselves into the Syr Darya and were drowned; others tried to make their way to the rear, only to be cut down by Timur's cavalrymen posted there. No quarter was given to the defeated troops as Timur's men plied their bows, war-clubs, swords and lances until their arms grew heavy with slaughter.

One of the few to escape the carnage was Airdi Birdi, secretary of state to Toktamish and a *bacchi,* as those secretaries employed by the Turco-Mongol rulers who wrote in Uighur script were called. He was forwarded to Timur who, after pumping him about the state of affairs in Toktamish's realm, pardoned him and enrolled him in his own service in a senior position.

Though Timur had given Toktamish a smart rebuff, the latter returned to pillage and loot the area north of the Syr Darya. Timur again took up pursuit but Toktamish vanished into the inscrutable steppe.

Toktamish s depredations had made two things clear: (1) that Timur could not safely absent himself from Transoxiana while Toktamish was on the loose; (2) that the latter had to be flushed out of his lair. Timur accordingly decided to launch a great invasion of the Kipchak steppe. His war council, however, successfully prevailed upon him first to secure his flank against the Mogols to the east. The latter had also conducted raids into Transoxiana during Timur's absence in Iran.

Operational plans for the Mogolistan campaign called for a division of forces into a number of columns. These would carry out coordinated pincer movements by which various Mogol groups would be trapped and destroyed. Guides were assigned to each unit, which had precise written instructions as to the route it would take and the area it would occupy. Upon completion of their assignments, all units would then rendezvous in the Yulduz valley. Timur's columns then began to traverse the area to the east and northeast of Lake Balkhash. But Qamar ad-Din, as he fled eastward towards Turfan, always managed to keep clear of his trackers. Some of Timur's men penetrated almost to Turfan, but to no avail.

Meanwhile Khizr Khodja, a Chagatai prince who had been put to flight by Qamar ad-Din, took advantage of the latter's involvement with Timur to carve out a principality for himself in the Khotan and Lob Nor region of Sinkiang. Though Khizr Khodja was an implacable enemy of Qamar ad-Din, Timur nonetheless attacked him lest the Chagatai kingdom reconstitute itself under a new master. Khizr Khodja was routed and fled eastwards into the Gobi desert. Timur then, as planned, effected a juncture of all his forces at Yulduz (northwest of Karashar) where, amidst "abundant fountains and delicious pasturage"[5] they and their horses rested from their exertions.

Despite pitiless harrying, the pacification of the Mogols would require further efforts. This was, however, the last campaign against the Mogols which Timur personally directed. Soon after he returned to his hearth, disquieting news reached him that Qamar ad-Din had slipped back into the Ili river valley east of Lake Balkhash and had reasserted his authority over that region. In 1390 Timur sent a task force into the area to seize him. The latter beat a retreat in a northeasterly direction. The expedition pursued him to the Black Irtysh river at the southwestern end of the Altai range, where they learned their quarry had crossed the river "into the woods where sables and ermine[e]s are said to be found,"[6] there to meet an unknown end. The force tarried some days along the banks, burning inscriptions on pine trees to record their accomplishments. Some six months had elapsed. Low on provisions and suffering from the bone-biting cold, the expedition returned home.

During this period Khizr Khodja became khan of the Mogols. He did this under the aegis of Khoudaidad, the new Dughlat clan head who, unlike his uncle Qamar ad-Din, was a legitimist. Cessation of Mogol depredations and the militancy with which the new khan imposed the Islamic faith upon the Turkic Uighurs of the Turfan area induced Timur to conclude peace with Khizr Khodja. In 1397 Timur married the latter's daughter, an advantageous union since Timur's new wife was a Chingisid.

Though these developments lay in the future, Timur could, by reason of his 1389 campaign, feel reasonably secure on his eastern flank. He could now turn to his principal enemy, Toktamish. Since the threat here was not imminent, Timur could go about his preparations in a more leisurely, albeit deliberate manner. He spent the winter of 1389/90 at some ponds near Bukhara hunting swans. In the spring of 1390 he convened a kurultai which was attended by his officers and officials. The purpose of this assembly was twofold: to decrease the wealth of his officers who, gorged on the avails of previous campaigns of plunder, had become less responsive to his commands; and to increase the size of his army. Timur achieved both objects by announcing the number of additional warriors each commander would be expected to appear with at the next troop muster. These figures were set down in writing by Timur's tavachis. The kurultai was concluded with a gargantuan feast.

Late in January 1391 Timur mounted his great invasion of the Kipchak, using Tashkent as the jumping-off point. Before leaving he reviewed his troops to check their equipment and good order. All his infantry were provided with mounts. He improved his men's morale by distributing among them all the silver money in his treasury. Though Timur regarded the bitter cold of the season as a trumpery obstacle, snow and rain finally induced him to halt for a time at Karasuman, a town in the Kipchak steppe.

It was here that Timur received envoys from Toktamish, sent to ward off the brewing storm. Approaching Timur on the run and then throwing themselves at his feet according to Mongol custom, they presented him with a letter from their master as well as with nine swift horses and a falcon, its collar bedizened with precious stones. Though Timur took the bird on his wrist, he received the envoys coldly. He consented to the reading out of Toktamish's letter only after pressing solicitations from his familiars. In the letter Toktamish called Timur "father" and blamed all his past misdeeds on the influence of evil companions. Asking Timur's pardon, he promised to do all that was required of him. Timur then dilated on how Toktamish had bitten his feeding hand and how his word could not be trusted. However, he concluded, if Toktamish truly wanted peace he should send his man Ali Bek to nego- tiate. Ali Bek apparently was not sent, for on February 21, 1391 Timur resumed his advance.

The conqueror took a roundabout route. First moving northward via Yassy and Sauran, he then veered toward a more westerly direction.[7] Both horses and men suffered great fatigue and thirst. Three weeks passed before water was found. At length, in late April, the army reached Küchük dagh ("little mountain," literally) which separates the basin of the Sary-su from the Turgai river in Kazakhstan. Here Timur climbed the heights and viewed with admiration the vast verdant plains. At his command, a stone pillar was erected on which was placed an en- graved tablet recording the date of his passage. The tablet, found in 1935, now reposes in the Hermitage in Leningrad.

Grave difficulties attended the army's further progress. It had been on the march for several months and food was becoming a serious prob- lem. To alleviate the situation, Timur had the army carry out a great battue. The large number of animals slain satisfied the army's victual needs for some time. However, the men's spirits remained low. No sign of the enemy could be discerned, nor even of any cultivated land. To raise morale, Timur held a full review of his men. Wearing a ruby- studded crown and holding a mace shaped at the top like the head of an ox, he rode past tuman after tuman. Then he began a meticulous inspec- tion of each regiment and company to check into the condition, equip- ment and number of men in each unit. As he rode past, each com- mander, following Mongol custom, knelt beside his horse, reins in hand, and kissed the earth, after which he recited formal phrases of blessing and praise of his lord. All this consumed two days. After satisfying him- self that the emirs had complied with the instructions agreed upon at the kurultai at Kesh, Timur ended the review with harangues designed to inspirit his men.

Timur had every reason to be concerned, for his position now was precarious. He had not made contact with the enemy and did not even know its approximate whereabouts. Toktamish could have continued to entice him further into the depths of Siberia and then have fallen upon his famished and exhausted men.

Timur's men reached the sources of the Tobol river. His scouts crossed the river and discovered campfires, but no enemy. However, the chance capture of an enemy horseman—Lady Luck seldom deserted

Timur—brought news that Toktamish was located in the direction of the Ural (Yaik) river to the west. Timur's army immediately wheeled in that direction. Timur learned that thanks to his rapid mobilization and movements he had caught Toktamish off guard. Though Timur's force was already en route in February 1391, Toktamish did not learn about this until April 6 and then only because two of Edigei's retainers, fleeing Timur's camp, had brought Toktamish news that Timur's army, "more numerous than the sands of the steppe and the leaves of the forest," was headed his way. Badly shaken, he tried to put a good face on the matter by announcing that he would assemble a force twice as large as Timur's. Messengers were sent out in all directions with a summons to arms. The designated assembly point was Kryk-Kula, on the right bank of the Ural (Yaik) river. Timur's forces, however, advanced with such promptitude that the troops of Azov, the Volga Bulgar area and other locales did not have time to join Toktamish before his battle with Timur.

Toktamish's battle plan was simple: operating from Kryk-Kula, he would attack Timur while the latter was crossing the Ural river. Timur, however, divined Toktamish's intentions and instead made his way to the upper reaches of the river and crossed at an unguarded point where he was not expected. Toktamish beat a hurried retreat from Kryk-Kula. As a result, those of Toktamish's forces which arrived late, knowing nothing of Toktamish's recent movements, easily fell into Timur's hands.

Toktamish's new strategy, as indicated by the disclosures of captured POWs, was to draw the enemy forces ever farther toward the northwest and, after exhausting them with repeated river crossings, finally to give battle. Timur's men were forced to cross not only the Yaik but also the Sakmara, Samara and Sok rivers until the borders of the old Volga Bulgar kingdom were reached. From a military point of view, Toktamish's plan was unexceptionable, inasmuch as Timur's troops had been on the march for six months and were much weakened after a steady diet of short rations. Clashes had occurred between outriders of the two hosts, but sharp as these were, Toktamish could not be persuaded to stand his ground and fight. Finally Timur decided to precipitate events by sending Omar-Shaykh with a force of 20,000 men to make contact with Toktamish's main force at all costs. This task force moved so rapidly that on the next day the scouts of the two armies engaged in sparring. Timur immediately readied his main body and lunged at Toktamish, who decided at long last the the proper time had arrived to accept battle. Six days of prodigiously foul weather, however, postponed the mammoth battle which took place on June 18, 1391, near Kunduzsha, located between the present-day cities of Kuibyshev and Chistopol.

Despite Toktamish's failure to get all his forces to join him, the latter were in no way inferior to those of Timur numerically. Though the exact number is a much controverted question, it would appear that the two forces were approximately equal in number. Timur's army, which "resembled the troubled ocean,"[8] when it moved, has been estimated at 200,000 men.

Timurid historians make much of the novel way in which Timur divided his army for the contest. For the first time, he divided his forces into seven bodies: a vanguard, the main body, two wings each with its own vanguard, and a powerful reserve under his own command. Toktamish kept to the old Tatar battle array of a main body and two powerful crab-like wings, whose job it was to roll up the flanks of the enemy while the main body engaged the latter's attention.

Timur's choice of battlefield near the Kunduzsha river also told in his favor. At this point the river, turning from the northwest to a southeast course, joins the Sok, a left affluent of the Volga, before it falls into the Volga. The area, then, resembled a triangle. Toktamish, in case of retreat, would find the Volga at his back, against which he and his army could be pinioned and crushed. Timur, if he were forced back, could organize a solid defense along the Sok, a much smaller river.[9]

The battle, which began in the morning, soon went badly for Timur. The two powerful wings of Toktamish's army swept around Timur's flanks and threatened his army with complete encirclement. Ibn Arabshah, with his usual spite where Timur is concerned, pictures the latter at this point piteously crying out to Sayyid Bereke, the holy man who had prophesied his rise to power: "O my honorable Sayyid, my army is defeated!" Sayyid Bereke replied reassuringly: "Do not fear!" Then, climbing down from his horse, he grabbed a handful of dirt and remounted. Flinging the dirt in the direction of the enemy, he cried "Yagy Kochdy!" ("The enemy is overcome!"). Timur followed the plucky sayyid and with his stentorian voice which, according to Ibn Arabshah, resembled that of a camel-driver calling his thirsty beast to water, rallied his men. The latter, taking heart, repeated Sayyid Bereke's cry and with ferocious counterattacks drove the enemy back into headlong flight.[10] Ibn Arabshah has undoubtedly magnified Sayyid Bereke's role in gaining victory for Timur. A pivotal factor was the defection of some of Toktamish's emirs in the heat of the battle together with the forces under their command, a factor emphasized by Toktamish himself in a letter to Grand Duke Yagailo in 1393.

The enemy routed, Timur then detailed seven out of every ten men to pursue the enemy. The latter found itself boxed in between the Volga and its implacable pursuers. Only a few, including Toktamish himself, managed to effect their escape. Even some who took refuge on some islands in the Volga were captured. Toktamish's wife, children and all his property fell into the hands of Timur's men. The bodies of Toktamish's troopers lay helter-skelter over the battlefield, covering an area of forty leagues. The scholar Charmoy, in his study of this campaign, placed Toktamish's losses at 100,000 killed.

There are indications that Timur's losses also were heavy and that his army emerged badly shaken from battle. He permitted his men twenty-six days of uninterrupted feasting and carousing to forget the cares and fatigues of war. The time was also used to plunder the environs. The booty included prodigious numbers of horses, cattle and sheep, a grievous loss to the population of the Golden Horde. Timur also issued orders to have Toktamish's dispersed peoples rounded up and sent to Transoxiana. It was in this connection that Edigei, Timur-Kutluk and Kunche-oglan—three Juchid princes in his service—asked permission to fetch their own peoples so they could be resettled in Transoxiana. Timur assented, on condition that this be done quickly.

Earlier, Edigei had secretly advised his people to move to isolated places out of reach of Timur's men. Anxious to turn Toktamish's discomfiture to his own advantage. Edigei had no intention of returning. Timur-Kutluk, a grandson of Urus Khan, began to gather his people but was dissuaded by Edigei. Timur-Kutluk instead had himself proclaimed khan. Only Kunche-oglan brought some of his people to Timur's camp but, as soon as he heard what the other two had done, he departed for home at the first opportunity.

Belatedly Timur realized that he had been gulled, especially by the sly schemer Edigei. Ibn Arabshah gloatingly describes how Timur, to retrieve the situation, sent a messenger to Edigei asking him to return forthwith to discuss an important matter, only to meet with refusal.

Bek-Bulat, whose ulus was centered in the upper Don region, had proclaimed himself khan even before the flight of Edigei and his companions. By the fall of 1391 he even managed to get control of New Sarai. His defection from Toktamish's army during his battle with Timur played an important role in determining the successful outcome for Timur.

Timur did nothing further to bring the Golden Horde under his control. In the late summer of 1391 he left for Samarkand in such haste that he arrived in September. The bulk of his army, clogged with so much plunder that many animals had to be abandoned, did not reach Samarkand until late 1391. Timur's abrupt disinterest in further campaigning aginst the Golden Horde may have been prompted by the belief that he had left it in such a shambles that it no longer posed a threat. He must also have been mindful of the weakened condition of his own army, which needed to be rested, refitted and reinforced.

CHAPTER VI

The Five Years War–I
Persia and Mesopotamia (1392-1394)

> "How poor the nations that must suffer
> gloriously triumphant generals."
>
> —José de San Martín

In May 1392, after a sojourn in his capital city of only eight months, Timur embarked on a new campaign which Islamic historians have dubbed the Five Year's War. The mainspring of the new action, Sharaf ad-Din informs us, was word that revolts had broken out against Timur's rule in Persia, though an itch for further campaigning cannot be discounted. While Khurasan was, by 1392, solidly incorporated into Timur's empire, other parts of Persia had only been lightly assimilated. During his first descent upon Persia he had neglected to provide its local government with a solid armature of Chagatai administrators. In the meantime disturbances had occurred, especially in the Muzaffarid and Jelairid areas, which were prejudicial to the maintenance of even this tenuous authority.

The magnitude of Timur's projected campaign may be gauged by his instructions to his tavachis. They were to muster and equip troops for a war of five years. On May 10 when the weather had already turned hot, Timur left Samarkand with an army of eighty thousand. Grave illness forced Timur to stop and rest in Bukhara for several weeks until he recovered. On June 20 the invasion force resumed its advance in a southwesterly direction.

Timur's first destination was the province of Mazanderan, the eastern tip of which he had conquered in 1384. Mazanderan and Gilan to the west, located along the southern shore of the Caspian Sea, have a warm climate, heavy rainfall, and dense forests and vegetation. They are quite unlike the parched, barren mountain and plateau country of the bulk of Persia. Geographically Mazanderan may be subdivided into two areas: the low-lying coastal plain full of impenetrable swamps and jungle, and the elevated and forested foothills of the Elburz mountains to the south. Both areas are extremely difficult of access. To compound matters the weather, universally execrated, fluctuates violently, causing much illness among the local inhabitants.[1]

As usual, Timur sought pretexts for the invasion of this area. These were not hard to find. During the fourteenth century the area had come under the rule of a dynasty of Shiite imams or sayyids who combined lay and spiritual powers and were under the influence of the Serbedar movement. The inhabitants, in Timur's representation of things, were living under heretical rule. Moreover, they had committed depredations against merchants and travellers.

Timur's march from Astarabad to Sari, one of the chief cities of the Sayyid state, was a toilsome and arduous affair which took three months. His men had to cut a road through the thick undergrowth with their axes. Upon hearing of his approach the sayyids fled to the fortress of Mahanasar, located twelve miles from Amul, the chief city. Here they shared refuge with foreign merchants and native inhabitants. Mahanasar was a reputedly impregnable stronghold situated on an elevated promontory above the Caspian Sea. In turbulent weather, for which the Caspian is so notorious, the sea would close over the causeway, which umbilically joined the fortress with the mainland, making approach by land impossible. The fortress commander also had a sizeable fleet of ships. The besieging of this fortress, which would be the high point of this campaign, presented Timur with an unusual problem since the enemy, making use of its fleet to bring in provisions and reinforcements, could hold out indefinitely against an attack from the land side. Undeterred, Timur ordered the Amu Darya fleet, which had been constructed by his shipwrights, to be brought to the Caspian; throwers of Greek fire were also also assembled. Timur's use of his Amu Darya fleet indicates that after the Mongol conquest the Amu Darya made its way into the Caspian Sea and retained this course until the second half of the sixteenth century, after which time it again began to empty into the Sea of Aral. With his Amu Darya fleet Timur managed to catch the enemy fleet by surprise and to capture it. Placing soldiers aboard the captured vessels, Timur attacked the fortress. These newly formed marine units sent up a hail of arrows into the stronghold, accompanied by such a quantity of flaming pitch and tar "that it was said that the Caspian Sea was become a sea of fire" (Sharaf ad-Din). At length the besieged, finding their position insupportable, begged for quarter, which was granted.

Timur's first act was to berate the captives for their errors in religion. He exhorted the sayyids to accept Islam in its Sunnite form. After removal of the riches stored in the fortress, it was razed. Meanwhile Timur learned that there were many Fedais in the country, called Assassins by the Europeans. Hulagu Khan, who had effected the definitive conquest of Iran in the 1250s, had failed to extirpate this Ismaili Shiite sect completely, so that when Timur entered Mazanderan some of his men had fallen victim to their daggers. By way of reprisal, Timur ordered the execution of all the Fedais his men could lay hands on.

Sayyid Kemal ad-Din, the local ruler, and his son were put on a vessel and sent to Khorezm. Other sayyids were dispatched to Tashkent and to Samarkand; these three locales served as residences of various representatives of deposed dynasties. Since sayyids claimed descent from the Prophet Muhammad, they were spared. Not so the inhabitants of Amul, Sari and other places who were put to the sword as heretics. Word of the conquest of Mazanderan, which was effected by the fall of 1392, was then sent to Samarkand. Timur spent the winter of 1392/93 in Mazanderan.

If, as Sharaf ad-Din informs us, Fars and Iraq Arabi (lower Mesopotamia) had been chosen by Timur as his campaign objectives for 1393, he nonetheless began the year with another invasion of Georgia. His first campaign six years earlier had ended, as previously noted, with the capture of the Georgian king, Bagrat V, who won his release by feigning conversion to Islam. Timur left Georgia, however, without bringing Bagrat's son George to heel. The circumstances of this second Georgian invasion in 1393 have been variously explicated. According to one account, Bagrat, upon returning to his homeland as Timur's vassal, entered into collusion with his son George. This collaboration brought about the ambush and defeat of a large force of Timur's men.[2] Another version has it that Timur learned that George was lurking in the mountains of Georgia waiting for the right moment in which to break Timur's grip over the country – a resolve which even his father Bagrat opposed.[3] What is not in dispute is the savagery with which Timur and his host now descended upon the land. As in the first campaign it was the eastern part of the country which suffered the most, though even in the west people abandoned their homes and fled into the mountains. Fire and sword were directed against both the people and the land, as Timur's men tore up trees, uprooted grapevines and burned them. Churches and monasteries were prime targets. Included in the destruction was the famous cathedral of Sveti-Tzkhoveli ("The Living Column") at ancient Mtzkhet, the capital of the kingdom before Tiflis. Leaving the country in ashes and ruins, Timur withdrew southward.

Fars and Mesopotamia were Timur's next objectives. On the way south through the mountain passes he traversed the provinces of Luristan and Khuzistan where his troopers, radiating out in all directions, punished the local tribesmen for their inveterate brigandage. This was something of a military promenade since his enemies either capitulated or fled at his approach. Shustar was fixed as the point of rendezvous. At Dizful, one day's ride north of Shustar, Timur tarried to admire the bridge over the Ab-i Diz river. This magnificent construction is reputed to have been built by the Sasanid ruler Shapur the Great (309-379). The lower part was of stone and the upper part of brick; it contained fifty-six high and low arches in alternation.

Before detailing Timur's activities in Fars it would be well to give a capsule summary of events in the province subsequent to Timur's first visitation. As will be recalled, Timur, upon leaving Fars in 1388, had tolerated the continued rule of the Muzaffarid princes by appointing them as his governors in various cities. After his departure a vicious elimination bout broke out among them as each sought to establish his supremacy. It would be tedious to relate the base treacheries and revolting barbarities which these princes committed against each other. Suffice it to say, Shah Mansur, more agile and unwearied than the rest, had blinded his cousin Zayn al-Din and forced his brother Yahya to retire from Shiraz, over which he had personally been given authority by Timur, to Yezd. When Timur now reappeared, Shah Mansur held Isfahan, Abrecouh and Shiraz, which he had chosen as his capital. Shah Yahya held Yezd, Sultan Ahmed ruled Kerman and Sultan Abu Ishaq lorded it over Sirjan.

Timur viewed the growing ascendancy of Shah Mansur as a threat to his own rule. Moreover, the constant internal strife had brought ruin and desolation to the land. This played hob with Timur's policy of restoring peace and tranquility to lands which he had conquered and considered integral parts of his empire. Since Shah Mansur was regarded as the chief marplot in bringing on this turmoil, Timur wasted no time on the other Muzaffarids but lunged directly at him. In April of 1393, after reassembling his army at Shustar, Timur marched on Shiraz, Shah Mansur's capital.

Timur's first action in early May 1393 was not against Shah Mansur personally but against a certain Sadet, the governor of one of his fortresses which lay in Timur's path on the way to Shiraz. This stronghold, called Qal'ai-i-Sefid ("White Castle"), which Sharaf ad-Din termed one of the strongest citadels of Asia, was considered so impregnable that no one had ever tried to take it. Situated on a mountain top, with only one narrow, slippery path of ascent, its formidable natural defenses were augmented by walls. On the top lay a plain, a league long, where food was grown so that the garrison could not be starved out.

Despite these daunting obstacles Timur ordered a general attack, which did not prosper. By luck, one of his men — Akbulak by name — while clambering among the rocks above noted an approach to the fortress by a path considered by the defenders to be impracticable. The unexpected appearance of Akbulak threw the garrison into consternation. Seconded by some of Timur's men, he began an assault from that quarter, while other attackers stormed their way up the usual path of ascent. The garrison was at length overwhelmed; those taken alive were pitched from the mountain top. Sadet, the fortress commander, was ordered killed in retribution for the losses sustained by Timur. Zayn al-Abidin, blinded by Shah Mansur and immured in the fortress, was set free. Akbulak, who had discovered the alternate path of ascent, received wealth beyond his dreams. Leaving one of his officers behind as fortress governor, Timur resumed his advance upon Shiraz.

Shah Mansur, apprised of Timur's approach, fled to Pul-i-Fasa. Reproached by the people there for his lack of manliness and hardihood, he decided to return to Shiraz and hold his head up to Timur in what he must have known would be certain death.

The battle took place in the plain of Patileh outside of Shiraz. There Shah Mansur with a force of three to four thousand cavalrymen awaited Timur's force. Not only were the men encased in armor from head to foot, but even their horses were protected with covers of thick silk. Timur's men numbered thirty thousand picked troops.

Badly outnumbered, Shah Mansur opened the attack at the time of the Friday prayer — bad form for anyone professing to be a good Muslim. Shah Mansur made straight for Timur himself and so impetuous was his sally that he managed to strike him with two blows of his saber which were, however, unable to penetrate Timur's strong helmet. This unexampled bravery won the admiration of the astonished Timur. Early in the battle, however, two thousand of Shah Mansur's troops fled from the battlefield together with his chief emir so that even the prodigies of valor exhibited by Shah Mansur, such as the routing of some of Timur's regiments, proved unavailing. At lenth, troops led by Shahrukh hemmed in Shah Mansur, who had been wounded in the neck, shoulder and face but continued to fight vigorously, saber in hand. Timurid historians differ as to how this man met his end. Ghiyas ad-Din, in the far more

creditable of the two versions, states that Shah Mansur, after being top-
pled from his horse, identified himself and demanded to be brought
before Timur, but was killed by some of the latter's warriors.[4] Sharaf
ad-Din, on the other hand, declares that though Shahrukh was only seventeen at the time, he personally cut off Shah Mansur's head. This he
threw at the feet of his father with the salutation: "May the heads of all
your enemies be thus laid at your feet!"—much to the gratification of
his doting father. In the meantime, Shah Mansur's remaining forces had
been so unnerved by the death of their sovereign that they turned tail,
though they returned later during the victory celebrations to make one
last unsuccessful sally.

The citizens of Shiraz, not wishing to stand siege, threw open the
city's gates. Timur entered the city and set up headquarters in that part
of the city called the Selm, leaving the bulk of his army encamped outside the walls. Eight of the nine gates of the city were shut; only the
ninth, that of the Selm, was left open. Timur's men seized the riches of
Shah Mansur and those of his chief lords. In addition, a large ransom
was levied on the population in return for the sparing of their lives.

The other Muzaffarid princes now hurried to submit to Timur. He
accepted both their homage and their rare and costly gifts. The army
was diverted and refreshed by a month long bacchanalia at which musicians played on organs and harps and "the red wine of Shiraz was
served by the most beautiful virgins of the city" (Sharaf ad-Din). Timur
then turned to more serious matters. The misrule and turbulence of the
Muzaffarids had brought misery to the country, especially to the poor
folk who, in Sharaf ad-Din's words, "were the tennis-ball of misfortune
and misery." Timur conveniently received a delegation of Muslim
divines and other dignitaries who urged that an end be put to Muzaffarid rule. At once he acted upon this advice, ordering the seizure, in-
carceration and spoliation of the Muzaffarid princes.

Timur resolved to organize his conquests in Iran on a less makeshift
basis than before. Earlier, he had delegated his son Omar-Shaykh to
conduct mopping-up operations against the relics of Shah Mansur's
forces and against the robbers of Luristan, and to install governors and
garrisons in that province and thereabouts. Now Timur, after enacting a
tax cut for the population, appointed Omar-Shaykh governor over Fars
with Shiraz as his capital. Good troops and capable advisers were assigned
to him. The savants and artists of Shiraz were deported to Samarkand.

On June 18 Timur left Shiraz, proceeding northward. Twelve days
later he sent back an order to Shiraz requiring the execution of all the

Muzaffarid princes, save two who had been blinded by their kinsmen. These were allowed to live out their days in peace and tranquility in Samarkand. Thus ended the remarkable Muzaffarid dynasty.

Upon reaching Hamadan, Timur made further territorial arrangements for his empire. His son Miranshah received western Iran and the southern Caucasus, so that in the west his fief marched with the borders of the states dependent upon the Ottomans. The fief also included the area around Baghdad still in the hands of Ahmed Jelair. Timur, following Mongol custom, sealed the document of conveyance of this fief with the imprint of his hand dipped in red ink.

By now it was August. Making his way westward, Timur diverted himself with operations against Kurdish robbers and a group of Zoroastrians. At the same time he sent his son Muhammad-Sultan to the Derbent area of the Caucasus to bring that region under submission and to exterminate local brigands preying on travellers. Timur's main objective, however, was Baghdad, the seat of the Jelairid dynasty.

Sultan Ahmed Jelair soon learned of Timur's somewhat leisurely but inexorable advance. Timur halted to observe Ramadan in Akbulak, not far from the place where Alexander the Great, a millennium and a half earlier, had decided the fate of the Persian empire. Here Timur received an envoy from Sultan Ahmed who hoped to induce Timur to turn back by assuring him of his submission.

The ambassador, the great mufti and scholar Nureddin Abderrakhman Isferaini, was received honorably by Timur out of respect for his quality. Not so the Sultan's excuses and gifts, though the latter included deer, leopards and Arabian horses with golden saddles, nine of each, according to Mongol custom. The sticking point was the failure of Sultan Ahmed to mint coins in Timur's name and to include his name in the Friday prayer. Since the envoy was not empowered to concede these attributes of sovereignty, Timur dismissed him without further ado.

Up to now, Timur had been proceeding at the gait of an arthritic ox. Hoping to surprise Sultan Jelair in his palace, Timur disencumbered himself of his baggage and the ladies of the court, these being sent back to Sultaniya. Travelling lightly, he made such great speed that he all but outdistanced his own soldiers. Reaching a town eighty-one miles from Baghdad, Timur learned that the inhabitants had released carrier pigeons advising Sultan Ahmed of his approach. The townspeople were accordingly forced to send a new message apprising the Sultan that the dust clouds they had seen were actually those caused by Turkomans fleeing from Timur. Meanwhile the latter made such great haste that, upon the authority of Sharaf ad-Din, he covered the eighty-one miles without dismounting. Travelling day and night, more probably he rode all day and had himself carried on a litter at night.

Unfortunately for Timur, Sultan Ahmed did not believe the second message. Even so, he had so little advance notice of Timur's approach that he barely had time to destroy the bridge over the Tigris and retire to the right bank with such craft as could not be sunk. The inhabitants of the city, having no stomach for a siege, made no attempt to bar Timur's troops. Some of the latter found the royal barge named "Sun" on the right bank and brought it to the left bank for Timur's use in crossing the Tigris. A special task force of forty-five emirs—the soldiers being too exhausted to go on—managed to catch up with Ahmed who, with two thousand horsemen, was headed west. Not without difficulty was Timur dissuaded by his emirs from conducting the pursuit himself. A sharp skirmish took place on the plains of Kerbela between the emirs and two hundred of the Sultan's force, with heavy losses on both sides. At length the enemy was routed and much booty taken. Moreover, Sultan Ahmed's wives and son fell into the hands of the emirs. Sultan Ahmed, however, managed to effect his escape to Egypt where he received a warm welcome from Sultan Barkuk. Timur's wait for the royal barge had cost him much precious time, an error which he later recognized when he told his intimates: "If at the very moment that I arrived I had entered the water and had crossed the Tigris, Sultan Ahmed would have been taken. But as I have stopped, he had a respite, and [because of] the time that the soldiers took to get across, he had gained distance."[5]

In the meantime Timur sent Miranshah southward to seize Basra. Letters of conquest were sent out to all corners of his empire, even as far east as Kashgar and Khotan. The Baghdadis paid the customary ransom for having their lives spared, which Timur distributed among his emirs and men. In collecting the ransom precautions were taken to protect the population from outrage at the hands of Timur's men, though cruel treatment was meted out to those suspected of hiding their money. Timur spent two months diverting himself in the pavilions situated on the Tigris, though he denied his soldiery any alcoholic indulgence. On his orders all the wine found in the city was cast into the Tigris. We are told that the fish, bloated in their intoxication, floated on top of the water where Timur's men speared them without difficulty. On discovering that inundations of the Tigris had damaged the

57263

mausoleum of Ibn Hanbal, founder of one of the four great schools of Muslim Sunnite jurisprudence, Timur had it repaired.

If Timur played the role of paladin of Islam in Baghdad proper, curbing his men's appetite for violence, looting and lust, he certainly gave them free rein in the city's suburbs and in other parts of Iraq. Bands of Chagatais tied up and tortured those unfortunate enough to fall into their hands, carried off and violated girls in debaucheries, broke into and vandalized mosques, hanged imams and used medresehs as stables.[6]

The conqueror left Baghdad in October 1393, taking with him the men of letters and artists who had graced the Jelairid court. A certain number of captives of both sexes were also carried off, later to be sold into slavery. Since the country had been picked clean of food by Timur's foragers, famine stalked the land. Regarding Baghdad as an integral part of his domain, Timur left behind a governor with a garrison, under orders to strengthen the city's fortifications.

It was in this period that Timur entered into his first direct diplomatic contact with the Mamlukes in Cairo. An embassy was sent to Sultan Barkuk headed by Shaykh Save, a distinguished theologian. The gist of Timur's letter, which his envoy handed over to Sultan Barkuk, was that after the death of Abu Said, the last of the Il-Khanids, fragmentation of authority and infinite misery had become the lot of the common folk of Iran. However, now that Timur's possessions marched with those of the Mamlukes, he proposed peace and friendship between the two great empires. These contacts, his letter continued, could include regular correspondence "so that the merchants of both nations might travel with security."[7]

Any hopes Timur may have entertained that all fortresses in lower Mesopotamia would capitulate as readily as Baghdad had proved to be false. The major trouble spot was Takrit, a stronghold ruled over by a robber baron by the name of Hasan, on the west bank of the Tigris some one hundred miles upstream from Baghdad. Timur responded to the pleas of merchants and travellers who complained that the robbers of Takrit pillaged passing caravans "and especially those of Egypt and Syria, which were the richest of any," and killed travellers. Parenthetically, this reference of Sharaf ad-Din's to Egypt and Syria clearly attests to the commercial prosperity of the Mamluke state at this time. Some of the Chagatai emirs were sent out with an advance force to begin the investment of the famed fortress, which is thought to have been built by the Sasanids. In late 1393 Timur arrived on the scene himself.

Timur admittedly had his work cut out for him. Though previous besiegers had used battering rams and other siege machinery, their efforts to take the citadel of Takrit had been unsuccessful. Perched on a high rock overlooking the Tigris, the towering walls of the stronghold rested on solid bedrock or connected portions of the adjoining cliff. Timur was undeterred by the fortress' reputation for impregnability. As a preliminary he first had the outparts sapped and overthrown. During these operations he ordered "his tent to be fixed near the works, to animate the men."[8] Following this, battering rams and stone throwers were pressed into use and a general assault prepared. Timur's tavachis divided the space before the walls among the soldiers, marking with a red furrow the portion each regiment would sap. Fortifications built on rock are, it should be noted, much more difficult to sap than those resting on more or less soft earth. The sapping completed, the pitprops, pitch and other combustibles were ignited, causing parts of the wall to collapse. Then Timur's troops attacked, taking the fortress town by assault. A second assault had to be mounted against the inner citadel to which Hasan and his followers had retreated. Though in the end the lives of civilians were spared, the captured soldiers were tortured to death for their obdurate resistance. Towers were built of their heads as an example to would-be malefactors. Timur left a section of the walls standing so that posterity might admire his military prowess.

Repairing to the grazing lands between Takrit and Baghdad, Timur was joined by Miranshah and other commanders who, in the meantime, had brought under submission the lands straddling the lower Tigris. Both Wasit and Basra received garrisons. These cities were important caravan stops for Muslim pilgrims from this area bound for the Hejaz and its holy cities of Mecca and Medina. Timur's warriors, for the remainder of 1393, forgot the cares and fatigues of campaign in hunts and other diversions.

Timur's next objective was to bring the upper reaches of the Tigris and Euphrates — northern Mesopotamia — under subjugation. Early in 1394 he resumed his march, heading northwest. At first the new year began well. Timur looked in on Mosul, whose ruler had made his capitulation some months previously. Edessa (present-day Urfa in southeast Turkey), abandoned by its prince, surrendered. The going from this point on would be more difficult.

Timur was put to no small trouble in securing the capitulation of the city of Mardin, east of Edessa. Mardin was ruled by Sultan Isa of the Ortok dynasty; he sought to fend off incorporation into Timur's domains by evasive action. Early in 1394, while Timur was marching on Edessa, Sultan Isa contacted him, offering his services. Timur sent word to Isa that he should immediately join him with his troops, for Timur intended to descend upon Syria to make war against Mamluke Egypt. Despite his promises Isa failed to put in an appearance. Stung by this, Timur (in February) marched on Mardin. Learning of Timur's approach, Isa emerged from the city. Humbly contrite, he brought rich gifts and asked for Timur's pardon. Granting forgiveness, Timur pitched his camp not far from the city. Here he received the sad tidings that his eldest son Omar-Shaykh, governor of Fars, had been killed by an arrow in Kurdish country while en route to join his father. He was only forty years old when he died. Also, Timur's men, who had entered Mardin to collect tribute and purchase goods, had been openly insulted by the inhabitants. Timur, however, decided not to besiege the rocky fortress city "because there was not grass enough for the vast number of horses and winter was almost at an end" (Sharaf ad-Din). Accessible by only one route and amply supplied with water and arable land on which to grow food, the city's citadel proved too much of a challenge for Timur at that time of the year. Late in February he left the environs of Mardin. The great storms which barred his way caused his men much suffering.

If the inhabitants of Mardin thought they were rid of Timur, they were soon undeceived. In April he returned. The condition of his army had improved so much that he was now able to mount his infantry on horses. Timur's men, on the day following his arrival, attacked with such fury that they soon made themselves masters of the town. The defenders retired to the citadel but the attack continued with such intensity that they capitulated. Fortune smiled on the people of Mardin, for on the day following their surrender Timur received news of the birth of a grandson, the future scholar-prince Ulug Beg. In his joy, Timur not only spared the lives of the inhabitants but even waived collection of the customary ransom. Sultan Sale, brother of Sultan Isa, was appointed Timur's governor. Then, hearing that the people of Amid (Diyarbekir) were refusing to submit to him, Timur hurried off to that place.

Timur's subsequent activities in eastern Anatolia may be briefly noted. Amid, located on the right bank of the Tigris, quickly fell and was sacked. Timur also ordered its fortifications to be razed, but the strength of its walls was such that his men had to content themselves with breaking off the crenellations.[9] After capturing Amid, Timur moved into the Mush region where he again put to flight his old enemy Kara Yusuf of the Black Sheep Turkomans. By the end of 1394 he had swept past Lake Van for a third invasion of Georgia, to be dealt with later.

What is remarkable in detailing Timur's activities during 1394 is an event which did not occur, namely, war with Mamluke Egypt. After the fall of Baghdad, Timur, as we have noted, sent an embassy to Cairo proposing peace and friendly intercourse. Barkuk, at the prompting of Sultan Ahmed Jelair, to whom he had given sanctuary, had the envoy executed as a spy.[10] At this time Barkuk further cemented his ties with Sultan Ahmed by marrying his niece.[11] Though Timur's conquests had not yet penetrated Mamluke possessions, Barkuk felt that a collison was in the offing and that his best course would be to march out and meet his adversary. Early in February 1394, while Barkuk was in the midst of campaign preparations, a letter arrived from Timur, declaring that the latter was "sent by Heaven to execute vengeance on the tyrants of the world." Timur's letter bristled with threats and warnings of dire reprisals if the murderer of his envoy did not make his submission. Barkuk replied in a defiant and insulting message. He likened the stilted and overblown language of Timur's secretary (who drafted the message) to the rasping of a bad fiddle.[12] Referring to Timur as an "Angel of the Evil One destined for hell-fire," he asked rhetorically, "For you are infidels 'and is not the curse of Allah on the Infidel?'" (Koran, II, 83; XI, 31).[13] Setting his great army in motion, Barkuk entered Damascus on March 23, 1394. Here he received embassies from three other rulers who were anxious to halt Timur, namely: Toktamish of the Golden Horde, the Ottoman sultan Bayazid and Cadi Burhan ad-Din Ahmed of Sivas. Their proposals for an alliance were accepted.[14] From Damascus, Barkuk marched to Aleppo, though not before aiding Sultan Ahmed once more to slip into Baghdad. Timur's governor there, with only a force of three thousand Sebzevari warriors, was powerless to oppose this advance and retreated eastward toward Shustar.

The threatened confrontation between Barkuk and Timur, was not, however, in the cards. Mindful of the weakened state of his army, which had sustained large losses of horses and sumpter beasts in the difficult campaigning of that year, Timur decided to postpone a show-down with the energetic and formidable Barkuk. Timur's flank, moreover, was once more menaced by Toktamish, who had re-established himself as khan of the Golden Horde. Barkuk, for his part, was no doubt relieved that the great battle did not take place, for he lived in greater fear of the growing might of the Ottomans than of Timur. After waiting several months for Timur to make good his threats, he learned that the conqueror had departed for Georgia. In November 1394 Barkuk judged that tensions had abated and returned to Cairo.

CHAPTER VII

The Five Years War – II
The Golden Horde (1394-1396)

Timur's devastating campaign against Toktamish still left the Golden Horde with great military potential. Moreover, Toktamish's eclipse was only temporary. As soon as Timur left for home, the former reassembled his followers and began a struggle with his rivals Timur-Kutluk and Bek-Bulat. By 1392 he had ensconced himself in New Sarai, killed Bek-Bulat and seized the city of Solkhat in the Crimea. His liberality in bestowing grants of important privileges on members of the aristocracy did much to facilitate this political comeback. By early 1393 he had reimposed his rule over most of the Golden Horde. Even his old enemy Kunche-oglan now recognized his authority.

Toktamish now began elaborating a grand design against Timur. In 1393 he approached Yagailo, the Lithuanian ruler, with the following proposals: (1) the resumption of tribute payment for the Russian lands held by Lithuania which had once pertained to the Golden Horde; (2) the establishment of commercial relations between the two states; (3) the conclusion of a new military alliance.

In order better to understand Toktamish's relations with Yagailo and his cousin Vitovt, we might consider briefly the Grand Lithuanian Principality. The Lithuanians, though at that time a pagan people at a rude stage of civilization, in the thirteenth and fourteenth centuries expanded south and east, incorporating large portions of what is now Byelorussia and the Ukraine. Meanwhile, their hard struggle with the powerful Teutonic Knights of East Prussia prompted them to seek military aid. This led to the conclusion of the dynastic Polish-Lithuanian Union of Krewo (1385) and the marriage of Yagailo with the Polish queen, Jadwiga. Vitovt, Yagailo's able cousin, led a faction which disliked this union, especially the Polish magnates' extravagant interpretation that, by it, Lithuania had become incorporated into Poland. In 1392, as the upshot of this opposition, Yagailo recognized Vitovt as co-regent and practically the ruler of the Grand Lithuanian Principality. Toktamish would, accordingly, have dealings with both.

Toktamish also turned his gaze towards Mamluke Egypt. The Golden Horde's interest in Egypt had deep historical roots. Both the Golden Horde and Il-Khanid Persia had belonged to the Chingisid empire. It was Il-Khanid Persia, however, which directly threatened Mamluke-held Syria and, ultimately, Egypt itself. The Mamlukes were, in fact, forced to beat back several Il-Khanid invasions. Meanwhile, the Golden Horde and Il-Khanid Persia came into conflict. Mamluke Egypt therefore adopted a policy of supporting friendship and military alliance between itself and the Golden Horde.

The death of Janibeg in 1357 had brought over twenty years of internal strife into the Golden Horde. Since the various rivals had little time for foreign relations, diplomatic contact with Mamluke Egypt practically ceased.

After he became khan of the Golden Horde in 1380, Toktamish decided to reactivate its foreign relations. In the spring of 1385 envoys arrived in Egypt from the Golden Horde. Significantly enough, their presents included some from Timur. The latter apparently wanted to show the Mamluke sultan that he considered himself Toktamish's "father," i.e., suzerain.[1] Iran's fragmentation after 1335 had done much to diminish Mamluke Egypt's need for an alliance with the Golden Horde. Timur s advance into Iran and his potential threat to Syria, however, encouraged a renewal of the old Golden Horde-Mamluke alliance. By associating himself with Toktamish's mission, Timur may have hoped to undercut such an alliance by indicating to the Mamlukes that Toktamish was beholden to him. Toktamish's marauding descent on Tabriz in the winter of 1385/86, which so angered Timur, occurred after the dispatch of the embassy to Egypt. The return embassy sent by Egypt in 1386/87 did not apparently offer any concrete proposals. However, when Toktamish sent envoys to Egypt in 1394/95 proposing military alliance, the proposal was received favorably. Now that Timur was master of Iran he was viewed as a much greater threat than before.

In his quest for allies, Toktamish dropped his policy of balancing off the several Russian principalities against each other in favor of "making concessions to the strongest duchy — that of Moscow."[2] Financial stringency played a part in the démarche. Toktamish was desperate for money and Moscow had the cash. It thus acquired the cities of Nizhni Novgorod, Gorodets, Murom, Tarusa and Meshchera.

We have indirect indications that Toktamish was negotiating an alliance with the Ottoman sultan Bayazid. He also began secret negotiations with the king of Georgia.

Timur's unsleeping suspicions with regard to the Georgians sparked off, in 1394, his third invasion of that unhappy land. While Timur was thus involved, Toktamish sent a force by way of Derbent which threatened his rear. This forced Timur to give up his plan to seize the strategic Daryal Pass through which the Georgian Military Highway now runs. Toktamish also mounted an attack upon Shirvan, but this was easily repulsed.[3]

Toktamish's depredations and elaborate diplomacy directed against Timur convinced the latter that he must make another, and this time a definitive, campaign against his erstwhile protégé. But the onset of winter and the need to make preparations for an enterprise of this magnitude caused him to postpone action for a few months. Timur made camp on the plains of Mahmudabad, a city now in ruins, located on the littoral of the Caspian Sea in what is now Soviet Azerbaijan. Timur, in his second great invasion of Toktamish's empire, this time picked the route through the Caucasus—one of the rare occasions that the southern Russian plain has been invaded from this direction. He was apparently influenced in his choice by three considerations: the traumatic remembrance of the privations suffered by his troops and the near disaster of the 1391 campaign through the Central Asian-Siberian steppe; secondly, the route through the Caucasus would be shorter, more direct, and would put him within easy striking distance of the lower Volga cities and the Crimea, from which the Golden Horde derived much important economic sustenance; furthermore, since Timur was faced with an alternative—to move against Toktamish or to attack the Mamlukes in Syria—he could, by sojourning in the Caucasus area, keep his options open until the last moment.

Even so, both Timur and (later) Toktamish made diplomatic efforts to stave off the impending collision. In the winter of 1394/95 Timur sent negotiators to Toktamish asking him to cease his hostile acts and to acknowledge Timur's suzerainty. Shami ad-Din Almalik, his ablest and most articulate negotiator, in handing over his master's letter, delivered such an impassioned and eloquent speech that Toktamish was momentarily won over, only to be dissuaded by his entourage "whose interest it was to make war" (Sharaf ad-Din). In consequence, Toktamish sent back a letter full of rude and coarse expressions which so angered Timur that he gave the order to begin operations.

In the meantime, internal strife in the Golden Horde had reached such an impasse that a bloody battle had taken place among some of the leading princes. Though the causes of this dissension remain obscure, it weakened Toktamish's position. Realizing the precariousness of his situation, he dispatched an embassy to Timur with peace proposals in a desperate bid to appease the latter's wrath. Whether this embassy ever reached Timur is a moot point. Some sources claim that Timur received the embassy south of Derbent but considered Toktamish's explanations inadequate.[4] Other sources state that when the envoys reached Derbent they learned that Timur was already on the march and approaching Toktamish's borders. They thereupon abandoned their mission and, in great fear, rushed back with the news to Toktamish.[5]

Timur's campaign, launched in the spring of 1395, came at a bad time for Toktamish. Quite apart from the recent dissension, the Kipchak still had not recovered from the 1391 invasion. To meet Timur's advance, Toktamish hurriedly dispatched a large vanguard led by one of his emirs. Timur, however, threw this back in an engagement near the river Kui in the North Caucasus. Toktamish, with a large army, then entrenched himself in a camp protected on all sides "by great bucklers and waggons which serv'd for walls" (Sharaf ad-Din). Toktamish, in the disposition of his forces, put himself in a false position: Timur could easily push his forces back against the nearby Terek river. Realizing his mistake, Toktamish struck camp and, in the teeth of enemy opposition, rafted his forces across the river. There he positioned himself behind hastily thrown up fortifications. The river now separated the two armies. A struggle for the river crossing—the only suitable one in the vicinity—went on for three days. Timur, under cover of night, finally forced his way past the barricades and gained mastery of the river passage. The stage was set for the second mammoth encounter between the two adversaries.

On the eve of the battle Timur inspected his men's battle gear: swords, lances, bows and arrows, chain mail, maces and nets for catching men. Again, as at the battle of Kunduzcha, he divided his soldiers into seven bodies, assuming command of the reserve himself.

The battle began on the night of April 14, 1395 when Toktamish attempted unsuccessfully to outflank Timur's forces. On the next day the same tactic was repeated, but in vain. Toktamish's left flank was sorely beset by Timur's powerful reserve. Before the battle resumed on the 16th Toktamish reinforced the left wing by detaching troops from his right wing. This did not redeem the situation, however, for again the left wing sustained heavy losses. Quarrels broke out among the emirs of the right wing. According to Ibn Arabshah, one of the emirs, Aktai by name, asked Toktamish's permission to kill another emir then and there. Toktamish promised to give him satisfaction but only after the battle was over. Aktai, in a huff, withdrew from the battlefield with all his followers.

The remainder of the right wing refused to rush to the aid of the sorely pressed left wing but began of its own accord to retreat towards Azov. This decided the outcome: Toktamish, together with a small number of his adherents, abandoned the battlefield. Despite Timur's ultimate victory it was nip-and-tuck until the very end, for the enemy put up a tremendous fight. At one point, Timur, reduced to fighting as a common soldier with only his sword, his arrows expended and his half-pike in shatters, was rescued from his predicament only by a bit of derring-do by one of his emirs with a band of fifty men.[6]

Toktamish's diplomatic contacts with Mamluke Egypt in the end availed him naught. We have seen how Sultan Barkuk in March of 1394 had given a positive answer to Toktamish's request for an alliance. Then Barkuk learned, in the fall of 1394, that Timur had returned to his own posssessions, and the anticipated great conflict was averted that year. A firming up of the alliance with Toktamish was then a less pressing matter for Barkuk. He did, however, respond to Toktamish's embassy by sending one of his own. This arrived in New Sarai while the battle of the Terek was taking place. Fearful of falling into Timur's hands now that Toktamish had been badly beaten, the envoys returned home. This was the last Mamluke embassy to Toktamish.

After the battle of the Terek, Toktamish, with Timur's men nipping at his heels, crossed the Volga and headed for the old Bulgar kingdom. Timur's warriors killed a number of Toktamish's followers, but Toktamish himself eluded capture. While the Bulgar state had been harried by Timur's men in 1391, this time they did a more thorough job. Though Timurid historians fail to mention it, it was Timur, evidently, who obliterated the Bulgar cities (Bulgar, Zhukotin, Kermenchuk, etc.) and not the Muscovites as is usually thought.[7] The destruction of Bulgar, a city of 10,024 homes, was so complete that only its name and ruins have survived.

Timur next made his way to New Sarai. Profiting by past experience, he decided to set up a new puppet khan. Even before reaching New Sarai he declared that Toktamish had forfeited the throne. Upon arrival he set up Koiradzhak, son of Urus Khan, as the new khan.

Crossing over to the right bank of the Volga, Timur set about subjugating the western segments of the Golden Horde (the lower Dnieper, the Don and the Crimea). In the meantime the emirs of the right wing of the Golden Horde had proclaimed their own khan, one Tash-Timur-oglan, a descendant of Juchi. Timur turned to deal with this new threat to his plans. Operating in the environs of Akkerman in the Dniester river estuary, his troops brought most of the local people into subjection. Tash-Timur-oglan and Aktai, however, saved themselves by flight. After plundering Akkerman, Timur crossed the Perekop isthmus and marched into the Crimea. The centerpiece of his operations there was the taking of the city of Caffa after an eighteen-day siege. The city was sacked and its Christian population enslaved. Other Crimean cities also felt Timur's destructive fury.

The conqueror now moved north toward the upper stretches of the Don into the Russian principality of Riazan, southeast of Moscow. Here he destroyed the city of Yelets, an event mentioned in the Russian chronicles. At this point we encounter a historical conundrum—did Timur continue northward and take Moscow? Sharaf ad-Din, anxious to glorify Timur and mindful that his great adversary Toktamish had taken Moscow, albeit by guile, avers that he did. This statement has been accepted as true by a number of historians.

This is flatly contradicted by the Russian chronicles. According to these, Timur, after harrying the principality of Riazan, suddenly stopped and remained immobile for two weeks. Then he turned his banners south, never again to threaten Russian possessions.

The people of Moscow, on Timur's approach, were filled with terror. The city's churches were open from morning to night, filled with people praying for deliverance. Metropolitan Kiprian, head of the Russian Orthodox Church, was unable to quiet the fears of the most faint-hearted. Hearing of this, Grand Prince Vasilii I, who had posted himself with his troops on the banks of the Oka river southeast of Moscow to bar Timur's advance, sent to the city of Vladimir for the revered miracle-working icon of the Virgin Mary.

The Russian chronicles tell us that Timur, asleep in his tent, had a nightmare on the very day (August 26) and hour that the Muscovites received the famous icon. In this dream he saw many church dignitaries with gold staffs and above them a woman of indescribable radiance surrounded by ten thousand warriors, the entire host rushing toward Timur in a frightening manner. Timur awoke trembling, and asked his intimates the meaning of his dream. The majestic woman, replied the wisest of them, was the Mother of God, defender of Christianity. "And so we will not prevail over them," commented Timur,[8] giving the order to retreat southward.

Should we dismiss the story of the nightmare as completely fanciful? The French scholar Jean Aubin offers evidence suggesting that Timur possessed the power of precognition or second sight, and that he had premonitory dreams.[9]

Timur's favorable opinion of Muscovite military capabilities requires some explanation. Let us go back to 1382. That year Toktamish was able, thanks to his stealth and cunning, to get within 56 miles of Moscow before its inhabitants realized their peril.[10] Moreover, Russian princes at odds with Moscow were aiding Toktamish with intelligence and men. Though the city had the only walls and stronghold of stone in northeast Russia[11] as well as cannon, a shortage of troops caused Grand Prince Dmitri "of the Don" (as he was called after the battle of Kulikovo in 1380) to repair to the city of Kostroma to recruit more troops, leaving behind his wife and children. They and the metropolitan Kiprian were allowed to leave the city only after much wrangling and unpleasantness. Men of wealth tried to do the same. The city folk, banded together in their *veche* or popular assembly, resolved to defend the city themselves. In the end their heroic efforts were of no avail. After three days of unsuccessful siege, Toktamish managed to insinuate himself into the city with false promises. He then ordered a savage sacking of this rich and populous city.

Many Muscovites felt that they had been shamelessly abandoned by their grand prince and the aristocracy. The proper lessons were learned, however. In 1390 an agreement was worked out between Grand Prince Vasilii I, the next ruler, and his relative, Prince Vladimir Andreyevich, by which in time of war one of them would remain in Moscow to head the city's defenses while the other led the army sent out to oppose the enemy.[12] This agreement was implemented in 1395. This time, too, the Muscovites were not caught napping. Scouts were apparently sent out systematically, for we know that the Muscovites received daily reports concerning Timur's activities in Riazan principality.[13]

Additional factors may have prompted Timur's withdrawal on August 26. The season of rain and foul weather was approaching. He would be campaigning in a northern land, for the most part forest, with few flocks of animals to feed his warriors and with numerous enemy troops barring his way. He had, moreover, only part of his troops with him.

Timur's withdrawal to the south took him to the mouth of the Don river. His chief operation there was the sacking of the port city of Tana or Azov, located near the site of the ancient Greek colony of Tanais.

Tana at that time had a large colony of merchants from Venice, Genoa, Catalonia and Biscay. The merchants of the city thought it prudent to send an embassy bearing gifts and seeking benevolence. A Venetian merchant living in the city at the time has left us an account of what took place.[14] According to this perhaps somewhat exaggerated description, Timur's camp covered eighty miles, while his personal head-quarters was located in a tent city of silk and gold sprawled over three miles. The latter was so large that it encompassed a river with a crossing. The envoys, after taking off their shoes and berrettas, were allowed an audience with Timur, who was seated on a golden throne. They presented their gifts and asked that the merchants of the city be allowed, after Timur took the city, to retain their trading privileges. Timur also graciously listened to the remarks of two Franciscan friars with them.[15] Timur was soothingly reassuring, inviting the ambassadors to a banquet at which he toasted them with his jewelled cup and acceded to their requests. Timur attached one of his senior officers to the envoys when they returned to the city, ostensibly to engage in trade with the merchants. Actually the man was a spy who, while in the city, carefully examined the merchants' warehouses and the ships in the harbor. Some of the merchants, not gulled by Timur's display of amiability and scenting danger, took asylum in the ships anchored in the harbor. By fortunate coincidence the Venetian galleys happened to be in the port on one of their regularly scheduled calls. The arrival of Timur himself a few days later was accompanied by various excesses. Though the Muslims were segregated and spared, the Christians saw their goods, their homes, churches and warehouses set afire while they themselves were made captive. A large number perished in the conflagration. Others succeeded in purchasing their freedom on payment of a ransom, while those who had taken refuge on ship escaped by sea. Once Timur left, a determined effort was made by the city's surviving inhabitants to recover from the carnage and destruction. Venice rapidly repaired the damage done to the Venetian quarter. Its competitors presumably did the same. Yet Timur's depredations in Azov and nearby commercial entrepots took a lasting toll.[16]

The next to suffer were the Circassians of the Kuban region, followed by other peoples of the Caucasus. Timur himself set up winter quarters in northern Daghestan.

Though Timur made Koiradzhak khan of the Golden Horde, he nonetheless appointed his own men as governors of its cities. Their citizenry, especially in Astrakhan and Sarai, did little to conceal their hostility. When Omar i Tabani, his governor in Astrakhan, reported the open enmity of Muhammad, the city elder, Timur felt that the Astrakhanis must be set an example. Despite the severe cold and heavy snowfall, in the winer of 1395/96 he made his way to Astrakhan, situated at the mouth of the Volga. Its citizens, learning of his approach, constructed a rampart of ice around the city. Notwithstanding, when Timur reached the outskirts and demanded that Muhammad present himself before him, the order was complied with. Muhammad was immediately seized and later shoved into a hole in the ice. Timur then let the people believe that upon payment of a ransom they would be spared further vexations. When this was collected he ordered the sacking of the city. The population was evacuated and the buildings set on fire. The devastation was so thorough that when it was later rebuilt another site was chosen some twelve kilometers away.

Timur detailed his grandson Pir-Muhammad to mete out a similar fate to New Sarai, capital of the Golden Horde. The city was duly taken, plundered and burned to the ground. Archeological excavations bear mute testimony to the unspeakable cruelty with which this was conducted. Piles of bodies without heads or limbs were revealed, and even some of the bones had been minced into little pieces.

Old Sarai, Solkhat, Baldzhiman and other cities were also destroyed. Though the nomadic population suffered substantially, the destruction effected in the cities was immeasurably greater. There was a reason. Timur sought to undermine the most cultivated and developed provinces of the Golden Horde to such an irreparable degree economically, especially commercially, that it could never again become a great state. In this he succeeded to a considerable degree.[17]

Timur's devastations would also seriously crimp the Golden Horde's ability to make war. His removal of artisans from cities such as New Sarai—some of whom were highly skilled metal workers—would give the Russians an edge in weaponry, specifically cannon (these were making their debut in the Near East and Central Asia). The ruin he brought also lowered the cultural level of life for the Golden Horde.

Though Timur, because he had looted and set fire to several Russian cities in 1395, is depicted in Russian chronicles as a malign figure, he unwittingly performed a great service for Russia earlier the same year by his defeat of Toktamish on the Terek river. He so weakened the Golden Horde that for some years after, Muscovy remitted little or no tribute payment to the latter.

The devastation of the Kipchak was so complete that during the winter of 1395/96 Timur's own men suffered from an acute scarcity of victuals and of fodder for their animals. "As a consequence of the great cold and frost the army of Timur grew weaker and their spirits fell," wrote Sharaf ad-Din, adding that the greater part of the cattle perished. In the spring of 1396 Timur hurriedly withdrew his army southward through the Caucasus. The Avars, Lesgians and other peoples of Daghestan in the eastern Caucasus rose up against him. These freedom-loving mountaineers were brought to heel only after several months of fighting. No one in the medieval period — not even the Mongols before him — made such a deep penetration into the wild mountains of Daghestan. Cutting down trees and pushing through roads, Timur pitilessly harried both valley and mountain dwellers. At length he continued his way southward by way of Derbent into Iran. He returned to Samarkand in the summer of that year (1396) where, as Ibn Arabshah puts it, "he shook his bags and emptied his pouch of the booty from Dasht" [i.e., the Golden Horde].[18]

Though Timur had gravely weakened the Golden Horde he failed to keep it entirely quiescent and biddable. His puppet khan Koiradzhak soon found himself unequal to his position. At first Toktamish, who had established himself west of the Volga, succeeded once again in setting himself up as khan. Other contenders, notably Timur-Kutluk and his associate, Edigei, undermined his position. The internecine struggle brought further ruin to the country. In the end Timur-Kutluk established his paramountcy. Deeming it prudent to have himself accepted as Timur's client, he sent an embassy which was favorably received on August 17, 1398. Edigei, who could not be khan because he was not a Chingisid, supported Timur-Kutluk.

Toktamish, meanwhile, made his last great bid to regain power. He concluded an agreement with Vitovt by which he relinquished all claim to Russian territory held by Lithuania and promised to aid Vitovt in securing the remainder. In return Vitovt would remit annual tribute to Toktamish and would help him acquire the Crimea, Azov, Kazan and Astrakhan.[19]

Initial successes were followed by several setbacks. Then on August 12, 1399 came the great battle of the Vorskla, a left affluent of the Dnieper, in which Toktamish and Vitovt were defeated by Timur-Kutluk and Edigei. This ended Toktamish's dream of again becoming khan of the Golden Horde.

Timur-Kutluk paid a very heavy price for his victory. Losses on his side were great and he had been badly wounded, expiring soon afterward. Edigei installed Timur-Kutluk's brother Shadi Beg (ca: 1400-1407) as khan. Toktamish led an adventurer's life for several years. Making his way to Tyumen in western Siberia he bethought himself of his former mentor Timur. He sent an embassy asking Timur to help him recoup power in the Golden Horde. The envoys reached Timur at Otrar in January 1405 while the latter was en route to invade China. Timur, anxious to curb the growing power of Edigei by supporting a rival, promised to help when he returned home. However, Timur died a few weeks later. Toktamish himself perished in Tyumen at the hands of Edigei's son. In 1419 Edigei, in turn, was killed by one of Toktamish's sons. Edigei had reunited the entire Ulus of Juchi for the last time. With his death the Golden Horde passed into irretrievable decline and final disintegration.

CHAPTER VIII
Descent into India

After two years of repose (1396 to 1398) in Samarkand it was India which next engaged Timur's attention. His motives for invading India have been variously assessed. One recent biographer believes that he wanted to secure his border on the south before becoming involved in any major conflict, either with China or with the Mamlukes.[1] The distracted state of India at this time, however, makes this more than doubtful. Historically, too, while the northwest frontier has been the ancient corridor of attack upon India, the Indians themselves have been little inclined to cause trouble beyond their own frontiers. Timurid historians, such as Sharaf ad-Din, assert that Timur had learned that the Muslim rulers of the Sultanate of Delhi were overly tolerant towards their Hindu subjects. He had, moreover, become aroused by those pages of the Koran calling for holy war against the infidels and wanted to become a *ghazi* or fighter for the faith. Elsewhere, Sharaf ad-Din avers that Timur's chief intentions in his wars were "to exterminate robbers, tyrants and infidels, to put a stop to their disorders, and give peace and tranquility to the people."[2] Subsequent events would give the lie to these pious professions. What led Timur to invade India was a desire for plunder, opportunities for which had been denied his followers during the relatively long sojourn in Transoxiana; a desire for more martial glory; and a wish to emulate his model Chingis Khan, inasmuch as the latter had invaded India. The time seemed opportune, for the Sultanate of Delhi, founded in 1205 in the wake of the conquest of north India by military adventurers coming from Central Asia, Iran and Afghanistan was by now in an advanced state of decay.

The Mongol threat to the northwest frontier had indirectly played an important part in the earlier expansion of the Delhi Sultanate. In the early 1220s Chingis Khan had penetrated as far as Multan in the western Punjab. Later, Mongols would periodically swoop down from Afghanistan and plunder the cities of Multan and Lahore. On several occasions they even laid siege to Delhi itself. Though the Mongol raiding parties were too small to effect permanent conquest, the Mongol threat forced the Sultanate of Delhi to maintain a large army and to improve measurably its discipline and organization.[3]

The subsidence of these raids in the first quarter of the fourteenth century, as the Chagatai realm declined, allowed the Delhi Sultanate to use its 350,000-man army to expand southward so that around 1335 it comprised almost all of India.

By the middle of the century, however, centripetal forces increasingly prevailed as local governors ignored Delhi and set up autonomous Muslim and Hindu kingdoms. Firoz Shah Tuglak (1351-88) was the last great ruler of the Sultanate. After his reign the state ceased to be an all-India power. His death ushered in a succession struggle which disfigured the decade prior to Timur's invasion. The area under the effective control of Mahmud Shah and the noble who controlled him, Mallu Iqbal Khan, included Old Delhi, Siri and some nearby districts. Nusrat possessed the districts bounded by the Doab (between the Jumna and the Ganges rivers), Sambal, Rohtak and Panipat. In fact, both Shahs were marionettes controlled by ambitious emirs. A confused struggle took place between the rival groups in which both the rural and urban populations suffered from the depredations and rapine which followed in its wake.

It was Pir-Muhammad Jehangir, Timur's grandson, who began the invasion of India. In 1392 Timur had appointed him viceroy over the Afghan area which abuts the northwest frontier of India, namely: Kunduz, Ghazni, Kandahar and Kabul. In the fall of 1397 Timur ordered his grandson to begin the invasion of India. By the end of the year Pir-Muhammad had probed deep into the Punjab, had attacked and taken the city of Uchha, and had invested the city of Multan.

In early 1398 Timur convened a kurultai. In his harangue he dilated on the disorders in India and the favorable opportunities these presented. The emirs were asked about their reactions but no one attempted dissuasion. A large army of some 90,000 men, combining both cavalry and infantry, was mustered from throughout the empire though "all of the chiefs, and the greatest part of the companys [sic] who were in posts of consequence, were Tartars."[4] On August 15, 1398 the expedition got under way.

In his invasion of India, Timur took a south-southeasterly course through Afghanistan. On reaching the formidable Hindu Kush mountains, he crossed via the Khawak Pass (11,640 ft.), used previously by Alexander the Great.[5] At Andarab, in northeast Afghanistan, near the axis of the Hindu Kush, Timur received complaints from the local Muslim population that it had been persecuted by the infidel Siah-Posh or Black Robed Kafirs (unbelievers).[6] The origin of the Kafirs is still a matter of conjecture. Popular tradition has it that they are descended from stragglers left over from the army of Alexander the Great. There is, however, good reason to believe that there were Greeks here before. Timur, detaching three out of every ten men in his army, assembled a task force to deal with these enemies of the faith.

The wild tangle of mountains in which Timur operated against the elusive Kafirs is, even today, one of the most inaccessible parts of the world. Leaving the excess baggage and most of the horses at Khawak, Timur began crossing the mountains. The going was very bad. A warm wind made the abundant snow so spongy and slushy that the men had to confine their movements to nighttime when the snow was once again frozen hard. The Kafirs were nowhere to be seen. They had, indeed, hidden themselves in caves and covered the entrances with snow. Upon reaching the tops of the mountains, Timur's men found no other way to descend than either to let themselves down by ropes or slide on their backsides to the bottom over the snow and ice. For his own descent, Timur had a wicker basket prepared, to which were attached strong cords. Five times the basket was lowered to previously prepared platforms before the bottom was reached. The lowering of the horses by ropes went much less successfully, however. Only two of the mounts escaped being dashed on the rocks below. Timur mounted one of these, leaving his emirs to walk along with their men. In places, staff in hand, Timur walked on foot.

At length Timur made contact with the enemy, apparently in the valley of the upper Alishang river near Najil.[7] Timur's men attacked the Kafirs, even though the latter had climbed to the top of the mountain. After a struggle lasting three nights the Kafirs begged for quarter. In an unusual lapse from his ordinary cruelty, Timur granted it on condition that the Kafirs agreed to become Muslims—a stipulation which was accepted. That night, however, the Kafirs treacherously attacked Timur and his men. Timur's anger now knew no bounds; captured Kafir warriors were slain and their women and children enslaved. Towers of heads were erected on mountain tops and near the scene of the attack. Timur also ordered that an account of this engagement be engraved on marble so that posterity would know of his valor.[8] This tablet pleased him mightily since not even Alexander the Great had defeated the Kafirs. Subsequent operations against the Kafirs, led by subordinate commanders, met with indifferent success. One force was ambushed and defeated, though a second force managed to put the enemy to flight.

Rejoining his army, Timur arrived at Kabul in August and made camp in a meadow outside the city. He received envoys from Edigei and Timur-Kutluk of the Kipchak, asking forgiveness for past misdeeds and pledging submission. Khizr Khodja, now khan of Mogolistan, sent an envoy with a similar message. Both missions were received warmly.

In September 1398 Timur resumed his march. On October 7 he reached the Indus where he halted until a bridge of boats and reeds could be made. Meanwhile, he dismissed the various envoys accompanying him, including one from the prince of Kashmir whom Timur ordered to await him with his army at Deopalpur. On October 11 (1398) Timur crossed the Indus, a feat not attempted by Chingis Khan who, at that point, had turned back.

Though Timur's primary objective was Delhi, some 600 miles away, he detoured somewhat in the direction of Multan. Pir-Muhammad had taken the city after a six month siege but then found himself in various difficulties.[9]

When Timur reached the Jhelum river he learned that the local Hindu ruler, who was named Shihabuddin Mubarak Tamin, was one of those who had repudiated his earlier capitulation to Pir-Muhammad. Hearing of Timur's approach, Shihabuddin shut himself up in his citadel which was protected on all sides by a deep moat. Even so, Timur's men took the citadel, which they burned down. However, Shihabuddin managed to escape.

Next on the line of march was the town of Tulamba, located near the confluence of the Jhelum and the Chenab, some 52 miles to the northeast of Multan. Up to this point Timur had encountered no real opposition. Many of the local rajahs and chieftains had sent presents to propitiate the conqueror. At Tulamba, too, events at first went smoothly. The large ransom demanded by Timur from the local population (save the Ulema and the Shaykhs, who were excused) was almost collected. Timur, in the meantime, was informed that his men lacked provisions. He therefore gave them authorization to enter the town in search of food. However, his soldiers soon transformed this into a general license to plunder, an action opposed by the townspeople. In the ensuing melee all the houses were burned and the population massacred or enslaved. Only the Shaykhs and Sayyids were spared. Timur made no attempt to take the town citadel, since it might have required a long siege. Because of the Tulamba affair "The unscrupulous conduct of the invader opened the eyes of those who had already submitted to Pir-Muhammad. They now changed their mind and became hostile toward him."[10] Tulamba was revealing in another important way: it presaged the fragility of Timur's hold over his men during the remainder of the Indian campaign. During battle, the latter would still willingly submit to strict discipline; however, they would take amiss any attempt to curb their appetite for plunder and rapine. Tulamba prefigured the savage sack of Delhi.

The following day Timur resumed his march to a "great and populous" town called Shahnavaz where he collected additional grain, burning what he could not carry. Then, moving along the Ravi river, on October 25 he reached a fordable point at a village called Jaijen. It was here that he received a full account from Pir-Muhammad of his plight after taking Multan. The torrential rains of the summer monsoon season had caused so many of his mounts to perish that he moved his troops, many now without horses, into the city. The local inhabitants, seeing his predicament, invested the place and interdicted supplies so that the number of mounts was reduced even further. The excessive humidity and the omnipresent mud further dispirited Pir-Muhammad's men. Timur quickly dispatched thirty thousand horses which enabled Pir-Muhammad to extricate himself from his difficulty.

The next objective was Bhatnir, reputedly one of the strongest fortresses in India. Timur's troops covered fifty coss in less than twenty-four hours (a coss varies from one to four miles). Even at its smallest computation the march was an extraordinary feat. A number of refugees from Deopalpur had sought protection at Bhatnir. Deopalpur was in bad repute with Timur since its citizenry had killed Muzaffar Kabuli and his one thousand troops sent there by Pir-Muhammad. At Bhatnir the press of refugees was so great that half of them had to remain outside the fort.

The taking of Bhatnir by storm was Timur's most notable conquest of the Indian campaign. Though situated in the middle of a (waterless) desert, the fort itself had a reservoir which was replenished during the rainy season. The governor, Rai Dul Chand, commanding a doughty band of Rajput warriors, had made all preparations for the coming ordeal.

Timur first struck terror into the hearts of those in the fortress by massacring the refugees outside the walls. Then he ordered a general assault from all sides. Despite a valiant defense, in a few hours Timur's men seized the gates and the city, except for the citadel, the sapping of which was quickly put in hand.

In despair, Rai Dul Chand asked Timur for terms. The latter agreed, removing his men from the city. On November 8 Timur received the governor graciously, presenting him with a gold brocade robe and a richly ornamented belt and sword. However, he was soon to show his sterner side. To avenge the killing of Muzaffar Kabuli and his men, Timur ordered the arrest of all the refugees from Deopalpur and Adjouan. The adult males were executed, the women and children were pressed into captivity.

When he learned of this, Kamaluddin Main, Rai Dul Chand's brother, closed the city gates. Timur's anger was now thoroughly aroused. As a preliminary, he ordered the immediate execution of Rai Dul Chand, and renewed the attack in all its intensity. Once again the besieged asked for quarter. Timur demanded tribute in return (November 28). The sum required was apparently so high that disputes soon arose, upon which Timur ordered the destruction of the city and massacre of its inhabitants. This prompted a common stand by Hindus and Muslims. As Sharaf ad-Din recorded: "The Guebres [idolaters] set fire to their own houses, casting their wives, children and goods into the fires; and those who called themselves Mussulmans cut their wives' and children's throats. And thus the men of these two sorts uniting together, put themselves in a posture of defence, being resolv'd to die sword in hand. They fought in a cruel and obstinate manner."[11] Timur followed up this bloodbath by burning the palace and other dwellings in the city.

The stench of dead bodies was so intense that Timur left Bhatnir on November 30 (1398), heading in the general direction of Delhi. In order better to carry fire and sword to the provinces of Multan and Lahore, he divided his army into numerous flying columns. As his units approached Lahore, Timur ordered that a general rendezvous be made at Kaithal, some thirty-four miles from Samana. His march from Bhatnir had been a military promenade. The populace fled in panic at his approach, leaving their possessions behind, while the cities did not choose to stand siege.

The chief victims of Timur's advance from Bhatnir to Delhi were not Hindus but Muslim Jats. But since the latter had engaged in highway robbery, he had a good excuse to harry his coreligionists.

From Panipat Timur crossed the Jumna into the Doab region in order better to provide his horses with forage. The fort of Loni, seven miles north-northwest of Delhi, was taken by storm and the garrison

slaughtered. From Loni Timur made his way to the magnificent palace
of Jahannuma, constructed by Firoz Shah, some six miles from Delhi.
At this point Timur could have immediately marched on Delhi. However, his approach was one of great caution. Guards were posted at all
fordable points on the Jumna river, cutting off Delhi from the Doab.
Timur sent out troops to ravage the country to the south and southeast of the city. Meanwhile, with a force of seven hundred, he crossed
the river to reconnoiter the terrain outside the city with a view to
picking a suitable battlefield. Mindful of the six months it took to take
Multan, Timur was anxious to avoid a siege, hoping instead to entice his
opponents out into the open to do battle on a field of his choosing.

The news that Pir-Muhammad and then Timur had invaded India
should have caused the rulers of Delhi and Firozabad to cease their
strife and form a common front. Help should also have been forthcoming from the rulers of adjoining regions. Nothing of the kind occurred,
so that Mallu Iqbal and Sultan Mahmud stood alone. So far these two
had done nothing to oppose Timur. Mallu, who had been watching
Timur's movements, seeing him within striking distance and accompanied by only a small force of seven hundred men, thought that a provi-
dential moment had arrived. Masking his movements behind trees and
orchards, he suddenly attacked with a force of about four thousand horsemen and five thousand foot, together with twenty-seven elephants. Not
having time to organize his battle line properly, Timur confined himself
to a rearguard action until relief forces arrived. The attackers were then
repulsed and sent fleeing back to Delhi. During the rout one of the elephants collapsed and died, an event hailed by Timur as a good augury.

This skirmish was the catalyst that touched off one of the bloodiest
tragedies of Timur's career. While en route to Delhi, his forces had
taken an enormous number of captives, both Muslims and Hindus. It
was reported to Timur that when Mallu and Mahmud had suddenly attacked him the captives had seemed very pleased. Other emirs warned
that during any battle to come, the captives would break their bonds
and enter the fray, though how they woud accomplish this is not clear.
On December 12, after mulling this over, Timur ordered that all persons
with Indian slaves were to put them to death forthwith. If they dis-
obeyed they themselves would be killed. It took less than an hour to
carry out the order. Even Maulana Nasir ad-Din Umar, one of the most
venerable scholars in Timur's retinue, "who cou'd never consent so
much as to kill a single sheep,"[12] had to order the slaying of his fifteen
slaves. The number of captives killed has been much exaggerated, how-

ever. Almost all accounts accept Sharaf ad-Din's figure of upwards of 100,000. The historian K. S. Lal, however, has convincingly demonstrated that 50,000 is a more accurate figure.[13] Nonetheless, even this figure for the slaughter of POWs seems worthy of an entry into a satanic edition of the Guiness Book of Records.

After the massacre Timur moved his forces closer to the city, hoping that Mallu and Mahmud would oblige him by emerging to do battle. His astrologers and soothsayers, however, were troubled by the omens. If their dire prophecies and doubts became known to Timur's men, who were not immune to the dark and nameless fears of a grossly superstitious age, their morale might be gravely impaired. Timur roundly told his seers "that neither joy nor affliction, adversity nor prosperity, depended on the stars" but on the will of Allah.[14] Though Timur consulted astrologers, he was only interested in favorable auguries. At the public prayer held the next morning Timur ordered that the Koran be brought forth. Opening the book at random, he chanced upon a passage "which predicted the destruction of a people by a wonderful effect of the almighty providence."[15] Interpreting this prophecy to his own advantage, Timur showed the passage to his army, greatly raising their assurance of victory.

On December 14, 1398 Timur crossed the Jumna river unopposed and camped on the plain of Firozabad, just outside the city. Here he set up a fortified camp. All kinds of shields, palisades and other barricades were thrown up around the encampment, while buffaloes and camels, their feet and necks trussed together, were placed in front of the ditch which formed the outer defense perimeter. The object of these dispositions was twofold: to break the force of any charge of the dreaded elephants, and by this seemingly extravagant display of caution and trepidation, to lure the emboldened enemy out of the city.

As usual, Timur's calculations proved out. Mallu and Mahmud debouched from the city's gates with a force of 10,000 horse, 40,000 foot and 120 elephants. The latter were protected with armor and on their backs were wooden towers bristling with crossbowmen, archers and javelin-throwers. According to Sharaf ad-Din scimitars smeared with poison had been placed between the tusks of the elephants, though this may have been a flight of fancy on his part "for poisoned weapons were not a feature of Indian warfare."[16] Throwers of Greek fire and melted pitch marched alongside the elephants as well as rocket-men, whose charges were designed to frighten the horses of the enemy. "The use of naphtha and Greek fire were known [in India] from early times.

Incendiary arrows and javelins, as well as pots of combustibles were hurled against the enemy." The Delhi army used grenades, fireworks, and rockets against Timur.[17]

Despite this dazzling array, there were grave deficiencies in the Indian army's situation. Timur's army, numbering 90,000 men, was almost twice as large. Mallu and Mahmud had set too much store by the ability of the elephants, "the animate tanks of medieval India" (Lal), to break the enemy ranks and to disperse his cavalry. Mahmud's foot soldiers, recruited from the peasantry and even from robbers, were of poor mettle and indifferently armed. While the appearance of the Indian troops did not disconcert Timur's men, they were very nervous at the sight of the elephants. It was bruited that arrows and sabers had no effect on the hides of these ponderous beasts and that they could toss a horse and rider a great distance into the air with their trunks.

Timur took a number of precautions to allay his men's fears. He entrenched his front line behind a ditch, in back of which was a rampart and bucklers. Buffaloes, whose necks and feet were bound together with leather thongs, were placed close to one another to break the charge of the elephants. The infanty was issued three-pronged iron hooks (called caltrops), which Timur had fabricated for the purpose, to place before the elephants. According to Sharaf ad-Din these contrivances were not used since victory was achieved before they were needed.[18] Nevertheless, the psychological effect of all these precautions must have reassured Timur's troops. Not so the scholars accompanying Timur who, when asked where they would like to be during the battle, answered: "If it please your majesty, we chuse to be near the ladys" (Sharaf ad-Din), a reply which earned a smile from him.

The battle array of both sides consisted of a vanguard, center, reserve and two wings.[19] The leaders of both sides led their centers. At the last minute Timur, at the suggestion of some of his emirs, strengthened the right wing and vanguard by detaching soldiers from the main body.

The battle began with an ear-shattering din. As Sharaf ad-Din relates: "So frightful a noise was never heard: for the cymbals, the common kettledrums, which were beat on the elephants' backs, the bells which the Indians sounded, and the cries of the soldiers, were enough to make even the earth to shake."[20] Ferishta, a Muslim historian of India who died in 1626, asserts that the Indians fought slackly, that in a short time they were "totally routed, without making one brave effort to save their country, their lives or their property."[21] This is not borne out by either the battle account of Sharaf ad-Din or by that of Ghiyas ad-

Din. The latter states flatly that "the enemy showed [much] steadfast-ness on the field of battle."[22] Timur's vanguard, as the enemy vanguard advanced, succeeded in hiding itself behind the right wing and at the opportune moment caught the enemy vanguard in the rear, mauling it severely. Meanwhile Pir-Muhammad, with the right wing, attacked the enemy left wing, first with a shower of arrows followed by the thrust of cold steel, and drove it back. He then had his swiftly moving cavalry attack the slow and lumbering elephants, most of whose drivers or ma-houts were dismounted by the first charge. The elephants fell back in panic on the Indian left wing (when terrified, elephants are apt to trample both friend and foe), causing further havoc in the enemy ranks. Meanwhile Timur's own left wing routed the Indian right. The task of dealing with the Indian center, or main body, which advanced in good order with its elephants, fell to Mirza Roustem, leader of the reserve. An all-out effort was made to put the elephants out of action. Lances were hurled at the mahouts and others mounted on the elephants' backs, while the beasts themselves were wounded in diverse places. In a short time, Sharaf ad-Din tells us, the battlefield was strewn with ele-phant trunks. Casualties among the outnumbered and outmaneuvered Indians also were heavy. In the words of Ghiyas ad-Din: "So many thousands of Hindus, with faces black as soot, and with bodies, as if covered by pitch, were killed, staining with a red color the sabers of our bahadurs [brave warriors], that their number exceeds any descrip-tion."[23] Even the bloodbaths in Isfahan and Sistan, the author adds, pale in comparison.

The discomfiture of the Indian main body sparked a rout as the sur-vivors, including Sultan Mahmud and Mallu, made a dash for the gates of Delhi. After managing to slaughter a large number of these before they reached the gates, Timur fixed his headquarters near the city walls. Mahmud and Mallu, not trusting the city's massive walls to keep Timur out, furtively fled the city that midnight, each going out a different gate. Upon hearing of this Timur, after conferring with his emirs, im-mediately sent out a unit in pursuit, but to no avail.

The stage was set for one of the greatest disasters ever to befall Delhi, the capital and the largest city of the Sultanate. Girded by walls five meters thick, the city was well equipped for a siege. In the walls were accommodations for guards, caches of weapons and storehouses for the keeping of grain in the event of a siege.[24] Even so, the inhabi-tants of Delhi, abandoned by their leaders, deemed resistance futile. They ceded the gates of the city, and Timur's horsetail standard soon was raised over the battlements. At first there was no intimation of impending tragedy. Entering one of the quarters of the city, Timur had the satisfaction of playing at emperor by sitting on the throne of the Sultan of Delhi and, at the imperial pavilion erected at one of the gates, of receiving a procession of civil and religious dignitaries. One of them extracted from Timur the pledge that the city would be spared from plundering and massacre upon payment of a ransom. All the elephants and rhinoceroses in the city were brought before Timur. The 120 elephants fell down humbly before him and simultaneously made a great cry as if they were asking for quarter.[25] Timur took some back with him to Samarkand, while others were distributed among his sons, grandsons and vassals in the various parts of his empire. Two days after his arrival in the city, on a Friday, Timur had Maulana Nasir ad-Din preach in the great mosque. His names and titles were mentioned in the *khutbah*. Curiously enough, no coins were minted.

Timur's men fully expected to sack Delhi as a reward for their great victory. Soon some of them slipped into the city and began molesting the inhabitants. Although he ordered his emirs to put a stop to this, they were unable. One source states that the city magistrates appointed by Timur to help collect the ransom asked for help in dealing with some rich citizens who had barricaded themselves in their homes and refused to pay their share. The troops sent got out of hand and began plundering.[26]

To compound the confusion, the ladies of Timur's court wanted to go into Delhi to see the sights, especially the famous palace of a thousand columns built by Alauddin Khalji in 1303.[27] The women and courtiers negligently left one of the gates open, allowing 15,000 men to slip into the city. By this time even the number of those authorized to enter was large. They included: (1) the emirs and comptrollers of Timur's divan charged with collecting the ransom; (2) soldiers sent to seize all refugees, since Timur's amnesty covered only natives of the city; (3) soldiers sent to collect grain and sugar for the army. Quarrels inevitably arose over the amount of ransom to be paid, the rigor with which the search for refugees was pursued, and over food requisition. There was more plundering. The inhabitants, in despair, set their possessions afire, threw their women and children into the conflagration and then rushed out to attack their tormentors.

This resistance only goaded Timur's men into increasing their depredations and killing. The emirs, in an attempt to contain the disorders, closed the city gates. That night, however, the soldiers within the city

reopened the gates so that by the next morning all of the army had
entered. According to Sharaf ad-Din, the emirs could no longer control
their men.[28] The next two days were spent in plundering, burning and
slaughter in Siri and Jahanpanah, which with Old Delhi comprised the
city of Delhi. Each soldier took at least twenty captives and some as
many as fifty or a hundred. The booty included precious stones and
jewels of all kinds, choice fabrics, vases, gold and silver cups and silver
money. On the 19th the troops turned their attention to Old Delhi
where a number of Hindus had taken refuge in the great mosque. A
force of five hundred men, led by two emirs, made their way there and
massacred everyone. Old Delhi was sacked the same day. Those who
escaped death were enslaved. These included a number of artisans.

During the first days of the disorders Timur was ensconced in his
quarters outside the city, and was so deep in his cups celebrating his
victory that, according to Ghiyas ad-Din, no one could acquaint him
with the events taking place. It was only later, when flames wrapped
the city, that Timur supposedly fully appreciated what was happening.
His reaction ran true to form: he raged not against his own mutinous
soldiers but against the hapless citizens of Delhi who had the temerity
to resist when subjected to the most appalling outrages. Whether Timur
could have restrained his men, who had run amok two months before at
Tulamba, is a moot point. By ordering the massacre of the Indian prisoners on the eve of the battle outside Delhi he had deprived his men of
their booty; the sack of Delhi was an indemnification. The assertions of
Timurid historians that he had no inkling as to what was happening in
the city until it was too late must be viewed with suspicion.

Timur's remaining activities in India, which consisted in perpetrating
further barbarities, may be briefly related. Before leaving Delhi he
ordered the assembling of the members of the city's Muslim establishment in the great mosque, where he posted a guard over them "to protect them from the insults of the soldiers, whom victory had render'd
insolent."[29] From Firozabad, a few miles from Delhi, he struck off in a
northeasterly direction and on January 4 (1399) he arrived at the important fortress city of Meerut. Its Muslim governor, after burning the
Hindu women in the rite of *jauhar,* put up a desperate though unavailing resistance. After the reduction of Meerut, Timur's men set fire to
the city and slaughtered the inhabitants.

At this juncture, Timur decided to divide his forces. Emir Jehan
Shah, with the left wing, proceeded to the upper stretches of the Jumna
river while Timur, with the remainder, moved on to harry the banks of

the Ganges. On January 13 Timur reached Hardwar, a major center of Hindu pilgrimage, on the banks of this holy river. Not far from here water flows from under a rock shaped in the form of a cow venerated by Hindus as the source of the Ganges. Here the Hindus came to fling the ashes of their dead, perform ritual ablutions and cast gold and silver into the stream. Though this was pretext enough for a self-styled champion of Islam to pillage it, the presence of a large number of Indians in the vicinity with great riches in cattle and moveables made the prospect of killing and looting that much more agreeable.

At Hardwar Timur left the Ganges and headed for the Jumna to join Emir Jehan Shah. He then moved with his recombined force into the Siwalik hills. In the course of a month's campaigning (January 23–February 22, 1399) in this mountainous, wooded country Timur fought twenty battles and took seven fortresses. According to Ghiyas ad-Din, the inaccessibility and natural defenses of these redoubts were even superior to those of Mazanderan in northern Persia where Timur had encountered so much difficulty. Timur gave further proof of his cunning in the taking of one of these fortresses. Though the governor of the fortress capitulated, the defenders refused to pay the usual ransom and barred Timur's entry into the citadel. He then hit upon the idea of offering large sums of money for weapons, even rusty and defective ones Out of greed, the inhabitants sold him their arms. Then Timur asked that forty of them come to serve in his forces. Upon their refusal, he attacked the citadel, which was soon overwhelmed.

From Siwalik Timur made his way to Jammu, the Hindu ruler of which was taken prisoner. Timur had his wounds carefully treated, since ransom might be paid for his release. Later on, whether by conviction, fears or threats, he was brought to see the beauties of Islam. He recited the credo and ate cow's meat, an abomination to his Hindu co-religionists. This apostasy brought its due reward, for Timur spared his life and made him his vassal.

The arrival on March 20 of a messenger from Miranshah in Tabriz brought news concerning conditions back home. This intelligence, it appears, was sufficiently disquieting for Timur to decide to wind up his affairs quickly in India. The next day he dispatched Hindu Shah, his treasurer, to Samarkand to announced his impending return. And two days later he issued marching orders to his officers. Before leaving he assigned Lahore, Multan and Deopalpur to Khizr Khan, a local potentate, as fiefs. Some historians claim that Timur made Khizr Khan his viceroy in India, but this cannot be substantiated. Timur freed most of the prisoners taken in Delhi save the artisans, craftsmen and others with special skills. These he took with him as well as blocks of stone and other building materials. Hunting rhinoceroses, tigers and other exotic animals and birds on the way, he crossed the Indus on March 19 "after inflicting on India more misery than had ever before been inflicted by any conqueror in a single invasion."[30]

Famine and pestilence swept the land. Timur's troops had destroyed stores of grain and standing crops; the myriads of putrefying corpses infected the air with their noxious emanations. Scarcely less appalling was the ensuing confusion and anarchy. Though Timur had awarded fiefs to Khizr Khan and other local lords, he made no real attempt to organize his Indian conquests and left no troops behind to enforce what dispensations he did make. According to Sharaf ad-Din, although one of his objects in invading India was to bring an end to anarchy, he left the country in even worse disorder than before.

Another of Timur's professed goals in invading India was to suppress Hinduism and to advance the Islamic faith. Yet the sources do not mention the destruction of Hindu temples. Nor did the defeats he administered to the local Hindu rulers who (except in Rajputana) were small-time landowners, do much to promote the Islamic cause in those parts.

Indeed, it is arguable that Timur's invasion did far more harm than good to the Islamic cause in India. His devastation of Delhi was so thorough that only in the sixteenth century under the Moghuls did it again recover something of its former importance. Though admittedly the Delhi Sultanate was already in a bad way, the shattering blows Timur dealt it effectively eliminated any possibility of a comeback. In 1425 this pitiable remnant of a past glory finally passed from the scene. Muslims as well as Hindus perished in the desolation Timur brought to the land. Understandably, Muslim historians of India have dubbed as martyrs those of their coreligionists who fought Timur, while the latter himself is branded as an infidel.

Timur did manage to seize great booty and in this way please both himself and his warriors.[31] His conquest of Delhi and the Punjab were to furnish his descendant Babur (1483-1530) with the legal and moral pretexts for his conquests in India which would result in the creation of the vast Moghul empire. And the Indian artisans and craftsmen whom Timur transported to Samarkand left their imprint on the arts of Central Asia. Timur, finally, could preen himself in the knowledge that he had penetrated India farther than had either Alexander the Great or Chingis Khan.

CHAPTER IX
Timur against Bayazid I Yildirim

Despite old age and recent illness, Timur did not tarry long in Samarkand. The first order of business was to dispose of some of the booty seized in India. This was distributed among the Muslim dignitaries and other worthies so "that every one might partake of the benefits of his conquests.[1] In an empire founded on plunder it was important not to overlook those left behind.

Timur also decided to construct a new cathedral mosque, to be financed out of the avails of his Indian campaign. The old cathedral mosque no longer met the needs of an expanded city population. Moreover, with his advancing years, Timur may have viewed the mosque as a partial atonement for his sins. Grandiose in scale, it was intended to beggar in size all other mosques in the Muslim world. Begun in May of 1399, its construction was pressed with frenzied speed. Two hundred masons and numerous other artisans worked on the mosque itself; five hundred men labored in the mountains of present-day Soviet Tadjikistan cutting stones which were transported to Samarkand by ninety-five chains of elephants.

Despite the tempo of construction, most of the work was done while Timur was away on campaign. The mosque complex — for it included a number of structures with an inner court surrounded by a rectangular wall — covered an entire city block.[2] The mosque itself was the largest ever built in Central Asia, and was also one of the largest in the Muslim world. It was the most grandiose and magnificent of the many buildings Timur constructed. Massive foundations were laid to counter any settling of the building or the action of earthquakes in this earthquake-prone region. Timur's demands on his architects, which included great spans of vaults and domes, exceeded their technical capabilities. Stone columns, moreover, are not suitable in an earthquake belt. The great haste and constant revision of architectural plans also contributed to the jerry-built nature of the buildings. By the seventeenth century the condition of the mosque became so dangerous that a new cathedral mosque was constructed in the Registan, or public square. Despite the rasure of time, enough remains of the main mosque, portal, etc. for them to loom over the low adobe houses of the modern Uzbeks. The now truncated portal, for example, equals in height a modern ten-story apartment house. The ruins are artistically most impressive, and bear witness to the extraordinary achievement of the numerous artists and artisans who worked on the project.

The complex is usually called the Bibi Khanum mosque. According to local legend, Timur's young and beautiful wife Bibi Khanum, daughter of a Chinese emperor, built the mosque as a surprise for him while he was away. However, Timur never married a Chinese princess.[3] Possibly Bibi Khanum is a corruption of Sarai-Mulk-Khanum, Timur's senior wife, who acted as patroness of the project, and who was anything but young.

††††††

The considerations impelling Timur to cut short his Indian campaign have already been noted. His progeny, ruling in the west, had by their follies brought such disorder there that a firm hand was needed. In Fars, Pir-Muhammad, son of Omar-Shaykh, was reportedly trying to poison his brother Roustem and others. He also showed an aversion to going out on military campaigns when ordered to do so by Timur. (Parenthetically, he should not be confused with Pir-Muhammad, son of Jehangir.) Much more disquieting was the situation in Azerbaijan where Timur's son Miranshah was exhibiting signs of insanity after a fall from horseback while out hunting. In 1398 he had descended upon Baghdad, where Sultan Ahmed had re-established himself, though his advisers sought to dissuade him. After two days he lifted the siege, upon learning of a conspiracy against him in Tabriz. The expedition, carried out in the torrid heat of summer, had been a grand exercise in futility. Other earnests of Miranshah's addled and disoriented brain were his squandering of the treasury and his destruction in Tabriz of the mausoleum of the famous physician, statesman and historian Rashid ad-Din, author of the encyclopedic *History of the Mongols of Persia,* a mother lode of information on Mongol history, customs and mores. Miranshah had the body exhumed and interred in the Jewish cemetery, although Rashid was a Muslim convert. Moreover, Miranshah had goaded Sharif Ali, ruler of Sheki and head of the Erlat tribe, into revolt. Though he too was a Muslim, Miranshah had plundered his principality, located in what is

now northern Soviet Azerbaijan, destroying cities and villages and rob-
bing and persecuting the population. This gratuitous cruelty caused
local inhabitants, in a play on words, to call Miranshah "Maranshah" or
"reptile-king." Sharif Ali was joined in this revolt by the Georgians,
who took advantage of Timur's absence in India. To meet the Georgian-
Erlat threat, Miranshah dispatched a force led by his son Abu-Bakr.
Though Sharif Ali was killed in a battle fought outside the walls of the
fortress of Alinjak, besieged by Timur's troops since 1387, the Georgian-
Erlat forces prevailed. This victory enable them to lift the siege of Alinjak for some time and to liberate Sultan Ahmed's son Tahir, who had
taken refuge in the fortress. In summing up Miranshah's actions, Sharaf
ad-Din declares that he had become a "lunatik." While in this mentally
deranged condition he quarreled with his wife Khanzade. Fleeing to
Samarkand, she informed Timur, just back from India, that his son was
planning to revolt against him. Then too, there was the matter of the
Ottoman sultan Bayazid I whose eastward expansion across Anatolia, to
be dealt with later, posed a threat to Timur's western frontiers. Finally,
Timur had a score to settle with the Mamlukes of Egypt and Syria and
the time seemed auspicious. All these factors galvanized Timur into action, even though he had returned from India only four months earlier.[4]

Timur's first military objective was to restore order in Iran. Once
this was done, he may have thought that the war with Bayazid and his
allies would be a lengthy one. Or, after dealing with Bayazid, he may
have intended to invade Egypt and then Europe. In any event, he issued
mobilization orders for a war of several years; Muslim historians have
accordingly dubbed this the "Seven Years War." The loot he had seized
in India provided Timur the wherewithal to reward his followers and to
finance the coming war, recalling the adage that "War supports war."

On October 11, 1399 Timur left Samarkand on his last and greatest
adventure in the west, leaving his grandson and heir-designate Muhammad-Sultan, son of Jehangir, in charge of the caretaker government in
Samarkand. His route southward to Iran took him to Kesh, Termed,
Balkh and Herat. En route he stopped off and paid his respects at the
tombs of sundry local saints and distributed alms among the poor. Tra-
versing northern Iran, he then made his way northwestward to Tabriz,
the capital of Azerbaijan and of the viceroyalty of his son Miranshah.
The latter, on Timur's arrival, was persuaded by his advisors to go out
and meet his father, but received a frosty reception. Two of Timur's
emirs had been sent ahead to restore order and to audit the treasury accounts. Finding that much money had been squandered, they refused

to pass the accounts. Though Timur was at first so enraged with his son's conduct that he wanted to have him executed, he at length relented. Like so many doting parents before and after him, he placed most of the blame for his son's conduct on the influence of bad companions. Miranshah's favorites, especially his musicians, were ordered hanged. These included the poet Muhammad Kuhistani, accounted the wittiest man of his time. Additional taxes were imposed on the population to replace the sums in the treasury frittered away by Miranshah; simultaneously, pensions were granted to members of the Ulema to help them forget about Miranshah's affronts to the Muslim faith. Miranshah nominally remained ruler over the former Il-Khanid possessions, but the real authority was entrusted to his son, Abu-Bakr. Despite his mentally disturbed condition, Miranshah was to accompany Timur on his march westward. Interestingly enough, Clavijo, who visited Miranshah in 1404, did not note anything out of the ordinary in his behavior.

Order was also restored in Fars, where Timur did not have to appear in person. Again bad companions were blamed for having corrupted one of Timur's progeny. The mixers of poison, mostly Persian, were hanged on Timur's orders.

The conqueror then took the road for Karabagh, whose broad and pleasant plains northeast of Nakhichevan had at one time been a locale much favored and frequented by the Il-Khans when they ruled in Iran. Here he was met by Shirvanshah Ibrahim. Ibrahim, who stood high in Timur's favor, begged him to pardon Sharif Sidi Ahmed, ruler of Sheki, whose father Sharif Ali had made common cause with the Georgian rebels. Timur obliged, confirming Sidi Ahmed as ruler of his possessions. Ibrahim, to honor his lord, prepared a great banquet for which so many horses and sheep were slaughtered that the camp cooks could not roast all the carcasses. This was supplemented with diverse entertainment and a barbaric profusion of gifts for Timur: exotic animals, "beautiful boys and girls," fine textiles, gem-encrusted gold belts, finely wrought arms and armor and six thousand choice horses.

Though Timur decided to pitch camp in the Karabagh in the winter of 1399/1400, festivities and relaxation were not the only things on his mind for, as we have noted, he had a score to settle with the Georgians. With a detachment consisting of three out of every ten of his men, Timur decided to seek out the Georgian rebels. Both Ibrahim and Sidi Ahmed were required to aid in the punitive foray. Making his way northward, Timur began operations. Axes and saws were plied to cut a road through the dense woods. Homes, shops, churches and other buildings in the invaders' path were soon only smoking, calcined ruins. Knowing the Georgians' addiction to wine, Timur ordered that all vines be torn up by the roots. Trees were cut down or stripped of their bark. For one month Timur's men engaged in the ruination of the countryside as far as the Aksai river in Daghestan. But though many Georgians were slain, others effected their escape. Meanwhile, Timur's men and horses began to suffer terribly themselves from the intense cold and snow. So Timur cut short his fourth campaign against the Georgians and returned to winter quarters at Karabagh.

With the coming of spring the conqueror decided to break camp. At a kurultai of his senior officers and princes of the blood, he secured unanimous agreement to give top priority to a resumption of the war against the Georgians.

Timur's route northward to Georgia took him through Berda, a city now in ruins, located in the center of what is now the Azerbaijan SSR. Here he was met by Taharten, ruler of Erzinjan, who brought nine times nine gifts. Timur singled him out for special favors; he was presented with a horsetail standard and two kettle drums and was again formally invested as vassal ruler of his principality. Taharten, we may note, had earlier made his submission to Timur in 1387 at a time when the Ottoman threat was still no larger than a man's hand. Dramatic changes had occurred in the meantime. The Ottoman Sultan Bayazid was making great gains in Anatolia and Taharten's possessions lay athwart his path of eastward expansion. Taharten's renewal of his subordination to Timur would be a bone in Bayazid's throat, since he coveted this area. Timur knew this; before dismissing Taharten he gave him instructions as to how to defend his territory against any Ottoman incursion.

Upon arriving at the borders of Georgia, Timur sent a message to King George VII demanding that he surrender Prince Tahir, son of Sultan Ahmed Jelair, to whom he had given asylum. Receiving a very uncivil reply, Timur launched a fifth "fire and sword" campaign against this doughty mountain people. Again terrible destruction was visited upon the land. The Georgians in their extremity fled from the valleys into the mountains, where no one had ever conquered them. Here, in their inaccessible fortified caves and houses perched on mountain crags, they had removed all the valuables they could carry.

In crossing the mountains of Afghanistan on his way to India, Timur had had himself lowered from great heights by means of a platform to which were attached long ropes manipulated by his men above. This device provided inspiration for a new method of attack against the Georgians. Climbing to the tops of mountains, Timur's men lowered their comrades down the sides of perpendicular cliffs with ropes attached to platforms or made-to-order baskets. Reaching the mouths of the caves, the soldiers first shot a rain of arrows and then jumped in to finish off those inside. Or, where this was not possible, flaming combustibles were hurled inside either to smoke the defenders out or to burn them, their homes and the wooden defense works. Fifteen Georgian strongholds were taken, including the capital (Tiflis), where Timur left behind some of his redoubtable Khurasani troops. In these proceedings Timur played to the hilt his role as champion of Islam in this Christian country. Captives escaped beheading only by embracing Islam. Mosques were built to replace burned churches and monasteries.

Though King George managed to elude capture by moving ever north, his nerves by now were badly frayed. He sent Prince Tahir, the immediate object of Timur's wrath, on to Ottoman territory to join his father Sultan Ahmed, who had fled from Baghdad upon news of Timur's approach. King George then sent an envoy named Ismail, apparently a Muslim, to plead with Timur. The king promised payment of the annual tribute, the sending of auxiliaries to serve with Timur upon call, and respectful treatment of all Muslims. Timur finally relented and agreed to pardon George. Before withdrawing southward, however, he harried other Georgians and destroyed seven more fortresses to give point to the pledge he had extracted from the king.

In his Georgian campaign of 1399/1400, Timur doubtless wanted to secure his flank before becoming involved with Bayazid and/or the Mamlukes. He had forced the Georgian king into submission. Kara Yusuf, leader of the Black Sheep Turkomans, had been driven from his possessions and forced to take refuge with the Ottomans. Ibrahim Shirvanshah, Sidi Ahmed, ruler of Sheki, and the White Sheep Turkomans were Timur's tributaries and their troops would later fight under his banners in the battle of Ankara. Finally, Taharten, ruler of Erzinjan, could be relied upon to comply with Timur's wishes.

North of Erzinjan lay the rather grandly named "Empire of Trebizond," formed by a Byzantine prince after the Crusaders had imposed their rule upon Constantinople as a result of the infamous Fourth Crusade in 1204. In securing his right flank, Timur could not afford to overlook this small state which, in the event of an Ottoman takeover, could be used by Sultan Bayazid as a springboard to attack him. (Early in the sixteenth century the Ottomans would use Trebizond as a base of operations for their struggle with Safavid Persia). Bayazid's borders marched with those of the Empire of Trebizond now that the cities of Sivas, Amasya and Tokat were in the Ottoman grip. The Empire's long seacoast and its port capital of Trebizond were vulnerable to attack by Bayazid's small navy. That Manuel III, ruler of Trebizond, was brother-in-law to Taharten, Timur's trusted vassal, only heightened the conqueror's interest.

We do not know precisely when Timur, to forestall Bayazid, descended upon Trebizond and reduced it to a vassal state. This probably occurred in the spring of 1400 following Timur's Georgian campaign.[5] Not considering the operation important enough to require his presence, he sent a task force under one of his divisional commanders. Manuel III at first thought he could stay the advance of this force by posting mercenaries in the mountain passes. These were quickly overwhelmed so Manuel prudently turned to diplomacy. Though our sources fail us as to details, he somehow successfully negotiated an agreement by which his empire became tributary to Timur, with its military and naval forces at the latter's disposal.[6]

Historians place the initiation of diplomatic contact between Timur and Bayazid at about the time that Taharten was paying homage to Timur. It was then that an embassy sent by Timur arrived in Adrianople (Edirne), the Ottoman capital, bearing rich gifts including a valuable robe and a letter. The subsequent Timur-Bayazid correspondence is beset with great difficulties for the historian because the letters often bear neither the date of their dispatch nor, in most, cases, the name of the place where they were written.[7] They also contain puzzling or unclear statements.

In his first letter Timur called Bayazid "son" and asked that the emirs whom he had dispossessed in eastern Anatolia, and who had fled to Timur's court, be reinstated. "Be contented with that which Allah has given you and with what you have seized from the unbelievers but give up immediately those provinces which you have stolen from other rulers so that Allah will be gracious to you. If not then I will be their avenger with Allah's assistance."[8]

Bayazid's reaction was one of unfeigned rage. Ordering the beards of the envoys shorn—a great insult in the Muslim Orient— he shouted at them: "Go back and tell your master that he should come at me quickly and I will be waiting for him. If he should not come then he should be separated from his legitimate wife."

Historians are inclined to put the blame on Bayazid for the exchange of epithets that followed, and which eventually led to hostilities. It is true that Timur recognized Bayazid as a great *ghazi* or fighter for Islam and was willing to leave him alone if he would but be content with the territorial gains he had made at the expense of the Christian infidels and cause no trouble. Yet Timur's approach was offensive. Calling someone "son" and giving him gifts of clothing were, in the ways of the Orient, actions resorted to when dealing with subordinates. Bayazid was stung to the quick when Timur did not at least treat him as an equal.

Insensitive to the hurt he had done Bayazid, Timur was greatly irritated by the failure of his mission. An animated and, on the whole, an increasingly abusive and minatory correspondence ensued, of which are preserved three more letters of Bayazid to Timur and four more of Timur to Bayazid, the former both initiating and closing this exchange. References will be made to some of this correspondence later on in the narrative.

At the moment Timur was concerned about the effect which further military operations would have on the morale and will to fight of his own men. Fighting fellow Muslims was no novelty; indeed, most of Timur's opponents belong to that faith. Now for the first time he would be making war against a Muslim who had scored great successes against the Christian infidel. Bayazid's reputation therefore had to be besmirched and blackened. This "smear campaign" was entrusted to the dervishes, with whom Timur had close ties. In making the rounds among his men, they branded Bayazid, his sons and high officials as sinful and degenerate; Timur, on the other hand, was represented as a paradigm of moral austerity and piety. In their opinion, war against Bayazid would be sanctioned by Allah, with Timur being "only a tool of Allah for the punishment of tyrants and the extermination of godless and immoral Muslims."[9]

†††††

Let us go back now a few centuries into history to understand better what followed. The first influx into Anatolia of pastoral nomadic Turkic tribes occurred in the eleventh century in connection with the rise of the sprawling ill-compacted Seljuk empire. In 1094 this mayfly of an empire collapsed in the wake of discords and internal strife. Branches of the Seljuks continued, however, in some parts of the Near East. In Anatolia the Seljuk offshoot was called the Iconia Sultanate; it was formed from former Armenian, Georgian and Byzantine provinces. By the early fourteenth century this in turn broke up into a number of independent emirates: Karasi, Karaman, Tekke, Saruhan, Hamid, Germiyan, Kastamonu, Menteshe, Aydin and Ertogrul. The last of these, named after its founder, the Turkish leader Ertogrul, was located in western Anatolia to the southeast of the Sea of Marmara. It was ruled by Osman Bey (1281-1326) who gave his name to, and is regarded as the real founder of, the Osmanli or Uthmanli (Arabic rendering) dynasty, of which the name Ottoman is a Western corruption. Both he and his successor Orhan (1326-1359) made conquests.

During the reign of Murad I (1359-1389) the Ottomans crossed over into Europe. After conquering eastern Thrace, Murad, who assumed the title of Sultan, transferred the capital from Bursa to the Thracian city of Edirne (Adrianople). He is also credited with creating the Janissary corps, the crack infantry force which the Ottomans possessed at a time when in Europe cavalry was still the "Queen of Battle" and infantry counted for little.[10] In 1389 Murad won a great victory over the Serbs at Kosovo, only to be struck down by a Serbian assassin. He was succeeded by his oldest son Bayazid. The defeated Serbs were, on balance, treated leniently. They became Ottoman vassals, obliged to pay an annual tribute and to furnish a stipulated number of heavy cavalry when called upon by the Sultan.[11]

Ottoman territorial expansion under Bayazid would take a quantum leap forward. In the early 1390s he annexed Aydin, Saruhan, Menteshe, Hamid and Germiyan in western Anatolia. In further campaigning to the east he conquered more territory or induced local rulers to acknowledge him as suzerain.

In 1394 Bayazid left Anatolia under the charge of his capable and energetic commander Timurtash, who busied himself with consolidating Ottoman authority in eastern Anatolia. Bayazid's main preoccupation now was the Byzantine Empire. Its emperor, Manuel II Palaeologus 1391-1425), has been aptly described as "heir not to a throne but to a desperate situation."[12] By this time it had shrunk to Constantinople and its environs, Thessalonika and a part of Greece. It had become a de facto Ottoman protectorate under Murad. In 1394 Bayazid decided to remove even this last lingering scrap of independence, to annex the city and make it his capital. Thus the long siege began.

The attack on Constantinople led to a final resuscitation of the Great Crusades, forcing Bayazid to lift the siege of the city. In September of 1396 he inflicted a crushing defeat on a large multi-national

Christian host at Nicopolis in Bulgaria. Panic seized Europe. Ottoman units reached up into Austrian Styria while other units ravaged Wallachia. Greece also suffered further assaults. And the siege of Constantinople was resumed.

Bayazid journeyed once more to Anatolia. The emir of Karaman had taken advantage of Bayazid's involvement at Nicopolis to resume hostilities. In 1397 he was defeated, killed, and his emirate was seized. Burhan ad-Din on the Sivas area, another old foe, had his possessions annexed the following year. Bayazid then moved to the upper Euphrates region of eastern Anatolia, then under Mamluke rule. Disregarding his earlier alliance with them against Timur, he annexed Malatya, Divrigi and Behisni (Besni). He would, by this action, alienate the Mamlukes.

Bayazid then returned to direct the ongoing siege of Constantinople. Whether it would have fallen but for Timur is one of the conundrums of history. Bayazid lacked a large fleet and heavy artillery, the two factors which enabled Sultan Mehmed II Fatih to conquer the city in 1453. Nonetheless, his siege was beginning to take effect. Famine stalked the city, while the price of a measure of grain shot up twenty gold pieces. Cadavers lay about unburied. France responded to Manuel's pleas for aid by sending out an expedition under Marshal Boucicault, a veteran of the Nicopolis debacle. Byzantium's fate was a matter of indirect interest to France. Of direct interest was the fate of the Genoese colony of Galata south of the Golden Horn,[13] in what is now the new part of Istanbul, since in 1396 Genoa had come under the rule of France. Manuel, at Boucicault's urging, decided on a trip to the West to make a personal appeal for more aid, leaving behind his nephew John as regent. And so in December 1399 Manuel, accompanied by Boucicault, set sail in the French ships, leaving behind some French troops under Chateaumorand, one of Boucicault's officers.

Manuel's journey as an imperial mendicant took him to Venice, Milan, Florence, Paris, London and then back to Paris where he and his suite were lodged in the Louvre. But though graciously received, he obtained little beyond fair words and vague promises. Constantinople seemed on the point of capitulating, while the trip of Manuel dragged on. Clavijo, during his sojourn in the city in 1403, learned that Regent John had concluded a treaty whereby he would cede the city, should Bayazid triumph in the seemingly inevitable war with Timur. Indeed, according to another source, in 1402 a delegation set out for Anatolia to bring Bayazid the keys to the city.[14] It was also widely believed by the city's population that the Patriarch Matthew had privily negotiated an agreement with Bayazid allowing him to remain on as head of the Orthodox Church when the city fell. These acrobatic negotiations also involved Timur. According to Clavijo, Regent John and the Genoese *podestà*, or governor, in Galata promised the conqueror that if he made war on Bayazid they would aid him by positioning armed galleys in the Dardanelles which would prevent Bayazid from transferring Turkish troops from the Balkans to Anatolia. "Further," Clavijo continued, "the Greeks [i.e., Byzantines] sent and promised Timur a subsidy in money."[15] The Genoese, moreover, hoisted Timur's standard over Galata Tower to betoken respect. Even so, Timur was concerned lest the Byzantines and Genoese capitulate to Bayazid. In August 1401 two of his emissaries arrived in Galata with assurances that Timur would soon make war against Bayazid and entreaties that the besieged continue to resist. One of the emissaries was a Dominican friar, Francis Ssathru (or Sandron). He, and possibly also his companion, was first sent to the area by the French king to help execute a Christian grand design wherein Timur would be used to bring Bayazid to ruin. The operation may have been the brainchild of Manuel II, then residing in Paris.[16]

The Ottomans, during this time, were also busy on other fronts. Worry was expressed over the fate of Modon in the Morea where Manuel II's family had been sent for safety, but which was now being threatened by the Ottomans. Finally, the Venetians, noting the gradual but implacable advance of the Ottomans in Albania, became concerned about the security of the nearby island of Corfu.

Though in 1400 Bayazid's main preoccupation was the siege of Constantinople, Timur's activities in the east did not go unremarked. While the latter was involved in the Caucasus campaign against the Georgians, Bayazid early in 1400 sent orders to his son Suleiman to resume operations in eastern Anatolia, using Sivas as his base. An envoy was sent to Taharten demanding that the tribute of Erzinjan, Erzerum and other of his lands be sent to Bayazid: i.e., Taharten was asked to switch his fealty from Timur to Bayazid, though the latter knew that Taharten was Timur's man. Taharten immediately penned a letter apprising Timur of this latest chess move.

Timur reacted to the challenge with his usual dispatch. Sending back the ladies of his household to Sultaniya, he arrived in eastern Anatolia in August (1400). On reaching Erzerum he was greeted by Taharten. On September 1 Timur entered Bayazid's territory with Sivas, the northeasternmost bastion of Ottoman Anatolia, as his objective. Suleiman, commanding an Ottoman force, engaged in some scrimmaging with Timur's men but, finding the enemy too numerous, thought it best to hasten to Bursa to obtain reinforcements. Mustafa, governor of Sivas, remained behind to direct the city's resistance. The fortress city, whose defenses had been completely rebuilt by Ala ad-Din Keikubad, the great Seljuk prince, was one of the most strongly garrisoned and best defended strongholds in those parts. The massive stone walls and bastions were protected by a moat on three sides. Timur built an embankment next to the west wall, the only one not protected by a moat. Battering rams, stone throwers and flame hurling machines began their fell work. Meanwhile sappers, boring like termites, were busy tunneling under the walls. As they finished, the wooden props in the tunnels were set ablaze, causing portions of the walls and bastions to collapse. Though the defenders fought manfully they could not stay the merciless attack of the enemy. After eighteen days of this nightmarish siege, and with the final storming of the city by Timur's troops close at hand, the inhabitants had had enough. Mustafa, the governor, apparently wanted to make a last ditch stand, but he was driven out of the city. A delegation of Muslim divines was sent out to Timur to plead for mercy.

The Muslims Timur agreed to spare and set at liberty, upon payment of a ransom. But the Armenians and other Christian noncombatants were enslaved. Since most of the 4,000 cavalrymen who had defended the city were Armenians, Timur decided that they should be buried alive. To make the torment of their martyrdom even more excruciating, Timur ordered that their heads be tied between their thighs "and they were rolled into pits in groups of ten like hedgehogs rolled up into balls."[17] To prolong their agonies wooden boards were first placed over them and only then earth. The impression Sharaf ad-Din gives, that Timur contented himself with enslaving the Christian noncombatants, does not tally with other sources. According to these Timur's men, upon entering the city, cut down every male they encountered, while the women and children, after being herded together in one spot, were ridden down with horses. Moreover, all the lepers who lived in a special quarter of the city were put to the sword.[18] Timur then ordered that the walls of the city be razed. Though Suleiman managed to lead reinforcements back to relieve the city, by the time he arrived it was too late. The fall of Sivas, the best fortified position in Anatolia, was a stunning blow for Bayazid, for it was the first serious setback he had received in his meteoric career. He then learned that Malatya had opened its gates to the enemy without a fight. Eastern Anatolia lay pinioned under Timur's boot.

Even while the siege of Sivas was going on, Ahmed Jelair and his ally Kara Yusuf of the Black Sheep Turkomans, who had slunk back into Baghdad, realized the dread implications of Timur's movements. Seeing that before long the corridor connecting them with their ally Bayazid would be closed, they decided to make a run for it. Timur, learning what the two were up to, detached troops to intercept them. But though Kara Yusuf s sister and Ahmed's other wives and daughter fell into Timur's hands, the two brothers-in-law managed to make their way safely to Bayazid's side. The latter's grant of asylum to these two implacable enemies of Timur would be another bone of contention between these two masterful and prideful conquerors.

The fall of Sivas was, as we have seen, accompanied by unspeakable bestialities. In these, however, Timur was not merely giving vent to his deep streak of cruelty. His campaign of terror was calculated to frighten Bayazid into being more tractable and entering into negotiations with a predisposition to yielding to Timur's demands. The latter were very stiff indeed, amounting to submission. Bayazid was to give back to the Anatolian emirs their lands. He was to deliver to Timur two thousand camel loads of butter and two thousand tents. Moreover, he had to proclaim Timur formally as sultan in his mosques and to recognize the latter's money as sole legal tender in his domains. Finally, he was to send his sons to serve with Timur.[19] Timur could hold the latter as hostages for the good conduct of their father. Bayazid's towering rage upon hearing of these demands might well be imagined. The Venetians, who were one of the best informed peoples of that time, learned that Bayazid's answer was to prepare for battle, massing troops in Anatolia and issuing calls to his Christian vassals in the Balkans for troops.[20] But by then it was far too late in the year to enter into such a distant campaign, so the collision between the two conquerors was averted for a time.

CHAPTER X
The Campaign into Syria

The taking of Sivas in 1400 gave Timur an excellent base of operations for a westward march across Anatolia against Bayazid. However, Timur was in no hurry to do battle with Bayazid. Mindful of his image in the Islamic world, he did not want to appear as the instigator of a war against a ghazi leader who had warred so successfully against the Christians. More importantly, he wanted to secure his flanks and rear before taking on such a redoubtable opponent. The Mamluke sultan might attack his lines of communication from Syria while he was involved with Bayazid in Anatolia. This would be especially dangerous in the event of reverses. The Mamlukes, in such an operation, would undoubtedly be aided by Sultan Ahmed Jelair of Baghdad. And the Georgians might dishonor their pledges of submission and open hostilities against his rear. Timur knew that Bayazid was unable to attack him straightaway. He doubtless surmised that Bayazid could not raise the siege of Constantinople, mobilize every available man throughout his empire, make the necessary logistical arrangements and traverse the several hundred miles to the upper Euphrates before the onset of winter when it would be impossible to engage Timur in the difficult mountain terrain of eastern Anatolia.

To play for time, Timur resolved to involve Bayazid in a lengthy correspondence and exchange of envoys. This might even induce Bayazid to make an accommodation, a welcome prospect, since Timur was not overwilling to take on such a formidable opponent. Indeed, Timur was far more interested in driving the Mamlukes out of Syria. In the meantime he could gather more information on the nature and composition of Bayazid's troops and his art of war. Also, Timur's agents could further undermine the allegiance of the emirs in Anatolia, dispossessed by Bayazid and pressed into his service.

While at Malatiya in southeastern Anatolia, Timur sent fresh envoys to Faraj bearing a letter which peremptorily demanded satisfaction for the murder of his first ambassador and the release of Atilmish. The latter, who was governor of Avnik and one of Timur's best generals, had been captured during a battle near Avnik by Kara Yusuf while Timur was campaigning in the Kipchak. Kara Yusuf had sent Atilmish to the Sultan as a gift; the Sultan had him thrown into prison where he now languished. When Timur's envoys reached Aleppo they were seized and imprisoned. When he heard about this, Timur became enraged and issued marching orders to his troops.

Timur's officers and principal lords remonstrated with him. They reminded him that his men had not rested themselves fully from the Indian campaign when ordered to make the very fatiguing march into Georgia. Now they were asked to press on to Syria and Egypt, a very toilsome and difficult business. The country was studded with towns and fortresses with high walls and strong citadels. The army of Syria was numerous. proficient and had everything needed to put up a vigorous defense. Unimpressed with these arguments, Timur replied that only God gives victory and that this had nothing to do with the number of soldiers. He reminded them of the seemingly impossible things they had accomplished in the past. The notables, seeing that their leader was obdurate, praised and applauded his decision.

Timur's southward progress on the way to Aleppo, which with Damascus was the most important city in Syria, was the usual blitzkrieg. The town of Behisni, the first stop, was quickly taken and devastated. The adjoining fortress was then attacked though it was built on a steep cliff. On October 7, 1400 the governor of the fortress, deeming further resistance futile, sent a delegation of Muslim divines with appropriate presents to Timur. Shahrukh agreed to act as intermediary. Upon the latter's supplication, Timur pardoned not only the governor but also all of the garrison. He then bypassed Kalaater which, according to Ibn Arabshah, he found too strong to take. The next stop was Aintab (the present Gaziantep) which opened its gates without offering any resistance. Timur placed a governor over it and added it to his domains. These conquests in southeastern Anatolia brought Timur to the Syrian border.

Meanwhile, the Mamluke governors in Syria were holding a council of war in Aleppo. The governor of Aleppo – Timurtash – called a traitor by the historian Ibn Arabshah,[1] played a leading role in the council's deliberations. In his address Timurtash laid great stress upon Timur's past exploits and record for invincibility, interlarding these remarks with examples. He urged submission to Timur, the coining of money in his name, the mention of his name and titles in the Friday prayer, and so forth. Though a few applauded these defeatist remarks, the majority opposed his counsel. Sudun, with great vehemence, even denounced Timurtash as a traitor. He belittled the strength of the enemy and extolled the might of the Syrian towns and military forces. In the vote that followed, a plurality opted for strengthening the defenses of the city and making a stand within its walls; no one was to leave the city to do battle with the enemy.

Timur, whose aim was to entice the Mamlukes out of the city, contrived to persuade them to abandon their plan to stand siege. In his march to Aleppo he exhibited great caution, going very slowly so that in two days only six or seven leagues were covered. Then his pace became almost glacial as the daily advance was cut to half a league. At each encampment a trench was dug around it and a rampart made with the soldiers' bucklers. It took Timur's men a whole week to cover the distance normally traversed in one day.

The Mamlukes, taking the bait, interpreted this exaggerated show of caution as cowardice and weakness. They sallied jauntily out of the city in battle order and pitched their tents in the open plains. Thus they jettisoned their original plan of standing siege in the city.

On November 8 Timur arrived in the environs of this arid, austere looking city. After two days of skirmishes and clashes the two forces prepared to do battle. In drawing up his battle array, Timur positioned his Indian elephants in a line out in front. The howdahs atop these bristled with archers and flingers of Greek fire. One corps was posted on a hill on the edge of the battlefield, to deal with the Syrians once they were routed and sent into flight.

The elephants, once battle was joined, played a decisive role. They plunged into the midst of the enemy and with their trunks tossed some of the soldiers into the air. Others were trampled underfoot. Panic seized the Mamlukes. Sudun and Timurtash, abandoning their soldiers, bolted for the nearest city gate. Their men, seeing this, dispersed. Most of them made for the Damascus road. They were pursued and slaughtered to such effect that only one horseman escaped to Damascus with news of the disaster. Others sought refuge in Aleppo. The result was a horrible press at the gates. Whole lines of fleeing men stumbled over one another and fell into the nearby ditches, which soon brimmed over with bodies. This only aided Timur's men in their grim task, for they were able to kill several men simultaneously with each thrust of the lance. Timur's troops then clambered over the piles of bodies and ascended the walls. Entering the city, they were given leave to sack it.

Neither the city's markets nor private dwellings were spared. Nor were women and children and old men proof against outrage. Everything was seized, including the women's rich ornaments and apparel.

During this violence Sudun and Timurtash were fleeing to the city's citadel. This was built on a mound of earth covered with freestone. The two leaders were confident that it could withstand siege. The small defending force hurled pots of flaming sulfur down on the besiegers together with stones and arrows. Despite this rain of missiles and combustibles, Timur's sappers began their work. To put a stop to this, the defenders lowered five archers down by rope. These unfortunates, however, were shot so full of arrows that when their bodies were drawn back up they bristled like porcupines. At length the badly outnumbered defenders met Timur's demand that they surrender. The two governors and their men were put in chains. Thereupon Timur sent an envoy to Cairo to propose an exchange of the two captives for Atilmish. Much booty was found in the citadel, seeing that the citizens of Aleppo had earlier carried their wealth here. Part of this was distributed among the soldiers.

Timur spent two days in the citadel admiring the prospect of the city and diverting himself by playing the learned casuist with the local theologians, whom he had assembled.[2] While his soldiers were torturing and branding people in other parts of the citadel, Timur, in his audiences with the theologians, sought to trap them with tricky or impossible questions so that he could order their execution or banishment. He posed a question which he said had stumped legal scholars in Samarkand, Bukhara, Herat and other cities he had taken, to wit: "Among those who died in the battle of Aleppo, who are the martyrs?" Ibn Shahana, the most learned scholar of the city, deftly side-stepped this one by quoting the Prophet Muhammad who, when asked a similar question by an inquisitive Arab, replied: "Those who are fighting for the word of God." Then Timur, in an allusion to his lameness, said, "I am half a man, but I have conquered Persia, Iraq, India and Tartary." To which Ibn Shahana, in his rejoinder, remarked: "Thank God for this and kill no one." Timur, coloring, retorted: "I kill no one, and I guarantee you the safety of your lives and possessions." Reassured, the shaykhs and professors began to unloosen their tongues and to talk freely until the chief cadi,* fearful of the consequences of this careless

----

*cadi = magistrate, judging according to the Shariat or Muslim religious law.

talk, called them to order saying, "Be silent and let this man [Ibn Shahana] speak, who knows what he is saying."

Timur's second question was to inquire what they knew of Ali, Muawiya and Yazid. It should be noted that Muawiya, the founder of the Umayyad caliphate in 661, had fought against the Prophet Muhammad's son-in-law Ali and when the latter died, took over as caliph in lieu of Hasan, Ali's son. Yazid, who succeeded his father Muawiya as caliph in 680, was implicated in the murder of Hussein, Ali's second son. For these actions both are regarded as criminal usurpers by Shiites, partisans of Ali and his line. The Sunnites, on the other hand, accept Muawiya and Yazid as rightful caliphs. But to recur to Timur's question. Before Ibn Shahana could answer, a Sunnite cadi rashly declared that Muawiya and Yazid were fighting the Holy War for the faith. Posing as a Shiite, Timur turned scarlet at this answer and bellowed: "Is that so! Muawiya was an oppressor and Yazid an evildoer, and you men of Aleppo are like the Damascenes who killed Hussein." Ibn Shahana quickly interjected that his colleague had merely repeated what he had read in books. Mollified, Timur ended the grim colloquy by praising the chief cadi and Ibn Shahana.

The next day Timur moved to the governor's palace where a prodigious banquet was in progress. Meanwhile, a saturnalia of destruction was taking place in the city, in which not even the mosques and medresehs were spared. Timur decided to bait the scholars with some more questions about Muawiya and Yazid. He badgered Ibn Shahana into admitting that Ali's cause was the right one and that Muawiya was not a lawful caliph. These extorted admissions so pleased Timur that he placed the chief cadi and Ibn Shahana under special protection. The following day he ordered the beheading of a certain number of townspeople, and the usual towers of heads were then erected.

But then the chief cadi and Ibn Shahana were again summoned. Timur's mullah* asked them to issue a *fetva* or religious opinion, legalizing the execution of the governor of Damascus who had killed Timur's first envoy. At this Ibn Shahana finally exploded, asking why so many Muslims were being beheaded without a fetva and despite the promise that no one would be killed without cause. At length an emir appeared and explained that only those guilty of manslaughter had been beheaded. Their heads would be used to erect a monument in

---

*In Muslim countries a mullah is a learned teacher or expounder of the law and dogmas of Islam.

Timur's honor, as was his custom. The theologians had misunderstood the order; they were now free and might go wherever they wished.[3]

After leaving Aleppo, Timur headed for Hama, one of the principal cities of Syria, located on the edge of the great Syrian desert. Here Timur stopped for twenty days to rest his men and horses. His emirs again urged a more leisurely gait. They suggested wintering at Tripoli, on the seacoast of Lebanon. Then, after a good rest, they could resume campaigning in the spring. Timur again rejected all arguments. The enemy, he declared, must not be allowed time to recover its balance. The army marched south to Emessa (Homs), which peacefully opened its gates. Baalbek, in Lebanon, was the next objective. While en route Timur detached forces to harry Sidon and Beirut. He quickly captured Baalbek, which is perhaps the world's oldest continuously inhabited city. Only a small, nondescript Arab town today, at that time it was a populous city. It contains one of the finest collections of Roman ruins extant. They must have been even more impressive then, before violent earthquakes shook the area in 1664 and 1750.

Timur examined the stupendous ruins.[4] These included the Temple of Jupiter, whose surviving six columns soar sixty feet into the air and are the highest in the world, and the massive Temple of Bacchus, still one of the best preserved ancient Roman buildings in the world, Rome included.[5] Baalbek is situated at the northern end of the elevated Bekaa Valley, the "breadbasket of Lebanon." Timur's men stocked up on vegetables, grapes and other comestibles.

The stay in Baalbek was not a protracted one. Situated aside the snow-covered Dar el-Baidar mountain, its air was bitingly chilly. Moreover, snow and rain began to fall abundantly. With the return of his men from Sidon and Beirut Timur was again on the move. His destination was Damascus, the chief city of Syria.

Timur had chosen well the time for his advance upon Syria. The authority of the thirteen-year-old Sultan Faraj was recognized only fitfully in Syria, while in Cairo the loftiest aim of each emir was to eliminate his rivals and claim the sultanate for himself. Timurtash, the Mamluke governor in Aleppo, who realized the danger after Timur took Sivas, sent appeal after appeal to Cairo. His reports of danger were, however, discounted. It was only after receiving intelligence that Timur was on his way to Aintab, a scant sixty miles from Aleppo, that the sultan convened a war council. In any event, even this alarum met with some disbelief, and it was decided first to send Asanbugha, one of the emirs, to Syria for confirmation of the reported threat from Timur.

Asanbugha left Cairo on September 25, 1400. Only after receiving a report (on October 14), signed by both Asanbugha and Timurtash and stating that Timur was marching toward Aintab, did Cairo begin preparing for a Syrian expedition. The towns and cities of Syria were ordered to send troops to Aleppo. The most important of the commanders obeying this order was Sudun, senior emir in Damascus, who came with a large army. Contingents also arrived from Palestine, Lebanon and Jordan, at that time appendages of Syria.

That Cairo waited so long to order full mobilization requires some explanation. Campaigns were usually launched in the spring when the weather was temperate. The Mamlukes complained bitterly if obliged to campaign in winter, especially into Syria.[6]

Faraj had, at great expense, readied an army that was magnificently equipped, "above all the cavalry, which was the best in the world" (Sharaf ad-Din). At Ghazzah the sultan was told that the Damascenes felt they could cope with Timur themselves. They were strong in numbers and full of determination and fight. Their city, moreover, had a year's supply of provisions. But the sultan and his party, not completely reassured, pressed on to Damascus, where they were joyously received by the inhabitants. Faraj immediately set in hand the strengthening of the city's defenses.

Meanwhile Faraj had sent to Timur an envoy dressed as a dervish and accompanied by two assassins, using the word in its original sense. (The Assassins first appeared in the late eleventh century as a fanatical offshoot of the Muslim Ismaili sect. By the fourteenth century, apparently, the Syrian Assassins had become secret agents of the Mamluke Sultans.[7] They used daggers smeared with poison in dispatching enemies.)

When Faraj's deadly embassy appeared before Timur, one of the latter's secretaries became suspicious. As a result the trio was seized and searched. Poisoned daggers were found in their boots. Interrogation revealed that Timur was to be stabbed while conversing with the envoy. The latter was killed with one of the daggers. The two assassins, after having their ears and noses lopped off, were sent back to Faraj with a message. Peace was still possible if Faraj would release Altimish and acknowledge Timur's suzerainty by minting coins in his name and mentioning him in the Friday prayer. A second envoy sent by Faraj promised the release of Altimish.

Timur marched to the north of Damascus and camped at the foot of a hill. As a precaution, he surrounded his camp with a trench and a barricade of bucklers and palisades. Scouts were sent out and, as contact with the enemy resulted, skirmishes occurred in which the Mamlukes prevailed. In revenge for Faraj's assassination attempt, Timur ordered Sudun and the other prisoners brought from Aleppo killed. Meanwhile, Sultan-Hussein, Timur's grandson, defected to the enemy after a debauch during which some seditious Persians persuaded him to rebel. The Syrians in Damascus, delighted with this morale-raising prize, received him warmly. Shaving off his long plait of hair, they dressed him in the fashion of their country. Sultan-Hussein then entered Mamluke service.

Upon hearing of his grandson's defection, Timur marched one league to the south side of the city. He protected his new camp with a wall built to the height of a man which in turn was surrounded by a ditch. At night infantry and cavalry units stood at battle ready, even though it was not the wont of the Mamlukes to fight night battles against foreign opponents.

Two days later Timur forwarded another embassy to Faraj. He was informed that despite his dilatoriness in returning Atilmish, Timur's anger would be appeased if he recognized him as suzerain. After a cordial reception the envoy returned with several of Faraj's emirs. The latter promised Timur the return of Atilmish in five days and full compliance with his other demands. Timur received Faraj's emissaries graciously.

After ten days of encampment, Timur took stock of the condition of his army. He decided to go to the green plains of Ghutah to the east of the city to fatten up his horses. The Damascenes mistakenly interpreted this as a sign of weakness, and the entire city population sallied forth confidently to do battle. Some of the civilians were armed with swords, others with sticks and stones. The cavalry and infantry, on the other hand, were well armed and equipped. According to Sharaf ad-Din, "and there was never seen before so great a multitude assembled."[8] Confronted by this host, Timur ordered his entire army to face the enemy, the cavalry dismounting to fight on foot. (The Mongols often resorted to this when in a tight situation.)

Battle was joined on January 5, 1401. Timur's two wings, together with the vanguard, led the attack, which was supported by his army's main body. The action proved to be disastrous for the Syrians, who had half of their number slain. During the battle the traitorous Mirza

Sultan-Hussein commanded the Syrian left wing. Captured alive, he was led into his grandfather's presence. The latter, so cruel to others, showed a remarkable indulgence towards his own progeny. Sultan-Hussein was chained and imprisoned as punishment for his defection. But, after being bastinadoed, he was soon released, Timur ordering that he never again darken his presence.

Timur then marched in order of battle towards the city. The elephants were placed in front to strike fear into the hearts of the city's population. The army, stretching from left to right wings, covered three or four leagues of ground. Despite the successful battle, Timur did not relax his precautions. He encamped on the bank of a deep rivulet, which served in lieu of a trench, and his men, using great and little bucklers, made a sort of rampart around the camp. Then the army, both infantry and cavalry, ranged itself in order of battle and crossed the rivulet.

Though Timur was still faced by a vast number of Syrians, they were by now discouraged and dispirited. The sultan went into conference with his emirs to decide what to do. Some plumped for a continuance of the war and for a second sortie. Others proposed deserting the city under cover of night. If the inhabitants were successful in defending the city, they argued, then the Sultan would still be its master. If not, then the Sultan would at least be able to extract his own force intact. The latter course of action was agreed upon. Faraj, at this juncture, was preoccupied with an even more pressing problem. Earlier, some of his emirs had made their presence scarce. Rumor had it that they had returned to Cairo to compass his deposition. Naturally Faraj was anxious to nip this plot in the bud.

Since he needed time to make his getaway, the sultan decided to deceive Timur. He sent him a letter which blamed the first sally on popular sedition. He proposed a one-day armistice, after which he promised to fulfill all of Timur's demands. Timur accepted. On the night of January 6, during the truce, Faraj and his principal emirs left the city by stealth. A deserter, however, soon informed Timur what had happened. A cavalry force was dispatched to intercept the sultan in flight. Though the pursuers caught up with and killed some of his men, Faraj and his emirs effected their escape and reached Cairo.

With the departure of Faraj and his emirs the inhabitants of the city, now a "shepherdless herd," were left to fend for themselves as best they could.[9] At first stunned by the news of the desertion, the Damascenes then began to argue among themselves as to their course of action:

defend the city to the bitter end, or ask Timur for terms. It was at this point apparently that Timur himself took the diplomatic initiative. On January 9, 1401, he sent two messengers who, approaching the high walls at a discreet distance, cried: "The Emir wishes peace, so send an intelligent man to discuss this with him." In the ensuing discussions, the counsels of those Damascenes who plumped for negotiations prevailed. Cadis representing the four schools of orthodox (Sunnite) Muslim jurisprudence agreed to act as the delegates. The Hanbalite Cadi Ibn Muflih was selected as leader since he knew both Turkish and Persian. Leaving the city was, however, not easy despite a safe conduct from Timur. Yazzadar, viceroy of the citadel of Damascus and as such answerable only to the Sultan in Cairo, opposed negotiations with Timur, and since the gate the negotiators intended to use was close to the citadel, was able to prevent them from using it. The four cadis therefore had to be let down from the city walls by ropes. Centuries before, St. Paul had escaped from the city to safety by having himself lowered down in a basket.

In a peroration to the cadis Timur presented himself as a liberator who had come to deliver the Damascenes from the yoke of the Christians and of the Mamluke Sultan. The Damascenes could indeed keep their city and their possessions. He asked only that the property of the Sultan, his followers and the merchants and notables who had fled the city be handed over to him. Most Damascenes, upon hearing these lenient terms, rejoiced and diligently sought out the arms, horses, mules and other items required. Those who had opposed the negotiations, however, remained extremely distrustful.

Then Timur's officials entered the city. Accompanied by city officials, they methodically went through every quarter, street by street, knocking on each shop door. If there was no answer the door was broken down and all goods were confiscated as punishment for mistrusting Timur's mercy. Shopkeepers responding had their goods inventoried so that, supposedly, Timur could indemnify them if their shops were looted by any of his men. Their keys were returned and they were told to resume business operations. The inventory takers were careful to note all cash on hand.

As a security precaution the Damascenes were adjured not to allow friends and relatives into the city. Concurrently the more important thoroughfares were closed off and the gates to the various quarters lowered to hinder passage. Timur's concern for the people's protection was the disarming explanation offered. Guards were posted at each gate.

Timur had some of his soldiers crucified for violence, which further re-assured the Damascenes. He told the city's merchants that he wanted to enrich them by opening up a great, well-guarded commercial highway between their city and Samarkand.

During the take-over of Damascus Timur had in attendance Ibn Khaldun (1332-1406), the great Arab historian.[10] A native of Tunis, he had settled in Cairo in 1382, where he came under the patronage of the Mamlukes. His diplomatic and other skills were so valued that he was asked to join Faraj's expedition againts Timur. He did this without en-thusiasm, for by now he was close to seventy.

On January 10, 1401 Ibn Khaldun left the city for Timur's camp. Prudence as well as natural curiosity prompted this move. He was among those who had urged negotiation with Timur. Since Timur's peace terms were received badly in some quarters, he felt he would be blamed and perhaps assassinated. For his part, Timur knew of his pres-ence in the city. Upon meeting Ibn Khaldun he was impressed with his distinguished bearing, distinctive Moorish attire, vast knowledge and cleverness. They saw each other frequently during Ibn Khaldun's thirty-five-day stay. This extended interview is one of the most remarkable in history.

The talks ranged over a number of subjects. From the beginning Ibn Khaldun stressed his Tunisian origin, probably to detach himself from the Mamlukes and thus appear in a better light. Timur, in turn, began to ask the most probing questions about the Maghrib (Northwest Afri-ca). In the end Timur pronounced himself dissatisfied with the answers. He bade his guest compose a work "on all of the countries of the Magh-rib, its remote parts as well as its near ones, its mountains and its rivers, its villages and its cities, so that I may clearly visualize them."[11] Ibn Khaldun, in view of his familiarity with the subject, was able to carry out the task in a few days of concentrated solitary effort. Timur ordered the work translated from Arabic into Chagatai or Eastern Turki, his own language. Unfortunately neither the original nor the translation (assuming that one was made) is extant. Whether Timur's interest was simply natural inquisitiveness or whether he mooted an eventual inva-sion of the Maghrib is not clear. Ibn Khaldun apparently feared the lat-ter for in further interviews he adroitly steered the conversation away from the Maghrib.

Some historians, following Ibn Arabshah, view the historian as some-thing of a prisoner and assert that Timur intended to press him into his service. Supposedly, he "escaped" from Timur via a wily subterfuge, stating that he would first like to return to Cairo to collect his books. Factually nothing of this kind occurred. Ibn Khaldun in his own account makes it clear that he was treated with kindness and consideration by Timur who, in the end, dismissed him under the most pleasant of circumstances and even concerned himself with the details of his journey to Cairo.

Though Damascus was now in Timur's hands, Yazzadar, governor of the fortress, resolved to defend it with his small garrison. So on January 14 the siege began. Sixty catapults, naphtha guns, ballistas and breachers began their work. Timur also used a wooden tower which was set afire by the defenders. He replaced this with another.[12] During the investment, part of the walls collapsed upon the soldiers of Khurasan and Sistan. The defenders quickly repaired the breaches. Meanwhile Timur's engineeers first diverted the water away from the moat and then tunneled under the walls. The pitprops in the tunnels were then soaked in naphtha and set aflame, causing portions of the walls to collapse. The citadel, as a result of all these actions, was ruined on all sides. The heroic defenders, after a siege of about one month, saw no recourse but to ask for an amnesty. Though Timur agreed, he had the governor put to death for his delay in capitulating. The garrison, consisting mostly of Mamlukes and Negroes, was enslaved. So were the women, children and old men, these being parcelled out among the mirzas and emirs. The artisans, craftsmen and scholars of Damascus were deported to Samarkand. These included workers in steel, producers of the world-famous damascene blades. Their skills took root in Khurasan and Persia but died out in Damascus. The deportees also included a twelve-year-old boy, Ibn Arabshah, who later in revenge would write an extremely hostile biography of Timur.

The conqueror replaced the old Syrian coinage of base alloy with newly minted coinage of silver and gold bearing his names and titles. Proclamations of his conquests, along with specimens of the new coins, were sent to Samarkand and the lesser capitals of his empire. Meanwhile his troops harried the Mediterranean littoral as far as Acre in northern Palestine.

The fall of the city's citadel set off a chain of events which would end in the fiery destruction of the city. Timur, in a further meeting with the cadis, declared that he had been disappointed in his expectations of finding a great trove of the Sultan's money in the citadel, which he had intended to give to his Chagai warriors. He therefore asked the cadis to help. Though the latter pleaded poverty, in the end they agreed to furnish 1,600,000 silver drachmas (the equivalent of 800,000 ducats). Four days later they brought the money. Examining the coins, Timur found a copper admixture of almost fifty percent. Affecting great anger, he denounced the Damascenes as iniquitous tricksters who had brought him worthless money. To make this point, he displayed some of his own coins. Of pure silver, each exceeded in weight a dozen of the proffered drachmas. Nearby, his commanders loudly clamored for a cancellation of the amnesty. Timur bade them be patient. Then taking aside the four cadis, who by now were ashen with fright, he pointed out his men's menacing demeanor and advised a quick settlement. The Damascenes agreed to pay 960,000 ducats.

A few days later Timur asked for an even larger sum for his more numerous Khurasani troops. At first refusing, the Damascenes at length gave in. Fobbing off his Chagatais and Khurasanis with fine speeches, he pocketed both collections. Plunged into despair, the Damascenes pleaded for permission to quit the city without their possessions, but this was refused. Timur now demanded a third exaction for the benefit of the people in his own domain. In the end he received as much as from the two previous combined collections.

At this point Timur announced that, being old and worn out, he was departing for home. However, he needed aid in meeting his expenses en route. Contemptuously rejecting an offer of a half million ducats, he stated that, barring a larger offer, he just might settle in the city permanently. At length he received a sum three times as large.

Even so he remained dissatisfied. Summoning the shopkeepers before him, he announced that since the sum collected fell short of his needs, he was forced to order them to redeem their goods and wares for cash; otherwise they would be burned. His officials, using their inventories, proceeded to implement this order. Then came the turn of the immovable possessions (shops, homes, estates, etc.). Great sums were collected in an operation which induced citizens to dip into their caches of money.

Finally, in a meeting with his senior emirs, Timur claimed that the worthless Damascenes had given him little. He thereupon invited them to take the last and greater part of the Syrians' possessions. Provided with the shop inventories, Timur's warriors went on a rampage. Not only were the goods seized, but men were tortured to make them disclose all remaining caches of money. Some unfortunates were tied to a piece of wood and rotated over a fire like a roast. Others were simply branded with a red hot iron. Soon the air was heavy with the smell of searing flesh. Huge sums of money were extracted in this ferocious manner.[13]

How the great fire in Damascus started is a matter of some dispute. De Mignanelli, an Italian resident of the city (but absent at the time), claims that on March 17 Timur ordered the city burned after first removing the people he wished to save. Sharaf ad-Din, in the more generally accepted version, avers that the fire broke out accidentally.

During the course of the siege Timur had visited the reputed graves of two of the Prophet Muhammad's wives, Umm Selma and Umm Habiba,[14] located near the city. Timur affected outrage at their unkempt condition, adding that despite the magnificence of the city there were no domes over these tombs.[15] He ordered his senior emirs to repair this omission forthwith. Though the marble domes displayed much fine chisel work, they were finished in but twenty-five days.

Even so Timur's anger remained unslaked. After the fall of the citadel he harangued his privy council. The Damascenes, he charged, had for eight hundred years allowed the tombs of the wives of the Prophet to lie neglected. They were also berated by Timur for having treated Ali and Hussein badly. After this choleric outburst, his council mulled the matter over. They then informed the officers who in turn told their men. The latter, according to Sharaf ad-Din, became so incensed over this that on March 28 they forcibly entered the city without orders. In fact, this was but an excuse to kill, loot and rape. And so the saturnalia began, though the ransom had been paid. More loot was seized than could be carried away. Women and young boys were sexually assaulted in public. Meanwhile, a fire broke out, possibly by accident. Despite efforts to contain it, the entire city was soon ablaze. Timur decided to try to save the Great Umayyad mosque, one of the glories of Muslim architecture. He entrusted the mission to one of his senior emirs. The intense heat of the surrounding conflagration, however, melted the lead covering the mosque's cupola so that it cascaded downward in fiery, molten streams. All that remained were the walls of the mosque and one of the minarets called the "Minaret of the Bridge." Though the latter was made of wood plastered over with lime, it miraculously escaped destruction, to the amazement of the Damascenes. Not so the thousands of people who had taken refuge in the great mosque, only to perish in the conflagration.

The city of Damascus burned for three days. De Mignanelli, on his return in the fall of 1401, found it "reduced to a mountain of ashes."[16] And though he considered the people of Damascus to be "a very bad lot," he grieved over the destruction of the city.

Timur's departure in March 1401 brought further afflictions. In that month and continuing into April, a great plague of locusts descended and ate all that was edible down to the "stalks, leaves and roots" (de Mignanelli). Consequently, no crops were harvested that year. Timur's army had destroyed the city's stocks of food so that the little available to the famished Damascenes was that brought from afar. The stench of the decaying cadavers was so intense that the inhabitants were forced to take refuge in some fortresses which had not been burned.

Yet Damascus rose phoenix-like from its ashes. The Mamlukes, who soon reimposed their control, reconstructed the city's walls and citadel. The city itself rapidly recovered its aspect as a rich and populous place.[17] But though commerce once more flourished, Timur's deportation of artisans paralyzed the handicraft industry for many years.

Damascus was the southernmost point reached by Timur in his Syrian campaign. According to some accounts, he was deterred from going into Palestine and possibly on to Egypt by the swarm of locusts which ate up every green thing.[18] As it happened, he marched his army north to Hama. Though this place had earlier been spared, its inhabitants in the meantime had perversely destroyed the buildings Timur had constructed during his stopover. In revenge Timur had the city looted and razed and its residents enslaved. Detachments were also sent to Aleppo to burn and harry that city and to make inroads in other directions. At length rendezvous was made with Timur on the banks of the Euphrates.

Timur crossed the Euphrates and reached Edessa, which escaped sacking by a timely capitulation. He then advanced upon Mardin. Its sultan had earlier been imprisoned at Sultaniya but had won his release by promising to join Timur in Syria with his troops. This he had failed to do. Conscious of his fault, he did not emerge from the city to pay his respects. The citadel of Mardin was perched on an almost inaccessible rock which was girded below by the homes of the city's inhabitants. Within the citadel were extensive gardens and springs of water. The garrison had no need of the outparts below to maintain itself. Here the city dwellers took refuge. Foiled in his attempt to take the stronghold quickly, Timur contented himself with destroying the buildings in the lower town. A force was left behind to blockade the citadel.

Once out of Mardin, Timur dispatched troops to invade Georgia. They proceeded by way of Alanjik which had finally fallen after a siege which had lasted (with interruptions) from 1387 to 1401. Upon arrival in Georgia the task force began to harry the land. Timur retracted his force only after receiving assurances from his old opponent King

George that the latter would pay his annual tribute, would send auxili-
ary troops and would be generally obedient to Timur.

In 1394 Sultan Ahmed Jelair had re-established himself in Baghdad
after the withdrawal of Timur's governor, who felt he had too few
troops to defend the city effectively. In 1400 Ahmed, learning that
Timur was on the prowl in eastern Anatolia, had fled to Ottoman territory. Faraj, one of his emirs, stayed on as governor. In May 1401, while
still at Mosul, Timur sent a small force to Baghdad to collect a war contribution. Encountering resistance, its leader sent back a request for
more men and siege equipment. Timur decided to come himself with a
small force of picked soldiers. The bulk of the army, under Shahrukh's
command, was to head for Tabriz. Upon arriving at Baghdad, Timur invested the city while his sappers began undermining the city walls. At
that point Faraj was curious to know whether the terrible Timur was
really present. So he sent an envoy who, after being well received,
brought back confirmation. Faraj refused to believe him in view of the
modest number of besiegers. Accusing the envoy of dissembling, he had
him cast into prison.

Timur soon realized that he had too few troops to take Baghdad by
siege. He therefore sent word to Shahrukh to join him at Baghdad.
Though the city measured more than two leagues in circumference,
Timur's now greatly reinforced army was able to surround it completely. A bridge of boats was built on the Tigris below the city. Archers
were posted to bar the escape of anyone who might seek to flee down
river. The upper part of the river was controlled by Miranshah and
Shahrukh. Thus, though the river ran through the city and the Baghdadis had a large number of boats, there was no way out.

The Baghdadis offered a desperate resistance.[19] As soon as a break
was made in their walls they repaired it. The siege was not the only
source of heat; the furnace heat of August further sapped the energies
of Timur's men. Despite this, they raised a high platform which over-
awed the city. From this they poured a ceaseless rain of great stones
from their projectile machines. Timur, hoping the city would surrender
so that he could receive it intact, refused to order a general assault.
Thus the siege continued for forty days while famine stalked the city.
One day the heat was so intense that at noon the defenders retired to
their homes. To deceive the enemy they positioned helmets on sticks
along the battlements. Then they withdrew to the cool of their cellars
for refreshment.

Perceiving this sham, Timur finally ordered a general assault. Scaling ladders went up and the city was soon in his hands. Because of prior measures there was no escape, though many died trying to flee by way of the river. Faraj and his daughter did manage to break through by boat, but soon had pursuers hot on their heels. Seeing his end at hand, Faraj cast himself and his daughter into the Tigris where they both drowned.

Since a number of his soldiers had been slain in the general assault, Timur ordered that towers of heads be constructed in various parts of the city. Each warrior was to bring in one male head. In the general killing that followed, neither children of eight nor old men of eighty were spared.[20] Soon 120 towers of heads were erected as a warning to any who would resist. Some of the Muslim divines, sayyids and dervishes succeeded in reaching Timur's pavilion where they were given food and clothing and sent on to a safe place. Only one in a hundred of the remainder of the population was spared, in order to be carried off into slavery. Timur then ordered the general destruction of the city, exempting only the mosques, medresehs and hospices. Yet the amount of damage effected has been exaggerated. His men lacked both the time and the technical facilities to do a proper job.[21]

Timur left Baghdad with the Tigris stained red with blood and the air infected with the stench of cadavers. This time he did not leave behind an experienced administrator to direct the work of recovery. Marching a league upstream, he visited the tomb of Imam Abu Hanifa, founder of one of the four great schools of orthodox (Sunnite) jurisprudence. Timur prayed for this divine's intervention. He next ordered Mahmud Khan to make inroads into the surrounding area. Mahmud pillaged as far as the Shiite Holy City of Kerbela in central Iraq, which contains the shrine of Hussein. Instead of harrying Kerbela, Mahmud Khan and his men made their devotions. Timur could easily have journeyed to this most sacred Shiite pilgrimage goal. Posing as a Shiite, however, no longer interested him, now that he was winding up operations in that area. Instead, he proceeded northward toward Karabagh where he intended to pass the winter. He had achieved much since the taking of Aleppo: rich booty, further martial renown, and the securing of his flank against attack either from Syria or from Iraq Arabi. He soon would be on the move again in operations which would culminate in the last and most famous battle of his career.

CHAPTER XI
The Battle of Ankara

While Timur was involved in Syria and points east, Bayazid, at the instigation of Sultan Ahmed Jelair and Kara Yusuf the Turkoman, dispatched an army led by his son Suleiman to attack Taharten, Timur's vassal. The conqueror received news of this enterprise while near Tabriz in the course of his northward march following his reconquest of Baghdad in the summer of 1401. Shahrukh was ordered to lead his forces into Anatolia to oppose Suleiman. His army was stiffened with detachments originally sent into Georgia to make inroads there. Suleiman's forces were routed in the Sivas area. With Timur and the main host in northwest Persia nearby, Bayazid decided to break off hostilities and to resume negotiations with the conqueror. Earlier in the winter of 1399/1400, during Timur's Georgian campaign, Suleiman had seized Erzinjan which pertained to Taharten. Suleiman also captured the latter's wives and children and sent them into custody at Bursa. Bayazid now asked Taharten to act as his intermediary in his contacts with Timur. Through his nephew, Taharten informed Shahrukh that Bayazid would soon send ambassadors to arrange peace between the two empires. Bayazid also promised that if the negotiations succeeded, Taharten would get back his family. Shahrukh passed this information on to Timur.

The latter, in the meantime, continued his northward march from Tabriz. Crossing the Araxes river, he made camp at Nakhichevan. During this time he received an apologetic and respectful embassy from King George of Georgia. News also arrived from back home that Sayf ad-Din Barlas, long one of Timur's principal aides, had died. On December 12 (1401) Timur arrived at his favorite winter quarters at Karabagh. He still had no immediate plans for a war against Bayazid. Instead, he planned to lead a third great expedition into southern Russia in the spring. Sharaf ad-Din tells how houses were built of reed for Timur and the mirzas and how tents and pavilions were put up in the camp's enclosures. "And," he continues, "as Timur's intention was to make war in the Kipchak in the spring, the face of the pavilions was turned

towards Derbent."[1] News of Timur's intentions soon percolated into
the Kipchak. Envoys appeared from there with assurances of the Khan's
submission and complete obedience to Timur. This appeased the conqueror and he granted pardon. Sharaf ad-Din's laconic paragraph is not
supplemented by information in other sources. The Khan in question
was apparently Shadi Beg, the puppet of Edigei. As will be recalled,
Edigei was determined to reunite the Ulus of Juchi. The defeat of Toktamish and his Lithuanian allies in the Battle of the Vorskla (1399)
marked a giant step in that direction. Timur, viewing Edigei's growing
power with concern, had decided to strike him down. The Karabagh
was a good base of attack. Edigei's propitiatory steps, however, caused
Timur to relent and to turn to Bayazid.

After a mammoth feast at Karabagh Timur took up the affair of his
grandson Mirza Iskender. Before leaving Samarkand, Timur had entrusted the government of Transoxiana to his grandson and heir-designate
Muhammad-Sultan, son of Jehangir. Upon Timur's departure his grandson Iskender, son of Omar-Shaykh and governor of Andijan, though
only a lad of fifteen, lost no time in turning the situation in Mogolistan
to his own advantage. First he advanced upon and pillaged Khotan;
then he took Kashgar, where he set up winter quarters. Though he sent
nine Mogol beauties to Timur and another nine to his first cousin
Muhammad-Sultan in Samarkand, the latter rejected them out of pique
over Iskender's impulsiveness and show of independence. Iskender was
supposed to have waited for Muhammad-Sultan and his army. The two
were then to have carried out a two-pronged offensive against Mogolistan. At Muhammad-Sultan's order Iskender was seized and bound,
while members of his entourage were executed. This was a presentiment
of the fratricidal strife which would break out upon Timur's death.
When Timur later ordered Muhammad-Sultan to join him with an army,
the latter brought along Iskender "bound like a criminal" (Sharaf ad-
Din). During the winter of 1401/1402 Timur ordered his divan to make
a full investigation of the matter. Judged guilty by the divan, Iskender
was bastinadoed according to the Yasa of Chingis Khan. His chains were
then removed and he was set free.

Early in 1402 Sultan Ahmed returned to Baghdad and began rebuilding the city. He also tried to reimpose his writ on the surrounding country. Upon news of this Timur dispatched four bodies of cavalry to
Baghdad, which were to travel by different routes. While passing
through Kurdistan they were to carry out a second mission—the extirpation of the Kurds. Timur had a score to settle, since they had robbed

some of his soldiers during his return from the campaign against Baghdad. By now it was the dead of winter. The snow was so deep that his troopers had first to lay down felts ahead of their mounts to give them secure footing. Since the Kurds had come down from the mountains to escape the cold, Timur's men were able to slaughter a great number of them. Then the force led by Abu-Bakr showed up unexpectedly one evening before Baghdad. Sultan Ahmed, clad only in a nightshirt, together with his son Tahir and some of his adherents, managed to escape, though closely pursued. Timur's men spent the rest of the winter harrying Iraq Arabi (i.e., Southern Mesopotamia) in all directions. In the spring they returned to the imperial camp.

The background causes for the war between Timur and Bayazid may be briefly summarized: the Turkish sultan had given asylum to Sultan Ahmed and Kara Yusuf, Timur's implacable enemies. He had attacked Timur's faithful vassal Taharten and had seized his family. He had despoiled the emirs of Aydin, Saruhan, Menteshe and Germiyan. These had fled to Timur's camp where they lost no opportunity to urge an attack upon Bayazid. Both Timur and Bayazid appealed to history in asserting their claims to paramountcy in Anatolia. In the thirteenth century the Chingisids had asserted overlordship over Anatolia. Beginning in 1399 Timur claimed that as their representative, these suzerain rights over all Anatolian rulers now devolved upon him.[2] This included Bayazid, whom Timur viewed simply as a march lord. Bayazid, on the other hand, regarded himself as the legitimate Seljuk heir. Timur was, for him, but a rude barbarian from the depths of Central Asia.

Bayazid had achieved great renown throughout the Muslim world as a warrior against the Christian infidel. Timur was therefore anxious to blacken this reputation by depicting him as a protector of impious bandits. Bayazid's failure to mend his ways was, in Sharaf ad-Din's presentation of the matter, the immediate cause of the war that followed. Kara Yusuf, he continues, was a great robber who had pillaged Muslim caravans bound for the holy cities of Mecca and Medina. He had then fled to Bayazid's realm "which was a sure asylum for all the robbers of Asia." Since it was a point of conscience for Timur to put an end to this, he resolved to make war against Bayazid. The latter's chief ministers urged him to make peace with Timur. Becoming fearful, Bayazid sent a letter replete with pledges of submission and obedience. This was brought by distinguished envoys to Timur's winter quarters at Karabagh. Timur, in his answer, again disclaimed any wish to attack Bayazid since he was fighting the infidels. He had, however, given asylum to

Kara Yusuf whom Timur called "the greatest robber and villain in the whole world."[3] Bayazid must either himself put Kara Yusuf to death, send him bound to Timur, or at least expel him.

Bayazid's envoys, while in Timur's camp, were put into contact with Father Francis who had jouneyed to his headquarters bearing messages from Byzantium. He informed the envoys that Timur had accepted the proposals of Byzantium and Galata that the tribute which they had formerly paid to Bayazid should now go to him. This is related in Timur's letter of May 15 (1402) to Regent John, preserved (in distorted version) in the Venetian chronicle of Marino Sanudo.[4] The letter also informs us that Timur hoped to coordinate his actions on land with sea attacks on the Ottoman coast. A diversion by sea would be especially useful in the event of a protracted campaign. Timur was also anxious to prevent Bayazid from moving reinforcements from the Balkans into Anatolia. To do this, he looked to the sea power of Trebizond, Byzantium and Galata. During his first visit, Father Francis had journeyed by sea to Trebizond and then overland to Timur's camp. Manuel III of Trebizond, wishing to remain neutral in the coming struggle and afraid that Bayazid would learn of these negotiations, had caused some trouble for Father Francis. Timur not only reprimanded Manuel but ordered that he prepare twenty war galleys and await further orders. He also was to come to Timur's camp with troops.[5] In his letter to Regent John, Timur instructed him to ready twenty galleys and to send them to Trebizond. The Genoese in Galata, we learn from other sources, received similar orders. Finally, we may note, in this survey of Timur's contacts with Christian powers, that one of his sons had received a mission from the Venetians, though we do not know the details.

Before dismissing Bayazid's envoys Timur held a battue on the plain to the far side of the Araxes river. Once the animals were hemmed in, the envoys were honored by being allowed to enter the circle in the company of Taharten and the mirzas to kill the animals. Timur further honored them at a feast with gifts of golden caps and belts. The departing ambassadors were accompanied by Timur's own envoy, Chempai El-Chikede. In the spring, Timur said, he would move to the Anatolian border to await Bayazid's answer. If the response were unfavorable, then the sword would decide who was in the right.

Ottoman historians, interestingly enough, do not mention Bayazid's mission, confining themselves only to the insulting contents of the letter borne by Timur's envoy.[6] That Bayazid would approach Timur in such a fearful, contrite and submissive manner does not accord with his character. Though busy mobilizing his troops in the Balkans and in Anatolia, he may have thought that a modus vivendi could still be arranged through a last minute effort. Or he may have wanted to deceive Timur as to his intentions. In either event, his emissaries would naturally appear more conciliatory than before. Sharaf ad-Din, to honor the conqueror, probably presented this complaisance in exaggerated terms.

Timur, while out hunting one day, noticed an old canal leading into the Araxes which was in such disrepair that it was no longer used. He spent the rest of the winter restoring this. Driven by his emirs, Timur's soldiers removed the silt and debris which had stopped up the canal. Timur named the restored canal the "River of Barlas" after the name of his clan. "And on its banks," says Sharaf ad-Din, "have since been built several towns, villages, mills, vineyards, gardens and pleasure-houses."[7] Ten leagues long, it was navigable by small craft. Timur undoubtedly used the winter to recruit additional forces from throughout his empire.

On the approach of spring, Timur, Sharaf ad-Din would have us believe, was still torn by indecision since Bayazid was making holy war against the infidel. He adds—and this is more to the mark—that "The vast extent of the Ottoman empire, the number and valor of its troops, who were perfectly skill'd in war, and prepar'd to defend themselves, did not a little contribute to keep up his irresolution."[8] Moreover, Timur's troops were very much fatigued after three years of campaigning. Yet his generals and emirs were reluctant to verbalize their feelings lest they be thought weak and cowardly. They therefore persuaded the influential Emir Shams al-Din to act as their spokesman. They asked him to tell Timur that astrologers predicted inevitable misfortune for the Chagatai army. As soon as he was tactfully apprised of these baleful prognostications, Timur summoned Maulana Abdallah Lesan, one of the most noted astrologers of the day. This worthy thereupon came up with the counter-prediction that Timur would be the victor and the prince of Anatolia would become his prisoner. At this time an unusually large, bright and fiery comet was sighted in the western sky, illumining the heavens for three months. This was observed by people from as far east as the Rhine and Tagus rivers. The Greeks, who named this comet "the lampbearer," declared that its appearance presaged bloody fighting in the east. Timur's astrologers hailed it as an omen of certain victory. Shortly before leaving winter quarters at Karabagh (April, 1402) Timur learned that a son had been born to Shahrukh, whom Timur named Muhammad-Juki. The birth of a grandson to Timur was regarded as the second auspicious sign.[9]

Clearing the board for action, Timur had the ladies of the imperial household return to Sultaniya by way of Tabriz. Timur himself was obliged to wait two months at Avnik for the envoys of Bayazid. Upon their arrival Timur sent a second letter to Bayazid demanding the surrender of the fortress of Kamakh, which Timur claimed was in his territory. Bayazid would, however, be allowed to keep his kingdom.

Timur had little expectation that Bayazid would meet his demand. He readily acceded to Muhammad-Sultan's request that he be allowed to attack the fortress of Kamakh, which Sharaf ad-Din calls "one of the strongest in Asia." Kamakh was located thirty miles southwest of Erzinjan; Timur retook this city and set up his camp there. Emplaced on a high steep rock, Kamakh was protected by a labyrinth-like gorge on one side and by the Euphrates and its affluents on the other. The troops sent by Timur from Erzinjan under Muhammad-Sultan's command besieged the fortress for ten days. During this time they filled in the gorge and cut off the water supply of the defenders. Then during the eleventh night Timur's mountain troops, carrying ladders made of rope, tried to climb the rocks and let down ropes which could later be used by the attackers. The aroused garrison foiled these attempts by hurling boulders down on the attackers. Early the next morning the signal for a general assault was given. Despite a robust defense in which Greek fire, arrows and boulders were showered on the attackers, they gained their objective. Timur presented his newest conquest to Taharten, owing to its proximity to Erzinjan. Timur's army then camped in the plain of Sivas. Here appeared Timur's envoy, Chempai El-Chikede, with the envoys of Bayazid. The latter brought an arrogant letter in which Bayazid demanded that Timur appear before him or else his wives would be separated from him three times, i.e., forever divorced, since Omar, the second caliph, ruled that a Muslim cannot remarry a woman against whom he has repeated the formula of repudiation three times. If, on the other hand, Timur came and did not find Bayazid on the battlefield, then the latter promised that he would, in turn, separate himself from his harem three times. The reference to his wives caused Timur to flush with anger, since mention of the harem among Muslims is considered surpassingly coarse and insulting. Timur was equally adrenal over the way the letter was written. Timur, according to Sharaf ad-Din, when writing to Bayazid had observed the niceties of diplomatic usage by having both his name and that of Bayazid appear on the same line. In his letter, however, Bayazid wrote his name in gold and Timur's in black ink on the line below. Timur concluded that "The son of Murad is mad."

The outraged Timur rejected the envoys' gifts. Even these violated Mongol custom since they included ten horses, not nine. The ambassadors were informed that only their diplomatic immunity precluded immediate decapitation. Recovering his self-possession, Timur darkly informed the envoys that war was imminent, war which their master had brought down on himself by his actions.

Before dismissing this embassy Timur held a review of his troops in the plain of Sivas, witnessed by the envoys on horseback. As each squadron passed before Timur in his reviewing stand on a nearby hill, its commander "advanced, fell upon his knees, and holding his horse by the bridle" made a little speech to Timur about the valor and devotion with which he would be served. The latter would then respond, exhorting the soldiers to show their bravery. Timur was especially pleased with the appearance, equipment and turnout of the units brought along by Muhammad-Sultan, whom he had earlier summoned from Samarkand. His grandson had assigned a color to each unit to differentiate it better in the heat of battle. Thus one unit's standards, weapons and equipment were all in white, another in red, another in yellow and so on.[10]

The review lasted from daybreak into the afternoon. To acquaint the envoys better with the quality of his troops, Timur had them conducted through their ranks. He calculated that the quickness of the movements of his troops, their well-turned-out and valorous aspect, their excellent armament, discipline and blind readiness to carry out his slightest order would produce an excellent impression on the envoys. He knew that the latter, upon their return, would relate their impressions; hopefully, these might produce a defeatist mood in Bayazid's camp.

After the parade Timur dismissed the envoys with presents and a speech indicating his willingness to pardon Bayazid if he would release Taharten's family and send one of his own sons as a hostage. Timur promised he would treat Bayazid's son well.

The conqueror apparently had little expectation that Bayazid would comply, for he attached emissaries to the returning embassy who were secretly to make contact with the Tatars,* of whom there was a goodly number in Bayazid's army, and talk them into defecting to Timur's side.

---

*Peoples of Turkic provenience. Originally referring to a group living in Mongolia, the word "Tatar" has undergone a number of changes of meaning.

These agents were to dwell upon the kinship and other bonds of the Tatars with Timur's own people. This seed of propaganda, as we shall see, was to fall upon fertile ground.

During the winter of 1401/1402, while Timur was at Karabagh, Bayazid busied himself with issuing orders for a general concentration of forces near Bursa. Drawn from all corners of his empire, these would include Christian contingents from Rumelia and Serbia. The siege of Constantinople was lifted. The strategies adopted by the two conquerors must be guessed at, since only glimmers can be gleaned from the sources.[11] Bayazid's strategy must have called for a quick decision rather than a lengthy campaign. First, there were considerations of geography and climate. Campaigns in central and eastern Anatolia, owing to the weather, could not be launched until spring, with mobilization orders going out in December. If troops were levied from all parts of the empire, time would have to be allotted for European contingents to make their way to Anatolia. Contact with the enemy, owing to the distances to be traversed, could not be made until late spring at the very earliest. This left only a few hurried months for military campaigning over poor and rugged terrain at the hottest time of the year. The feudal cavalry, the bulk of the army, was ordinarily dismissed and headed for home in October. "If," as Sir Charles Oman points out, "they were kept in the field so late as November their horses perished, and they themselves melted away or mutinied."[12] The growing shortage of fodder as snow and cold descended upon the land would adversely affect the many animals which ordinarily accompanied the Ottoman army. The Sultan, who at this time personally commanded the army in major campaigns, was accompanied by the Grand Vizier and other ministers of the central administration; it was not prudent for them to absent themselves from the capital for more than six months. Moreover, the Greeks and other subject Christians might draw fresh courage from a lengthy interruption of the siege of Constantinople, and revolt. It might even encourage the Europeans to organize a fresh crusade, despite the Nicopolis debacle. That Timur at the time was in contact not only with Byzantium and Galata but with other Christian powers, was doubtless known by Bayazid's excellent intelligence service. Bayazid's own diplomatic initiative had failed. In 1400 he had requested the Mamluke sultan to send him troops to use against Timur. Faraj, miffed over Bayazid's seizure of Malatya at the time of his father Sultan Barkuk's death, turned down this request for aid. He may also have been too unsure of the loyalty of his troops to let them be removed from his control.

Bayazid needed a victory that was not only quick but decisive. Partial victory would leave him at a grave disadvantage. Once he and the main army left for home for the winter, local governors with their garrisons would be in no position to continue the offensive. The enemy, in the spring, could overpower them before the Ottoman army could return. And to return so soon would be difficult. Campaigns at such a great remove were so exhausting for the horses that, as later Ottoman history would show, a year would often elapse before another effort could be mounted.[13]

To gain a quick victory Bayazid needed to take the offensive aggressively into enemy territory. This was risky, in that Timur could withdraw eastward, lengthening Bayazid's lines of communication and shortening his own. This, however, was a gamble Bayazid felt he had to take.

Since speed was of the essence, Bayazid must have broken camp at Bursa as soon as the weather permitted—probably not before April. He stopped off at Ankara, now the Turkish capital, which he made his main base of supply. Some writers feel that Bayazid should have remained at Ankara and, in a strong defensive position, have awaited Timur's attack. Bayazid was advised to do just this by Ali Pasha, his grand vizier. The assumption here is that Timur, like the crusaders at Nicopolis, would oblige Bayazid by allowing him to dictate the place of battle. Timur, however, did not fight his wars this way. Leaving Ankara, Bayazid continued his eastward march to Tokat. His plan, apparently, was to keep to the north while moving eastward. Bayazid hoped at some point to attack Timur from the north, hitting his right flank and rear.

In June Timur, while camped in the plain of Sivas, learned that Bayazid had reached Tokat, directly to the north. He had, moreover, occupied the ford over the Tosamly river which lay in the path of any invader. Thus only sixty-five miles of rugged, wooded terrain separated the two hosts. Even at this late date, a flurry of negotiations took place.

Despite the difficult terrain, Bayazid decided to attack Timur since it accorded with his general plan. However, Timur refused to accept battle and withdrew to the south. He too, possibly hoped for a quick showdown but he apparently reasoned as follows: if he marched out to meet Bayazid's advancing forces, his own troops, consisting largely of cavalry, would be operating at a disadvantage in the wooded,[14] broken terrain. Another possibility was to attack Bayazid before he was able to move out of Tokat. In such an event, however, Timur's army would first have to make tiring marches before attacking a well-rested enemy force in a prepared position and in possession of the ford over the To-samly river. In the event of defeat Timur's army would have to retreat via unfavorable routes and would most probably be destroyed. Agents had been sent to sow dissension among Bayazid's Anatolian troops. Since these approaches took time to take effect, Timur, in postponing the conflict by withdrawing, may also have been playing for time.

Timur could, of course, have himself remained at Sivas and awaited Bayazid's attack in a prepared position after harassing his forward troops with his horsemen. But in moving southwestward toward Kayseri and then northwestward via Kirshehir to Ankara he had something more elaborate in mind—the strategic discomfiture of Bayazid before the two armies ever came to blows. Execution of such a plan presupposed an intimate knowledge of the roads and terrain in the area. The Anatolian emirs who had defected to Timur doubtless provided this information.

Careful to mask his movements from Bayazid as long as possible, Timur expected that his opponent, as soon as he learned of them, would either quickly turn around to head for Ankara or thrust at Timur's flank from the north. In either case the advantage lay with Timur, for in skirting the course of the Kizil Irmak river, the largest in Anatolia, he not only had better roads but access to a plentiful food supply, now that harvest time was at hand. Bayazid, on the other hand, could expect only difficulties with both food and terrain.

In his roundabout march from Sivas to Ankara, Timur set a blistering pace, covering the distance in but twelve days. Bayazid, when he realized that Timur's ultimate objective was Ankara—his own main base of supply, acted with his usual impulsiveness. Marching his men with great exertion and privation, he even apparently tried to make contact with the enemy's right wing—Sharaf ad-Din mentions light clashes—but to no avail. Though Bayazid's route was shorter, he also failed to reach Ankara before Timur did. Immediately upon arrival, Timur called upon Yakub, the Ottoman commander at Ankara, to surrender. When the latter downrightly refused, Timur had his engineers divert the stream called Chibukabad, the fortress' source of water, while his sappers began to undermine the wall.

Meanwhile, Timur had ample time to prepare for battle. Setting up camp to the northeast of Ankara, directly in Bayazid's line of march, he fortified the camp with trenches and palisades. He also gave careful attention to the question of water—so vital to life. His camp had the Engirsu river to its back; he also had his engineers dig wells near the camp. Simultaneously, he had a spring to the east, accessible to Bayazid, destroyed and may very well have tampered with other water supplies.

Strategically, Timur had reversed the situation at Tokat, so unfavorable to him. By besieging Ankara he had cut Bayazid off from his main base of supply and left the latter no option but to fight the enemy's well-rested troops with his own exhausted and thirsty army at a spot selected and prepared by Timur. If Bayazid lost the battle his situation would be extremely precarious; if Timur met with misfortune he still would have a good line of retreat to the southeast. Had he wanted to, Timur could even have postponed the battle. Bayazid, on the other hand, had to push for quick results, for if he delayed Ankara might fall. Even more importantly, his troops could not hold out for long without water in midsummer heat which in this part of Anatolia exceeds one hundred degrees (fahrenheit).

As regards the size of both forces, we may reject the enormous numbers (hundreds of thousands) cited by various authorities for both sides, as absurd.[15] The victualling and provisioning problems in moving such prodigious numbers even at moderate speed make the mind reel. Yet both leaders accomplished prodigies in the celerity of some of their movements over the wretched roads. The German scholar Roloff, in picking his way through the labyrinth of improbable and discordant figures, arrives at a maximum of 20,000 for each side, though in the various sources Timur's army is invariably represented as much more numerous,[16] Roloff argues persuasively that at the beginning of the battle—before Bayazid's Tatar troops deserted—the two sides were fairly evenly matched numerically.

The battle of Ankara was, even at Roloff's dehydrated figures, a very large engagement for that time. In medieval Europe the number of effectives rarely exceeded ten thousand, even in the largest battles.[17]

Mention might be made of the infantry-cavalry mix in the two armies. While Timur had some infantry, it was basically a cavalry force. Despite the renown of Bayazid's Janissary infantry contingent, his army also consisted for the greater part of mounted men, though infantry did bulk larger numerically and qualitatively.

What of the morale and élan of the Ottoman troops? Some authors, such as von Hammer, make much of Bayazid's strictness and miserliness and the irregularity with which he paid his troops, all of which had an adverse effect on their morale. They take their cue from the Ottoman chroniclers who relate various colorful anecdotes to this effect. This must be viewed with caution. Apart from the Tatars seduced by Timur's agents, the Janissaries, Serbs and others in Bayazid's army were to fight manfully despite the furnace heat and wracking thirst.

Another hard-worked story that will not down is that Bayazid was no longer fit to lead troops in the field.[18] Flushed with an unending string of victories, blinded by pride and egotism, gargantuan in his appetites which included pederasty, Bayazid, in this view, presents a study in dissipation and overindulgence which recalls *mutatis mutandis* the cosmic contrast between Young Hal of England and his transformation into the sodden, bloated, besotted Henry VIII of the well known Holbein painting. Though conceivably Bayazid's character had changed, this picture is vastly overdrawn. No one in such a state of mental and physical decomposition could have acted with the energy, physical courage and decisiveness that the forty-eight-year-old Bayazid showed both before and during the battle.

One of the fabrications accepted by many historians about Bayazid's supposed bumbling and befuddlement concerns his behavior upon his arrival at Ankara. Blinded by pride, he intended to show Timur that he was unimpressed by his strength (the latter's crushing numerical superiority is assumed) by moving to the north and holding a hunt in the waterless highlands. After three days of sport during which five thousand of his men perished of heat exhaustion and thirst, Bayazid returned to find his camp occupied by Timur's soldiers and his only source of water polluted.[19] That one of the great campaigners of his time, faced by an opponent of Timur's caliber, should have indulged his pride and high spirits by sacrificing several thousand of his men strains credulity. Bayazid, upon arriving at Ankara, apparently did not immediately engage Timur in battle. Undoubtedly, he wanted to give his men some small rest—half a day according to the most trustworthy sources—before throwing them into battle. Such is the seed of truth in this diverting but improbable tale.

On the morning of June 20, 1402 the two armies drew up for battle, Timur moving out of his fortified camp where he had been ensconced in anticipation of a surprise attack by Bayazid. The battlefield, situated in the plain of Chibukabad, was in the same area where Pompey had fought Mithridates. Bayazid's army was located to the north of Timur's. He arrayed his forces in the usual manner, with the Janissaries dug in on a hill behind a screen of light cavalry. The sipahis and the reserves were posted behind the Janissaries. Bayazid's Anatolian troops (including the Tatars infiltrated by Timur's agents) were placed on the right flank under the command of his oldest son Suleiman, governor of Aydin, Karesi and Saruhan. The Serbs, led by Stephen Lazarevich, Bayazid's brother-in-law, were on the left. Bayazid took his place in the center with his Janissaries and his two sons Musa and Isa. Mehmed, Bayazid's bravest and most prudent son, led the reserve.

Timur's army presumably was also deployed in the customary manner with light cavalry covering the entire front, and behind them the main vanguard, center, reserves and, to both sides, the left and right flanks. Princes of Timur's family, assisted by the senior emirs, commanded the various units, save for the reserve led by Timur himself. The latter, it is interesting to note, assigned the troops of Shirvanshah Ibrahim, Taharten of Erzinjan and Kara Yuluk of the White Sheep Turkomans to his right wing, facing the Serbs on the Ottoman left wing. Thus the Christians (Serbs) of Bayazid were opposed by the Turkomans of Timur.

According to Sharaf ad-Din, Timur posted several ranks of elephants in front of his army "as well to intimidate the enemy, as to serve as trophys [sic] of the spoils of India."[20] Though their howdahs contained archers and hurlers of Greek fire they apparently played a minor role in the fighting.

A description of the battle must be offered with great diffidence — our sources obfuscate the tactics employed and, indeed, some of the statements made are grotesque and fanciful. Timur apparently initiated hostilities with attacks by his light cavalry; these were followed by counterattacks by the troops of the right wing on Bayazid's left, consisting of Serbs. The latter, encased from head to foot in their heavy armor, offered doughty and rock-like resistance and could not be dislodged from their position. Timur then committed the remainder of his right wing, striking the Serbs on their left and rear, but they held firm. Timur's left wing was then brought into play against Bayazid's right, and here his action prospered. The troops of Aydin, seeing their old emir in Timur's ranks, switched sides. Their example was followed by the contingents of Saruhan, Menteshe and Germiyan as well as by the Tatars suborned by Timur's agents. Thus Timur's initial tactical advantage was now supplemented by numerical superiority — factors which decided the outcome of the battle. The remnants of Bayazid's right wing led by his son Suleiman, dislodged from their position, now began to fall back. Timur's efforts to drive a wedge between the Serbs and Bayazid and his Janissaries were, however, unavailing — indeed, the Serbs managed to cut their way through to Bayazid's side, causing Timur to cry out admiringly: "The wretches fight like lions!" Commiting the remainder of his troops to battle, Timur now forced back the Ottomans all along the line. Bayazid, however, repaired to a nearby hill where with his Janissaries, Serbs and other troops who joined him after being forced to retreat, he stood his ground. At length Stephen Lazarevich, seeing the battle lost, counseled retreat. Bayazid refused, deeming this unworthy, and determined to fight with his Janissaries to the bitter end. Seeing this, Stephen, as well as some of the other Ottoman leaders, left the field of battle. Even so, Stephen covered the retreat of Suleiman and his troops, enabling them to fall back in good order towards Bursa. Suleiman was taken out of the fighting by the Grand Vizier and the Janissary Agha, or leader. Bayazid's two sons, Mehmed and Isa, also fled; the first toward the northeast, the second in a southerly direction. Bayazid, deserted by his sons, viziers and many of his generals, fought on tenaciously with his Janissaries until nightfall. Both sides were taking heavy casualties. Only when Bayazid saw his men reduced to a pitiful remnant did he decide to flee. By a caprice of fortune, during the getaway his horse stumbled against a rock and unhorsed him. This enabled Mahmud, titular Khan of Timur's empire, personally to capture Bayazid and to present him bound to Timur. The emir of Germiyan, who in 1399 had fled to Timur in Syria after being held captive by Bayazid for nine years, aided the capture by pointing Bayazid out to Timur.[21] Bayazid's son Musa and his senior generals were also taken prisoner.

Upon the conclusion of a successful battle, the Mongol and Timurid art of war called for the prompt pursuit of the enemy lest it regroup and continue resistance. Here Timur faltered. He did, to be sure, detail his grandson Muhammad-Sultan to intercept Suleiman in the only pursuit organized. But though the former succeeded in reaching Bursa in but five days, Suleiman managed to slip out of the city in time, carrying off the greater part of Bayazid's treasury. Muhammad-Sultan seized the remainder of the treasury as well as a variety of gems, fine textiles, vessels and furnishings; these included a set of large double doors, one bearing the image of St. Peter, the other that of St. Paul. Of Byzantine manufacture, they were executed in gold, silver and blue enamel. These doors were later installed in Samarkand. Clavijo, who saw them there, admired their exquisite beauty.

Bursa was set afire and its wooden houses were quickly consumed by the flames. At Yeni Shehir Timur's men captured Bayazid's wife and two daughters. Later Timur permitted Abu-Bakr, who was with Muhammad-Sultan, to marry one of the daughters, thereby connecting the two houses by marriage. Abu-Bakr led a force to Nicaea (Iznik), site of the first general council of the Christian church, and then on to the shores of the Sea of Marmara, plundering and slaying along the way. Suleiman, deciding resistance was futile, crossed over into Europe.

Timur meanwhile had made his way westward to the cool and agreeable city of Kutahya, still famous for the colorful and distinctive tiles made there. Here for two months the conqueror and the bulk of his army rested and diverted themselves with feasts and other forms of entertainment, while elements of his army fanned out in all directions, killing, looting and destroying. One place which Timur's soldiers reached was the ancient city of Sardis, nestled in a fertile river valley due east of Smyrna. This had been a site of civilization since the later Stone Age. Subsequently it became the capital of the kingdo, of Lydia, and it was here that the fabulous King Croesus kept his golden treasury. Timur's men obliterated the last city to stand on this site. An American team from Harvard-Cornell, excavating the ruins since the 1950s, has been reporting many important discoveries.[22]

Initially there was fear that Timur would continue his path of conquest into Europe. According to one source, after the battle of Ankara Timur demanded that the Byzantines furnish him with some vessels with which to cross over into Europe.[23] "The lord of so many tomans or myriads of horse," Edward Gibbon remarks in one of his striking phrases, "was not master of a single galley." And it was mainly to oppose such a crossing that a league or alliance was formed at this time which included the Byzantine Emperor, the Venetians, the Genoese, the Knights of Rhodes and the Duke of Naxos in the Aegean islands.[24] Late in 1402 the league signed a treaty with Suleiman the son of Bayazid, who ruled over lands in the Balkans. We know from Clavijo that Timur by this time was extremely vexed with the conduct of the Byzantines and Genoese; accordingly, he began treating Christians in his realm with much severity.[25] Despite their fair promises to Timur, they had done nothing to prevent Turkish troops from crossing from Europe into Anatolia prior to the battle of Ankara. Later they made a packet by ferrying the fleeing Ottomans from Anatolia into Europe. The Venetians, arch rivals of the Genoese, had confined themselves to transporting Greek Christian refugees. In the end Timur, while at Kutahya, contented himself with summoning embassies from the Genoese at Galata and from Byzantium. Early in September these left for Timur's camp bearing rich presents. By the time of their arrival Timur had moved on to Tire in western Turkey by way of Ephesus (Ayasoluk).

Timur's last major military action in Anatolia involved the reduction of the port city of Smyrna (Izmir), the only important fortified city in Anatolia still in Christian hands. An ancient port, it was taken by Alexander the Great and is mentioned several times in the Bible. Largely Greek in population at that time, it had for forty-seven years been in the hands of the Knights of Rhodes (later called the Knights of Malta), a Catholic religious and military order founded during the Crusades. Under their rule the commercial importance of Smyrna was gradually restored, the Genoese playing a significant role in this commercial rival. Apart from booty, Timur's object in taking the city seems to have been a desire to undercut criticism to the effect that by defeating Bayazid, he had aided the Christians.

While at Tire, some thirty-six miles southeast of Smyrna, Timur dispatched envoys to that city demanding the conversion of the Knights to Islam. Failing this, they should agree to pay the tribute (*jizya*) and to fly Timur's banners from their battlements. Should they refuse then there would be a mass annihilation of the inhabitants as sanctioned by Islamic law. The garrison commander, Brother William de Mine, answered this ultimatum with a scornful reply. The Knights had good reason to believe themselves in an impregnable position. The city nestled like an amphitheater against the slope of a hill.[26] At the foot of it rose a fortress which commanded the sea approach. The city had successfully withstood sieges by both Bayazid and his father Murad. Bufillo Panizati, admiral of the Order, had in 1402 twice visited the city; by dint of his efforts the garrison had been increased to two hundred knights and the defenses shored up. Nor was the city lacking in munitions and victuals. And, unless Timur was able to close off the sea approach, additional supplies and reinforcements could be brought in.[27]

After the blunt refusal of his demands by the Knights, Timur arrived before Smyrna in early December (1402). Meanwhile, the columns sent out to harry western Anatolia had rejoined the main force. On December 6 Timur began a siege of the city. Towers were built on wheels, each holding two hundred men furnished with assault ladders. These were pushed next to the walls. Meanwhile ten thousand sappers began boring under the city's walls. Catapults for hurling boulders and Greek fire and battering rams were quickly constructed and put into action. Timur's soldiers then attacked the city on land from three sides. Despite the furious assault the defenders were able to beat back the first attack.

Timur then decided to tighten the noose around the city. On the land side it was encircled with a rampart of earth to prevent reinforcements from reaching the city. Simultaneously Timur took steps to close off the sea approach. His soldiers were detailed to drop off stones at the two ends of the breakwater which controlled the passage into the inner harbor. And though only one tenth of his men were engaged in this task, it was completed in one day. The galleys at anchor in the harbor barely managed to effect their escape before the trap was completed. Then giant platforms mounted on three-legged stilts were positioned next to one another in the water and planks were laid so that one could walk from one part of the crescent-shaped shore to the other as though on land. Large shields were constructed to protect the besiegers on this gigantic scaffolding as they pummeled the city from the sea side with a variety of projectiles. Meanwhile on land sappers were busy undermining the walls. The besieged offered stubborn, desperate resistance, showering Timur's men with pots of flaming naphtha, arrows and stones. During all this time it rained so hard that, in the words of Sharaf ad-Din, it seemed that a second Deluge was at hand.[28] Even this torrential downpour, however, failed to extinguish the flaming containers of naphtha. Finally, when the sappers had completed their troglodytic work, Timur ordered the wooden shoring in the tunnels which had been impregnated with naphtha set afire. This caused the collapse of sections of the city's walls and the deaths of a number of the defenders. A general assault was then mounted; Timur's men burst, swords in hand, through the yawning breaches and debouched into the streets. A handful of knights, led by de Mine, somehow managed to force its way through the enemy cordon to the shore and to swim out to the galleys. Some of the Christian city folk also managed to swim out to the galleys and, clinging to anchors, ropes or oars, begged to be taken on board. Those on ship, however, pushed them away with their spears. Smyrna itself was given over to general destruction. At Timur's command its entire population, including women and children, was put to the sword. Pyramids of heads were erected, though with one modification from Timur's usual practice. To stretch out their relatively small number they were alternated in such a way that one skull grinned out between every two stones. Several days after the taking of Smyrna a new squadron of ships sent out from Cyprus by the Knights of Rhodes to succor the city arrived in the harbor. Timur ordered these bombarded, not only with Greek fire, but also with the heads of the slain defenders. The galleys departed in haste. Sharaf ad-Din gloatingly observes that Timur took Smyrna in just a fortnight, whereas Bayazid had unsuccessfully besieged it for seven years.

The Genoese governors of the nearby ports of Ancient Pocaea (Focea Vecchia) and New Phocaea (Focea Nuova), at present the small, comatose Turkish seaside villages of Focha and Yeni Focha, hurried to make their submission, menaced as they were by Muhammad-Sultan's troops. The islands of Chios and Lesbos, which were also Genoese commercial outposts, did the same.

The taking of Smyrna was Timur's last military action in Anatolia. The rejoicing in Europe and especially in Byzantium at Bayazid's defeat was not shared by the Christians of Anatolia. They had suffered doubly, first at the hands of the Ottomans, then even more so from the men of Timur.

By crushing the Ottomans Timur was able to bring Mamluke Egypt to heel. Late in 1402 he sent a mission to Cairo to demand recognition of his suzerainty. Specifically, Sultan Faraj was asked to pay tribute and to insert Timur's name in the Friday prayer and on the coinage. He was also asked to release Atilmish and to execute Sultan Ahmed Jelair and Kara Yusuf, detained in Syria by the Mamlukes. Faraj, who was preoccupied with internal difficulties, agreed to these demands and, after releasing Atilmish, sent an embassy to Timur.[29] Rich presents were exchanged. Timur's gifts included a crown, a royal mantle and a jewel-studded belt — gifts indicative of Faraj's vassal status.

Faraj regarded his subordination as a temporary expedient designed to ward off invasion by Timur. No Mamluke coins bearing the latter's name are known to us.[30] Nor did Timur obtain satisfaction in the matter of Sultan Ahmed and Kara Yusuf. Two years later in 1404, Timur, in dismissing the Egyptian envoys who had travelled to Samarkand, sent back a demand that Sultan Ahmed be sent to him bound and gagged along with the head of Kara Yusuf. The Emir of Damascus, however, allowed the two their freedom, apparently on his own initiative, since Faraj's authority in Syria was then in great disarray.

††††††

After leaving Smyrna Timur returned to Ephesus to pass the rest of the winter, while his men pillaged the countryside. Upon his return the Ephesians sent children out to greet him, hoping to soften his heart. The children quoted verses from the Koran, copies of which they held in their hands, and pleaded for mercy. "What are they bleating about?"

he asked his retainers. Upon hearing their explanations he ordered his cavalrymen to trample the children to death under their horses' hooves.[31]

Timur's treatment of the captured Bayazid has given rise to the most bewildering and diverse interpretations. Our sources are so discordant that it is unlikely this controversy will ever be cleared up. What seems credible, after peeling away the lest confidence-inspiring accounts, is that Timur at first treated Bayazid well. Then, after an unsuccessful escape attempt by Bayazid, the casual security measures taken to guard him were replaced by more stringent ones. These included closer guarding by day and chaining at night. When Timur was on the move Bayazid was conveyed in a *kafes*, a Turkish word which can be variously interpreted as a cage, a room enclosed with a grating, or a latticed sedanchair. Historians accepting the first meaning and relying on dubious sources later elaborated the story that Bayazid was transported about in a cage with iron bars like a wild animal. A close study of the sources does not substantiate this. What was involved was a sedan chair with lattices which was carried between two horses—a contraption used in the conveyance of ladies of the harem.[32]

Timur's expectation that one of Bayazid's sons would ransom him did not materialize. On March 8, 1403 Bayazid died at Ak Shehir where Timur had set up his headquarters. Exactly how he died is likely to remain a perennial controversy.[33] Some historians claim that he committed suicide; others, that he died of apoplexy. The nature of the Islamic faith militates against the suicide theory. Muslims are taught surrender to Allah's will; the word "Islam" itself means "submission." A suicide commits a mortal sin and forfeits Paradise.[34] Suicide is accordingly rare among Muslims. Possibly Bayazid lost the will to live, but that is another matter.

Timur, who showed much sorrow over Bayazid's death, permitted his son Musa to escort the body to Bursa, the old Ottoman capital and chief burial place. Four days later Muhammad-Sultan, Timur's favorite grandson and heir-presumptive, died of natural causes at the age of nineteen in Afyon Karahisar.

After leaving Afyon Karahisar Timur's route eastwards took him through Kayseri, Sivas, Erzerum and Kars. On the way he gathered up sixty thousand families of Kara or Black Tatars previously brought into Anatolia by Hulagu in the thirteenth century. He planned to use these people in his projected invasion of China.

While at Kars, Timur assigned Iraq Arabi to his grandson Abu-Bakr. Baghdad, its chief city, lay in ruins. Timur ordered it restored as a staging post for the Mecca caravans. There was one hitch—Baghdad and its dependencies had slipped out from Timur's control. Though a force sent there in the winter of 1401/1402 had chased Sultan Ahmed out, several months later, during Timur's involvement in Anatolia, he had skulked back in. Soon, however, his son Prince Tahir revolted in a bid to seize power for himself. Sultan Ahmed appealed for aid to his old ally Kara Yusuf. The two routed Tahir in a battle; the unfortunate son, while escaping, fell from his horse into a brook and drowned. Later Kara Yusuf turned on Sultan Ahmed and took Baghdad, where he was residing. Sultan Ahmed succeeded in escaping to Damascus.

Timur ordered Abu-Bakr's brother Roustem of Isfahan to help him. The two brothers, prior to the battle against Kara Yusuf in the fall of 1403, quarrelled over the tactics to be employed. At length Roustem alone engaged Kara Yusuf. The latter, who saw his brother killed and his wife captured, fled westward to Mamluke territory and joined Sultan Ahmed in his refuge. Since Timur had assigned the Iraq Arabi area to Abu-Bakr, it now became his. He promptly took steps to encourage agriculture and to rebuild Baghdad.[35]

As regards Anatolia, Timur contented himself with a general acknowledgment of his overlordship by local rulers. He apparently was actuated by what has been called the law of diminishing returns in imperialism.[36] The integral incorporation of Anatolia into his realm would have involved efforts entirely disproportionate to any material benefits to be derived. There is evidence, moreover, that Timur was too weak militarily to have brought this off. Casualties had been heavy. Even before the battle of Ankara he had been unable wholly to snuff out pockets of resistance.

Anatolia, however, could conceivably be used by a hostile power as a base of operations against Timur's western possessions. He took several measures in the event of such an eventuality. The first of these was a pitiless harrying of the land, which would for some years create problems of economic recovery. Secondly, Timur pared down significantly the areas under Ottoman control by restoring the emirs dispossessed by Bayazid. Thirdly, Timur did what he could to promote discord among the four sons of Bayazid who possessed portions of the remainder. A lethal and protracted struggle for supremacy then followed. Not until the reign of Mehmed II Fatih (1451-81) would the Ottomans be able to resume their advance into eastern Anatolia. Finally, Timur gave further grants of contiguous territory to his loyal march lords, namely Taharten of Erzinjan, Ibrahim of Shirvan and Kara Yuluk of the Turcoman White Sheep confederation. Here not pulverization of territories but consolidation into puissant border bastions was the end in view.

Timur's Anatolian campaign, despite his brusque withdrawal, had profound historical consequences. Both Byzantium and Trebizond received a half century of reprieve from Ottoman annexation; the area extending from Syria westward to Algeria received more than a century. Timur removed for all time the Ottoman threat to the empire he left his heirs; by the time the Ottomans resumed their eastward advance it would have passed into the dustbin of history. Finally, the news of Bayazid's dramatic defeat gave hope and courage to those states anticipating Ottoman attack in the future.

Timur's final irruption into Georgia in late summer of 1403 may be briefly noticed. Early in the summer of 1402 he had sent a punitive force to punish King George for his disobedience. The campaign had ended with the king's promise to fulfill all of Timur's demands. The king reneged on this and, moreover, had failed to journey to Timur's camp to congratulate him on his great victory over Bayazid. As a preliminary to his own arrival in Georgia, Timur had ordered Ibrahim Shirvanshah to make forays, during which the latter occupied some of the mountain passes.

King George, upon Timur's approach, sent an embassy bearing gifts. In his message the king professed astonishment that Timur should march against such a petty ruler. He promised to send money and soldiers to serve with Timur and to appear in person as soon as his fear had subsided.

Timur rejected both the message and the presents, insisting that the king appear in person. He apparently suspected that the king was stalluntil after harvest time, so he dispatched a force to harvest the wheat and pulse. These were ground into meal and transported back.

Timur himself then arrived before the fortress of Bintvisi (Kurtin), on the Algeti river, deep in enemy country. The taking of this redoubtable fortress would be the centerpiece of the campaign. Located on a steeep mountain, it was further protected by surrounding precipices. Only a narrow and sinuous path led to the top of the peak. Here the Georgians had built homes and laid up stocks of wine, food and rain water which they caught in cisterns. The mountain, moreover, was fortified on all sides. Protected by a strong garrison, the inhabitants had good reason to consider themselves safe. South of the fortress was an even higher rock which the Georgians ascended, using ropes and ladders.

Timur encircled the complex with fortifications or sconces. He also built a platform of wood and stone midway between his own camp and the fortress gate. In a week's time the platform had risen so high as to overawe the fortress. One night a mountain climber named Bikidgek managed to thread his way unobserved to the top of the peak south of the fortress which afforded access to its inner part, and to bring back the news. The next night four of Timur's mountain warriors returned to this route of ascent. Attaching ropes to a tree growing out of the rocks, they drew up ladders made of cord. Fifty of Timur's men used these to draw themselves up into position. At daybreak the attack was clamourously sounded. Despite stubborn resistance the small, intrepid band reached the fortress gate, which was meanwhile being pummeled by stone-throwing catapults positioned on the giant platform. At length the gate was forced; immediately, Timur's men poured in and took the fortress. Timur stonily rejected all pleas for quarter. The captured officers were pitched over the high fortress wall. The remaining defenders were beheaded and the women and children enslaved. Bikidgek and the other brave mountain warriors received lavish presents.

Timur resolved to carry out his depredations in Georgia as far as Abkhasia at its northwestern extremity. Flying columns fanned out, while Timur himself followed with the main host. In some locales axes had to be used to cut a road through the woods. The Georgians, pursued through the deep gorges, fled into the caves above by means of ladders which they drew up after them. Timur, to dig them out, had specially constructed baskets raised to the tops of the cliffs by means of ropes. These were then lowered down the steep mountain face. Upon reaching the mouth of each cave, the men in the baskets would discharge a shower of arrows and then jump inside with swords and lances in hand to kill the defenders.

Seven hundred towns and villages, as well as churches and monasteries, felt Timur's destructive fury. Even the trees were uprooted and burned. Some Georgians in Timur's service became so appalled at this that they sent messages to King George imploring his submission. In despair the king agreed. Envoys, with Timur's generals serving as intermediaries, approached the conqueror and promised rich presents, the annual tribute, and troop contingents to serve in his army upon call.

Timur remained unmoved. His generals persuaded his Muslim divines to broach the matter in the imperial council. The theologians unanimously opined that "since the Georgians consented to pay the tribute, and not to injure the Mussulmans, they were oblig'd by their law to grant 'em quarter, without doing 'em any further harm either by slaughter or pillaging."[37] This solid wall of opinion, Sharaf ad-Din avers, caused Timur to give way. Others give credit to Ibrahim Shirvanshah who used his influence with Timur to persuade him to grant peace, on condition that Georgia become a vassal dependency.[38] Though Timur had insisted upon the king's personal appearance, he may now have decided to settle for half a loaf since he was anxious to go on to other things. The Georgian envoys were dismissed with a favorable answer. In several days' time they returned with "a thousand gold medals struck in the name and august titles of Timur"[39] and a profusion of other gifts, including a giant ruby. They solemnly swore that the tribute would be paid. Timur accepted this submission. He withdrew southwards via Tiflis, though not before destroying more churches and monasteries on the way. Unlucky Georgia was now finally rid of Timur, but his repeated invasions, even more devastating than those of the Mongols, had baleful and enduring effects on the history of that country.

Since Timur's passion for destruction was matched by one for construction, he now became ridden with the idea of rebuilding the city of Bailakan near the confluence of the Araxes and Kura rivers in the central part of present-day Soviet Azerbaijan. Destroyed by Chingis Khan's Mongols in 1221, in Timur's time it was inhabited only by "insects, scritch-owls, serpents and scorpions."[40] The plan elaborated by his engineers and architects called for a "wall, ditch, four marketplaces, and a great number of houses, baths, caravanserais, squares, gardens and other commodious places."[41] Approved by Timur, the plan was executed with his usual love of speed. Though hampered by cold and rain, his entire army completed the job in a month. And since water was essential for irrigation and animal husbandry, his men dug a canal six leagues in length connecting Bailakan with the Araxes river — this also in one month's time. Thus Timur fulfilled his goal of restoring the lower Araxes to its full economic potential; work toward this end had begun during his winter sojourn of 1400/1401 in the area. The Araxes plain was the rice basket of Azerbaijan.[42] When Clavijo passed through Bailakan in 1405 it already had twenty thousand houses. At the present time the city is once more in ruins.

The town and canal completed, Timur pushed on to the lush pastures of Karabagh where thatched cottages had been prepared for him.

Here he spent the winter of 1403/1404 on matters of state, dispensing justice, receiving delegations and hunting. At night he diverted himself by arguing theological questions with his divines.

In the spring Timur broke camp at Karabagh for the last time and headed for Samarkand. His route took him through northern Iran. Here he fought the last battles of his life. He passed by Firuzkuh, 86 miles east of Teheran, which he took by storm. Following this he led an expedition to the northeastern littoral of the Caspian Sea to snuff out pockets of resistance. Continuing eastward to Meshed, he then veered off to the northeast toward Samarkand, which he reached in August of 1404. He had been away almost five years.

CHAPTER XII
A Diplomatic Interlude

> "In politics there are no
> friendships, only alliances."
> —John F. Kennedy

Timur's diplomatic contacts with Christian states would not be limited to the Genoese colony at Pera and Byzantium and Trebizond. Western interest in Timur was at first aroused when it became apparent that he, in his expansion westward, would no doubt ultimately collide with Bayazid who was expanding eastward into Anatolia. After the great conquests of the Mongols in the thirteenth century, the West sought alliance with them against the Muslims. They hoped thereby to take the latter in the rear. Now the West hoped that Timur could be used to the same end against Bayazid. There was also interest in stimulating commerce with the Orient, promoting the cause of Christianity, and curiosity with regard to Timur's power and intentions. England, France and Castile were all involved in missives and missions to the great conqueror.

Timur's contacts with Castile, one of the major states in fragmented Spain, came about indirectly. Henry III of Castile, in order to obtain firsthand information about the impending confrontation between Bayazid and Timur, sent Pelayo de Sotomayor and Hernán Sánchez de Palazuelos to Bayazid, who allowed them to accompany him in his march against Timur. They witnessed the battle of Ankara which ended with Bayazid's defeat and capture. Timur, upon learning of their identity, received them graciously. After questioning them about their country, he gave them gifts and bade them return home. Two lovely ladies whom Timur had liberated from Bayazid's harem were entrusted to their care. One of them, Angelica (or Angelina), was of Greek descent while the second, Maria, was a granddaughter of the king of Hungary. Bayazid had apparently captured them after the battle of Nicopolis in 1396. The returning Castilians were also accompanied by

Muhammad al-Kadi, Timur's own envoy, bearing a letter and gifts for King Henry. The letter's contents must have been encouraging, for Henry soon dispatched an embassy of his own to Timur. This consisted of court chamberlain Ruy Gonzales de Clavijo, master of theology Fray Alonso Páez of Santa María and a bodyguard by the name of Gómez de Salazar, who died en route. The trio, accompanied by Timur's envoy, left Spain from the port of Cádiz on May 22, 1403. Making landfall at Constantinople, they learned many interesting things during their stopover. Then sailing on to Trebizond, the party made its way overland passing through Tabriz, Rayy, Termez and Kesh. On September 8, 1404 they were received by Timur in Samarkand.[1]

Clavijo's activities in Samarkand are noted elsewhere. Leaving for home late that same year (1404), the Clavijo party's progress was so glacial that it did not reach Castile until March 1406. Clavijo's account of his three year journey is one of the most remarkable travel relations of the Middle Ages.[2] The diplomatic contacts between Timur and Castile were barren of result and the Clavijo mission has been treated as an isolated event by Spanish historians. It did, however, reflect that spirit of adventure, enterprise and curiosity which would later take the Spaniards into the New World.

During his sojourn in Anatolia, Timur also carried on correspondence with the French king Charles VI Valois (1380-1422) and with the English king Henry IV Lancaster (1399-1413). Both sovereigns played host to the Byzantine emperor Manuel II while he was in the West seeking aid against Bayazid, the enemy of Timur. Since a Dominican, John Greenlaw, Archbishop of Sultaniya, played a key role in these negotiations, the missionary activities of the Catholics in the east may be briefly noticed.

These involved two Catholic missionary orders, the Franciscans and Dominicans, both founded early in the thirteenth century. The Crusades imbued both orders with a desire to penetrate the Orient and to establish Catholic missionary outposts there.[3] The archdiocese of Sultaniya, created in 1318, fell within the purview of the Dominicans, while the Franciscans were active elsewhere. Under Uljaitu (1304-1316) Sultaniya became the capital of the Il-Khanid state. The obsessive goal of the Il-Khanids was the conquest of Syria and Palestine. This involved them in protracted warfare with the Mamluke sultans of Egypt. Since Mamluke Egypt was the great bastion of Islam at that time and the il-Khans of Persia were pagan-shamanists, the western states of Europe —Genoa, France, England and the Papacy—looked upon the latter as natural allies. This led to the exchange of several embassies in the period 1284-1303 as well as negotiations by which the Il-Khanids sought to involve the West in a joint "crusade" in Syria.[4] Though nothing came of these approaches they facilitated Catholic missionary activity directed from Sultaniya. Not even the conversion of the Il-Khanid ruler Gazan (1295-1304) to the Islamic faith disturbed this activity.

The collapse of the Il-Khanid state (1336) and the dismemberment of Persia into a number of Islamic kingdoms adversely affected missionary activity. Other blows followed: decimation of the ranks of the Catholic orders in Europe by the Black Death, reducing both personnel and resources available for work in the East; the "time of troubles" into which the Golden Horde was plunged after the killing of its ruler Jani-beg (1359); growing Muslim fanaticism in Central Asia as Islam consolidated its position; the advance of the Ottoman Turks; and finally, an anti-foreign national Chinese resurgence as the "barbarian" Mongol or Yüan dynasty was supplanted by the native Ming dynasty (1368). This was accompanied by a closing of routes to China via Central Asia used by missionaries and merchants alike.

For a time the wars of Timur also adversely affected missionary activity. By the end of the century, however, things seemingly took a brighter turn. As Timur forged his great empire he became increasingly concerned with the stimulation of international trade. Expansion of trade and missionary activity had gone hand in hand in the earlier period. Some of the Catholic missionary outposts had, indeed, ministered to the spiritual needs of the resident European merchants. Timur, moreover, in his involvement with Bayazid, was anxious to forge alliances with Christian states. Archbishop John of Sultaniya, deeming it licit to utilise one infidel to ruin another, was only too anxious to lend a hand. He accompanied Timur on his progress through Asia Minor. Possibly he had been sent in 1398 to Genoa and Venice bearing letters from Timur.[5] His travels as an intermediary would also take him to France and England.

Timur's correspondence with the kings of France and England gives us much trouble since only some of the letters have been preserved and not all of these in the Persian original. Moreover, the allusions in these are often far from clear.

Only the first of the two letters sent by Timur to Charles VI of France is extant in the Persian original. It is dated August 1, 1402, with Sivas as the place of venue. The nineteenth century French orientalist Silvestre de Sacy believes, on the basis of internal evidence, that Timur held the French king in small esteem.[6] In his short message Timur acknowledged the earlier visit of the preacher monk Francis bearing letters from Charles VI. In return Timur was sending Archbishop John to put him in the picture with regard to his own activities. In conclusion, Timur proposed that merchants from both states be given free access to the markets of the other "for the world is well provided for thanks to the merchants."

Timur's second letter to Charles, bearing the same date and venue as the first, has come down to us in a Latin translation. Though containing some of the same information, it is longer and different in form. The letter's salutation and references to the French king are much more flattering. Moreover, Archbishop John is singled out as a knowledgeable person, "worthy of trust, except for religious matters," with whom Charles could converse on all topics. Timur also professed pleasure at hearing of Charles' animosity towards Bayazid who, according to law and religion, should have been as one with Timur. However, Bayazid had failed to observe his treaty obligations and Timur, aroused by the Christian friars and preachers and by the promises of the king's subjects, had accordingly deposed him.

The absence of the Persian original of Timur's second letter in the French archives suggests that the Latin version is in fact the original and that it was written by Archbishop John prior to his departure for Europe. Archbishop John, in his letter, did all he could to massage the pride of the French king and to heighten the importance of the mission entrusted to him by Timur.[7]

We learn from a French chronicle that Charles VI received Archbishop John in Paris in May 1403 in the presence of a brilliant concourse of dukes and other notables. John disclosed the goals of his mission to be the following: (1) to give information concerning Timur's great victory over Bayazid, the capture of the latter and Timur's liberation of Bayazid's Christian captives and resolve to free any others he came upon; (2) to witness the majesty of the French court and to acquaint the latter with the brilliance of Timur's realm. Archbishop John dilated on the opportunities his embassy offered to promote mutually profitable trade. This could be further secured by the conclusion of a trade treaty.

While in Paris the archbishop discussed Timur's career with many people. Much interest was shown in this, for not only was John Timur's envoy but he was also a high-ranking Catholic prelate who had spent time at his court. John further satisfied this curiosity by preparing a brief memoir on Timur in French.[8] He was careful to present him in a good light where Christians were concerned. The bestialities committed by Timur in Smyrna were simply not mentioned.

Charles VI's letter to "Temirbey" bears the date 15 June 1403. In it he thanked Timur for informing him of his great victory over Bayazid and declared his readiness to accord Timur's subjects trading privileges in all French possessions on, at the very least, a reciprocal basis. He also thanked Timur for the benevolence and many kindnesses that he had shown Christians. The king also stated that he had discussed many other matters with the archbishop, who would give Timur an oral report.

The form and phraseology of Charles VI's letter indicates that it was composed by Archbishop John. Charles had written to Timur before but, unfortunately, we do not have copies of his letters; in fact, we do not even know if Timur received Charles' last letter. The former returned to Samarkand only in the summer of 1404. Possibly the letter was handed to him while en route. In de Sacy's view Timur's two letters of August 1, 1402 and Charles' answer are not of great moment and historians who assess this as a true embassy or political negotiation are wide of the mark.[9] He believes that the first letter to Charles was probably written mainly to indulge the Catholic missionaries, especially Archbishop John. He dismisses Timur's second letter as the handiwork of the archbishop. Subsequent historians, however, believe that what we have in view is a diplomatic correspondence looking toward the conclusion of a trade treaty.[10] Timur's interest in stimulating trade is well attested. France, for its part, had vital commercial interests to foster, including the safeguarding of the outposts of the Genoese now that the latter were French subjects.

England's contacts with Timur's realm have received far less attention from scholars. English archives preserve copies of replies made by Henry IV to letters of Timur's son Miranshah and of Timur himself. The originals have not come down to us.

It was possible that Miranshah might succeed his aging father as supreme ruler. He had, moreover, shown open favor to Western traders and missionaries. Quite naturally, he became the object of attention on the part of Western rulers.

Henry's reply to Miranshah's letter was sent from Hertford (year not given).[11] Calling Miranshah the "patron of the Catholic religion," the king thanked him for the friendship and protection he had afforded to its adherents and clergy. He also thanked him for ensuring the safety

and welfare of Christian merchants. He had learned of this from Archbishop John and from a series of letters. References to the latter indicate that the initiative for the establishment of friendly relations came
from Miranshah. Henry declared his wish to pursue this matter further
and authorized the archbishop to negotiate on his behalf.

In his letter to Timur, Henry IV states that he had learned of Timur's
friendship for England from the archbishop though England had done
nothing to merit it. This the king valued highly. England also was interested in stimulating commercial contact with Timur's empire which
would involve the subjects of both states. The king expressed joy and
relief at the news of Timur's victory over Bayazid. In closing, Timur was
informed that Archbishop John would not only bear the royal message
but would acquaint him orally with the king's "deeds and doings."

There is much that is puzzling and obscure in some of the references
made in Henry IV's letters. We do not know when they were sent. The
most likely surmise is that Archbishop John, who left France for England in June 1403, took with him Charles VI's letter for Timur. He was
then also entrusted with Henry IV's letters to Miranshah and to Timur.
The archbishop thereupon departed for the Orient furnished with letters of protection from Henry IV. Though it is not certain that Miranshah and Timur ever received Henry's letters, this correspondence is of
interest as marking England's first efforts at contact with two Central
Asian potentates.

Conditions in Central Asia, France and England militated against any
further development of relations. Timur's death early in 1405 brought
in its wake a succession struggle and other perturbations. In France
Charles VI, beginning in 1392, was subject to recurring bouts of insanity
during which power was disputed by rival factions. Also the threat that
England would resume hostilities—the Hundred Years War had still a
half century to go—hung over France like a thundercloud. In England
Henry IV, a usurper, was distracted by rebellions and kept on a short
financial tether by Parliament, which parsimoniously doled out funds
to him in return for checks on the royal authority. By 1412 he had
measurably improved his position, only to be afflicted by a debilitating
illness which forced his withdrawal from an active political role.

CHAPTER XIII
"The Napoleon of Asia" !

> "War is the domain of physical exertion and suffering. If one is not to be overcome by these features, he must possess a certain physical and mental strength, native or acquired, which makes him indifferent to them."
>
> — Clausewitz, *On War*

Though many references have perforce been made to the organization, weaponry, strategy, tactics, leadership, etc. of Timur's army, an overall summary has been deferred almost to the end, for two reasons. First, Timur after his assumption of supreme power in Transoxiana in 1370, spent the next 35 years in almost uninterrupted war. In such conditions he could not but make efforts to improve his army's fighting capabilities, so that important modifications were continually introduced. Insight into the way he waged war can be better provided when some specific military actions already described are alluded to. Second, now that the general lineaments of his reign are known, the role of his army in the state he created may be better appreciated.

Much nonsense has been written about Timur's army, primarily because military historians have almost to a man accepted and drawn upon the spurious "Institutes" and "Autobiography" of Timur, which describe with a prodigality of detail the table of organization of his army and the tactics and strategy which he supposedly employed.

The organizational structure of Timur's army was patterned after that of Chingis Khan with but one important difference, namely, that the infantry played a more important role in Timur's military operations. This is understandable when it is remembered that Timur, from the very first, had under his rule both nomads and settled peoples.

Chingis, on the other hand, started out with nomads and only later, after invading sedentary areas, impressed the people of the latter into his army. Timur's infantry was recruited quite naturally from among the sedentary population; the nomads furnished the cavalry. The sedentary areas also provided the artillerymen of the day—those who manned the stone-throwing catapults and fire-throwing apparatus, the arbalests and battering-rams as well as the crude cannon, which will be discussed later in more detail. The infantry also provided the corps of engineeers, the men who sapped fortresses, built platforms near the enemy's walls the better to attack him, and the hydraulic engineers who diverted streams either away from or towards the enemy as the case might require. On occasion the cavalry would dismount and fight on foot; or, conversely, at other times the infantry would be mounted on horses.

Unlike Chingis, Timur made some tactical use of war elephants acquired in the course of his Indian campaign late in his career. Chingis considered elephants too slow and cumbersome to be of use. Capturing some used against him while besieging Samarkand, he had them let out into the steppe to perish of hunger.[2]

Military campaigns were preceded by kurultais or assemblies attended by the senior commanders and officials. These were consent-building sessions at which military ardor for the campaign was aroused by Timur by skillfully contrived speeches. Once this object had been attained, plans were formulated for the conduct of the war. Timur would determine how many men he needed and the number each province was required to furnish. Tavachis or officials who were charged with the levying, organization and registration of troops and the transmittal of orders to units would then fan out into both the settled and the nomad areas and carry out the troop muster. Each province had to be ready to provide the basic levy and, if needed, a supplementary one. As in Chingis Khan's army (and in Turko-Mongol military formations in general) units were nominally based on the decimal system: tens, hundreds, thousands and ten thousands (tumans). In actuality units did not always correspond to these numbers. Thus the tuman could number fewer than ten thousand while the koshun or hundred might number as many as five hundred persons.

According to the fifteenth-century writer Abd-ar Razzak Samarkandi, each warrior, in presenting himself for the general levy, was required to bring with him provisions for one year and the following weapons: a bow with thirty arrows, a quiver and a shield. For every two nomad horsemen there was to be a third spare mount. Every ten men were to have a tent, two spades, a pick, a saw, an axe, one hundred needles, a rope for a lasso, one strong hide, a kettle and spare provisions. Timur held frequent inspections to make sure that his men were properly turned out and supplied. Thus, before the famous battle of the Terek, Timur examined the equipment of each regiment. Mentioned in the sources are swords, lances, bows, arrows, chain mail, clubs and pole-nets for capturing men alive. In cases of hard emergency the stores of victuals of all units would be merged and a system of rationing set in hand. The frequent hunts while on campaign not only honed the battle-preparedness of the men but added freshly killed birds and animals to the common larder.

In Western Europe at this time even the most successful and awe-inspiring commander was in constant fear lest his plans be disconcerted by the rash action of one of his headstrong barons or subordinates. This would have been unthinkable in Timur's army. Every unit commander knew his place and strictly adhered to it.

Timur's Chagatai warriors—the cream of his army—wore plaits of hair as had those of Chingis. And despite Timur's pose as a pillar of the Islamic faith he used Chingis' Yasa as his code of military justice and conduct. Sharaf ad-Din, for example, relates many instances of subordinates "punished according to the laws of Chingis Khan." The Chagatais, like the Huns, Avars and Mongols before them, unnerved their opponents, who were used to fighting peoples who at least looked like themselves, as much by their loathsome and horrid appearance as by their military prowess. Commenting on their repulsiveness, Clavijo writes: "All these wandering Chagatai folk appeared to us with faces so burnt by the sun that for ugliness they might well have come straight out of hell itself."[3] As noted earlier, the Chagatais originally were descendants of Turkic and Turkified Mongol nomad tribes who settled in Central Asia after the Mongol conquest. Gradually they adopted the superior economic-cultural tradition of the sedentary peoples of the area. The majority began to use the local linguistically related Turkic language. Some, however, adopted the Tadjik language. This was especially true of those groups who had settled around Samarkand, Bukhara and Khodzhent where the predominant language was Tadjik. In the fifteenth century the term "Chagatai" was extended to compass all Turkic peoples of Transoxiana. Included were tribes like the Karluks who had settled in the area in pre-Mongol times.[4]

As Chingis had done, Timur paid much attention to intelligence gathering whereby he was apprised not only of such directly military factors as the best roads for retreating and advancing, possible battle-fields, strongholds, the enemy's military capabilities, but also of the mood of the population, dissension, and the diplomatic situation in general. Timur had a special staff of intelligence officers to concern themselves with these affairs. Frequently dervishes and merchants were the agents who gathered this information; since travelling was a normal part of their activities, they were unlikely to arouse suspicion. Though the principal weakness of any espionage system is the fact that demand creates supply there is no evidence that Timur was ill-served or gulled by his agents. Even Toktamish, himself a past master in the gathering of intelligence, was surprised at Timur's knowledge of the strengths and weaknesses of his opponents. Nor was psychological warfare (as we call it) neglected. Here again merchants and dervishes were pressed into use to help shape enemy public opinion. Timur's propaganda ranged the gamut from ambivalent promise to persuasive sincerity. The object was to sap the will of the enemy to resist. Timur preferred to have cities and towns open their gates to him without fighting so that he could receive them intact. If a siege were necessary, Timur sought to persuade as many of the population as possible that if they abstained from aiding the defending force they would receive favorable treatment.

Like Chingis Khan Timur also had maps prepared of areas to be invaded, this at a time in Western Europe "when maps were nonexistent and geographical knowledge was both scanty and inaccurate."[5]

Water for his troops was another of Timur's preoccupations. As one American traveler on a trip made in the vicinity of Samarkand during the autumn of 1931 writes: "On the steppe and in the Zerafshan Valley were a number of curious, ancient-looking brick domes. These, we learned, were sardobas, or watering-places, built by Tamerlane in the 14th century, when his invading armies swept through the pass and across the steppe. The climate was so arid that he found it necessary to establish them in order to make travel possible. The domes cover wells, or cisterns, filled during the spring freshets. thus keeping the water clean. To this day they are in excellent condition."[6] Heat, as one noted German authority on military science has pointed out, is one of the greatest trials for a soldier in wartime. When, under such circumstances, water is in short supply "heat becomes a torture, making troops unfit for further marching or for battle."[7] The author adds that troops, after taking a village, will invariably rush for the nearest wells, heedless of the proximity of the enemy. Timur not only saw to it that his own men were well supplied with water, but he did whatever he could to deny water to enemy forces. Just prior to the battle of Ankara Bayazid's soldiers, it will be recalled, were wracked with thirst after long marches in great heat. Timur, by poisoning or blocking off the local water supplies, helped to ensure his victory in the great battle that followed.

Once the campaign was under way, each unit commander proceeded with his men in the position assigned him. The vanguard (mangalai), preceded by its forward guard, spearheaded the advance. Since at times the mangalai could number as many as several tumans, this was a powerful force. Reconnaissance patrols consisting of exceptionally brave soldiers were thrown out in all directions to prevent surprise, to ascertain the enemy's whereabouts and numbers and to offer the first resistance. Each unit was provided with guides whose importance may be gauged by the fact that Timur himself habitually distributed these among the army units.

If it was decided to strike camp near the enemy's defensive positions precautions were taken. A ditch was dug around the camp and towers which were apparently moveable and equipped with large shields with apertures, were put into position.

As mentioned before, Timur's troopers took their families, flocks and other possessions with them. When dangerous and difficult operations lay ahead, these would be left behind in a solidly entrenched camp with wagons placed around the perimeter. Women, dressed as soldiers, were sometimes used by Timur to trick the enemy into believing that he had not broken camp. In the maneuvering that took place against Toktamish in 1391 just prior to the battle of the Terek, Timur, according to Clavijo, "issued orders that all the women who marched with his soldiers should don helmets with the men's war gear to play the part of soldiers" and remain in camp while he and his men stole out of camp and marched against Toktamish.

It was precisely at this time that weapons using gunpowder as a propellant appeared in the Near East after making their debut in Europe between 1325 and 1350. Timur and his heirs were the first to use firearms in Central Asia. During his long military career Timur often found it necessary to besiege cities and strongholds. Rumors reached him about the existence of cannon and, given his penchant for making use of the latest techniques and weaponry, it is hardly surprising that he took steps to acquire some. The Soviet scholar A. M. Belenitsky has established on the basis of a little-studied fifteenth century chronicle that there were stone-shooting cannons in Timur's army as early as 1379 when they were used during the siege of Urgench; Nizam ad-Din

mentions such weapons in the siege of Damascus in 1400-1401 by
Timur. Though used mainly in the besieging of strongholds, they were
also employed as anti-personnel weapons. Cannon were, however, still
too primitive to be used extensively. The Mamlukes also acquired firearms during this period—cannon are thought to have been used in a
street battle in Cairo in 1389. Yet when the Mamlukes fought Timur in
Syria in 1400 "neither used firearms in open battle."[8]

The besieging of fortified cities and strongholds was carried out by
Timur with great precision. First a circle around the besieged point
would be marked off with a red substance into segments. Each segment
was then assigned to a particular commander who was responsible for
the siege work at that point. Large numbers of projectile and battering
machines were then employed. Sapping also was used extensively. After
tunneling toward the walls, sappers ignited the wooden shoring placed
under the foundations, causing the walls to collapse under their own
weight. The besiegers would then pour into the breaches. Fortifications
were, admittedly, somewhat primitive as judged by later standards. Indeed Vauban, who served under Louis XIV of France and was perhaps
the greatest military engineer of all times, attributed the astonishing
conquests from the time of Alexander the Great to Timur to a lack of
proper fortresses.[9] We know that the walls of the major cities of Iran,
where Timur did much of his campaigning, were made of mud brick.[10]

Timur's battle order is the best indication of the evolution and improvement he effected in his fighting machine as he went along. These
troop dispositions may be best understood by contrasting them with
the battle order obtaining at the onset of his career. His battle with
Ilyas Khodja in 1365 reflected the usual battle dispositions of that
time. The battle array of Timur then consisted of right and left wings
and a center. Both the left and right wings had a vanguard in front and
a flank guard (*kanbul*) as side protection. It was the task of the kanbul
to prevent the enemy from executing an enveloping movement around
the two flanks and hitting the army from the rear. In token of the importance of this mission the kanbul was made up of the bravest and
most battle-tested koshuns. The prime defect of Timur's early battle
order lay in the weakness of the center in relation to the two wings,
since it had neither a vanguard nor a reserve.

The salient innovation in 1391 was the strengthening of the center
by giving it both a vanguard (with the command post behind, and a new
body—the reserve—behind that), so that the center guarded both the
command post and the reserve. The latter was held in readiness to go to

that part of the battlefield where it was needed. Frequently its appearance clinched the outcome of a battle.

The infantry in the battle formation stood behind the cavalry. Heavily protected with armor, shields, swords and spears, these men played an exceptional role in those parts of the battlefield where the fighting took on a defensive character. Then, under the protection of their shields and towers, they took the lead in repulsing the enemy attack. Though Timur's battles are usually represented as cavalry actions, there are more than enough references in the sources to the important role played by the infantry. Timur's army also included special forces such as mountain troops and corps of engineers.

So far we have been mainly concerned with Timur's great talents as a military organizer. He was also one of the great military leaders of all time. As such he evinced traits common to a number of the great captains of all ages noted by the foremost military writers, such as Karl von Clausewitz.

First, there was a boldness in his strategical and tactical arrangements which old age did nothing to impair. More a Patton than a Montgomery, to put the matter in World War II terms, Timur was ever mobile, ever the prober. To be sure, he conducted most of his wars in enemy territory—a factor which allowed him to operate more venturesomely than if he were defending his hearth.

Timur well understood the importance of showing himself to his troops in the heat of military action. Sometimes he could be seen in the hottest part of the fray. During sieges he at times pitched his tent near a point of danger. It was this personal example of shared dangers and hardships which filled his troops with unstinting trust and carried them on to surmount the greatest obstacles. Like Alexander the Great and Prince Eugene of Savoy he was wounded on a number of occasions, though never as grievously as in the action which earned him the sobriquet of "the lame."

Timur was highly innovative, ingenious and resourceful when confronted with a new situation. Whether besieging a seaport without a navy to back him up, or fighting war elephants, or operating against an enemy such as the Georgians protected by dense forests and mountain strongholds located in eagle's eyries, Timur elaborated appropriate techniques to fit the circumstances. Nor did the vastly different types of terrain on which he fought—desert, steppe, mountains, woods, swamps and jungles—nor climate, whether the bone-biting cold of Siberia or the stifling, miasmal heat of India detain him. Nor did he apparently feel the need of an initial period of acclimatization for his troops before throwing them into action—a practice followed by U.S. forces in South Vietnam.

Great commanders such as Napoleon and Suvorov have often been highly articulate and have used this talent to inspire their troops. Timur shared this quality, and whether in war council or in haranguing his troops, he knew precisely the arguments to be used in winning over and rousing his auditors to the desired response.

A touch of the theatrical is often another common denominator. Timur's acceptance of the duel in front of his men offered by Hussein Sufi before Khorezm is a case in point. The elaborate military reviews staged by Timur again attest to this sense of the dramatic and appreciation of its value. Napoleon well understood this and, like Timur, held reviews while on campaign.

Napoleon had at least one advantage over Timur. He could appeal to the powerful forces of nationalism unleashed by the French Revolution, or in the case of his increasingly numerous non-French contingents, the Revolutionary credo of Liberty, Equality and Fraternity. Timur, to sustain the loyalty of his diversified ethnic followers, was driven to two expedients in addition to the carrot and stick technique of rewards and punishment: the power of his personality, and the inculcation of loyalty to one's unit. The words of the great German historian Mommsen with regard to the Carthaginian general Hamilcar Barca are relevant for Timur's army: "A great general is able to substitute his own personality in the eyes of his soldiers for their home country. . . . In the long years of war the soldier finds a second home in the camp; and as a substitute for patriotism he has his *esprit de corps* and his enthusiastic loyalty for his great leader."[11]

The way Timur made his personality felt has been duly noted. The development of group loyalty which lies at the basis of all morale is the other side of the coin. The Chagatai warriors in their actions functioned as one man even while not at war, something which made a strong impression on Clavijo. Speaking of the festivities arranged by Timur for the celebration of certain royal marriages outside Samarkand in the fall of 1404 he writes: "From their custom as soon as the camp of his Highness thus had been pitched all these folk of the Horde exactly knew where each clan had its place. From the greatest to the humblest each man knew his allotted position, and took it up, without confusion in the most orderly fashion. Thus in the course of the next three or four days we saw nearly twenty thousand tents pitched in regular streets to encircle the royal camp, and daily more clans came in from the outlying districts."[12] Clavijo then describes how everything needed to feed, supply and take care of the warriors, including the provision of bathing facilities had been organized.

Teamwork was not merely the result of the discipline imposed by Timur; it is inherent in the structure of nomadic life. Owen Lattimore has pointed out that the popular picture of the nomad living simply and independently is wholly without basis. "The truth is the other way around. Nomadic life requires tight organization, technically skilled division of labor to cover a wide spread of activities, close gradation of responsibility and authority, precise legal concepts of territory—what land belongs to what tribe."[13]

Timur stimulated his warriors not only by generous and prompt payment of salary while on campaign but by special rewards and battlefield promotions to individuals who had performed acts of exceptional bravery. On the other hand, leaders who were found wanting in the performance of their duties were court-martialed and punished.

Timur's method of waging warfare was far removed from that obtaining at that time in Western Europe, where membership in the Christian community and the pressure of the Catholic Church had led to the evolution of an unwritten code of gentlemanly conduct and behavior among the warrior caste (though much less operative where the lower orders were concerned). Were Timur's wars, then, conducted in correspondence with Islamic precepts? The answer must be a resounding "No." In Muslim theory a declaration of war was lawful only under carefully circumscribed circumstances and then only with some decent regard for humanity. Noncombatants, for example, were not to be harmed unless they aided in the war and there was to be no needless destruction of property.[14]

While on campaign Timur, like Chingis, brought terrible destruction not only to the people and buildings but to the land itself. The object was to demoralize the noncombatants among the enemy population. We see the same end object in view in the pitiless burning and harrying of the land in France by Edward III and the Black Prince during the Hundred Years War. The ends sought in twentieth century warfare by blockades, the dropping of napalm, defoliants and bombs from the air had to be attained in the fourteenth century on the ground. Timur, in areas he intended to keep, took measures to restore the fertility of the soil. Both Chingis Khan and Timur have been blamed for permanently destroying the fertility of some lands. Historians believe, for example, that the fabled fertility of Mesopotamia came to an end when first the Mongol invaders levelled the dikes and irrigation canals and then Timur finished this destructive work.[15] Recently, however, a geographer has stated that "it is now commonly believed that the desert was created by man's ineptitude in permitting the salt to permeate the soil."[16] He then goes on to describe the slow, molecular, often final process by which salinization takes place in this situation—a problem by no means surmounted by modern technology. It is easy—as well as colorful—to attribute the ruination of once fertile areas to the depredations of wild barbarians. It behooves us, however, to take a hard, close look to see if we have tarred the real culprit. As one Soviet work puts it in writing of Central Asia: "The silting up and salinization of the soil appeared as the constant scourges of the population of the agricultural districts, located around the city of Bukhara and other [nearby] places. . . The lower reaches of the Amu Darya were strongly silted up."[17] In this connection experts have pointed out that it is easier to construct a new irrigation system than to restore one where salinization has done its deadly work.

In Summary: Timur conducted wars in order to obtain the wherewithal to reward his warriors and also to ensure the loyalty of officials and members of the Muslim establishment in Transoxiana, who also received some of the booty. Heavy as the taxation and payment of tribute were, they did not suffice to meet this need. These wars at the same time allowed his warriors to drain off their martial energies in distant lands, leaving undisturbed the peace and tranquility of his own country. The huge military establishment enabled Timur to keep the peasants and artisans cowed and submissive. That not one significant peasant or artisan rebellion took place in Transoxiana while Timur ruled is not a matter of coincidence.

Timur's military machine[18] also allowed him to undertake great projects with scant regard for the feelings of those whose fortunes were affected, of which his demolition and reconstruction of one of the quarters of Samarkand is a conspicuous example. Never again would such power be extended and exercised over an area which comprehended both Central Asia and some countries of the Near or Middle East.

CHAPTER XIV
Samarkand

Before describing Timur's last adventure—his setting out to conquer China and his death en route—it behooves us to examine more fully and consecutively the fiscal, administrative and cultural aspects of his rule. The occasion is all the more opportune in that the Spanish envoy Clavijo — whose relation is such a vast mother lode of information — appeared at Timur's court precisely at this time.

Administratively, Timur broke his empire down into two main divisions: Transoxiana, which he ruled directly, and the much larger remainder which he ruled through his sons, grandsons, intimates and certain local dynasts as vassals. In connection with this second category of territory, extensive use was made of the *soyurgal.* This was a further development of the *ikta* or grant of land or revenues made by a Muslim ruler to an individual as a means of recompense for services introduced centuries earlier into the Near East.[1]

The soyurgal was a grant, usually of land, though it could also be something else of value. Only the general traits of a soyurgal can be noted, given the lack of clarity of our sources. Usually it consisted of one or more villages, although the area could be much larger. Like the ikta holder, the soyurgal grantee collected the taxes and imposts for which the people living on his grant were liable and kept all or part for his own use. Unlike the ikta holder he also enjoyed juridical and administrative immunity. The soyurgal grant might be permanent or it might be subject to annual review, after which it was either renewed or terminated. It could also be cancelled at any time for insubordination of the holder.

Initially the soyurgal was bestowed by Timur on individual commanders for exceptional bravery. Later, local rulers voluntarily submitting to Timur might get back their possessions in the form of a soyurgal. Another class of recipient might be the enemy of his enemy. Finally, Timur made soyurgal grants on a mass basis to deserving individuals during celebrations such as those marking the end of a successful campaign.

Timur also made wide use of the *tarkhan* charter. Tarkhan recipients had their lands, economic enterprises and other immovable properties exempted from the taxes and imposts ordinarily owed to Timur's treasury. The tarkhan charter, unlike the soyurgal grant, was given to persons who already owned property. The recipient also was immune from punishment for nine offenses, the tenth bringing punishment. Timur gave these out to a wide variety of persons: senior and junior military leaders, civil servants, court officials, sayyids and senior members of the Muslim establishment. The tarkhan was introduced by earlier Turkic and Mongol rulers.

In his lifetime, Timur appointed his sons and grandsons to be rulers of provinces, which might encompass huge areas. Both the holders of these appanages and of the larger soyurgals tended to build up their authority, creating centrifugal forces which would help tear apart Timur's empire after his death. Even while alive his authority was challenged at times, despite the draconian punishments meted out. Thus in 1375, when the Jelairs gave him trouble, he had their leader executed and the clan broken up and resettled. In 1388 he had several emirs executed in Samarkand upon learning of their disgruntlement. Even his sons and grandsons gave him difficulty, as we have noted.

The imperial administrative system is not without interest. In addition to the central administration each province had a *divan* or chancellery which carried out various governmental functions. These included the collection of taxes, the maintenance of law and order, the upkeep of public buildings, the proper function of the irrigational system and general surveillance over the mood and disposition of the population. Swift communications were provided by the postal system so that Timur got word of events on his borders in several days' time. Each divan maintained copy books recording income received and sums disbursed. Both the Chagatai Turkic and Tadjik languages were used in the copy books of the provincial divan and at Timur's court.[2]

Since Timur was away from his capital most of the time, control over this extensive administrative complex both in the capital and in the provinces posed a problem. Timur attempted to cope with this in diverse ways. Senior officials both from the capital, where he retained a caretaker government, and from various parts of his empire journeyed to his encampment of the moment to render accounts of their stewardship and perhaps also to bring receipts. Timur himself would periodically descend upon the capital and while there look into the management of affairs since his previous visit. In 1396, on his return from the Five

Years War, Timur conducted a grand inquest into the administration of affairs in Khurusan and Transoxiana. Clavijo reports that when Timur returned to Samarkand in 1404 after the Seven Years War he ordered great gallows to be set up and proclaimed that they would be used both "to gratify and give enjoyment to all the common folk" and also to "give a warning and example" to malefactors. Clavijo then reports how officials in the government of Samarkand or recipients of Timur's favor were tried, executed and their possessions seized, to the wonderment of the common folk.[3] Timur no doubt gained popularity by his execution of highly placed malefactors as well as replenishing his treasury.

Justices accompanied Timur on his travels. These not only regulated matters involving Timur's army and court but listened to complaints made by people living in the encampment area. Three departments of justice existed, according to Clavijo, each concerned with a particular type of case: (1) cases dealing with affairs or quarrels of consequence involving private litigants, (2) cases affecting the Treasury, (3) cases involving governors of outlying cities and districts. During an encampment three large tents would be pitched, to which litigants and defendants would repair to have their cases adjudicated. Sentences would then be handed down, but not before Timur was informed of the nature of the various cases. Judgments would then be executed in sixes and fours.*

In his zeal to repress corruption, abuse of authority and price gouging, Timur also ordered frequent inspections, audits of accounts and fact-finding missions. Harsh punishments were meted out to the guilty. Timur expected the Ulema to help him ferret out corruption and other abuses. While wintering at Karabagh in 1403/1404 he summoned Ulemas from throughout his realm to join him for conversations. He complained one day that though learned men should always guide sovereigns in their conduct his own Ulemas kept still. Hearing only praise and compliments in reply, he angrily informed his auditors that they knew better than anyone what was really going on locally. Encouraged by these words, they then filled him in on affairs back home. He thereupon selected a number of them and attached a senior official to each. The latter was empowered to indemnify poor persons mulcted by Timur's own officials and to mete out exemplary punishment to miscreants. A rigorous and extensive repression then followed.[4]

Timur showed concern for ordinary folk in other ways. In 1396, upon his return from the Five Years campaign, he exempted the pop-

---

*As Clavijo puts it: "de seis en seis, e dellos de quatro en quatro."

ulation of Transoxiana from ordinary taxes for three years. At other times money, grain and other comestibles were distributed among the poor. In areas ravaged by his armies he appointed capable administrators. Even sources hostile to Timur admit as much. Thomas de Medzoph relates that Timur's appointment in 1397 of a certain Shaykh Ahmed as administrator of the Van region of eastern Anatolia ushered in eleven years of prosperity.[5] According to Nizam ad-Din, Timur in quitting Baghdad in 1393 left behind an experienced administrator who devotedly attended to the needs of the poor and suffering.[6] As Sarton finely put it, Timur was able "to think of the common good as soon as he himself was satisfied, and to protect the common man against greater gangsters than himself."[7]

If local rulers made quick submission they might be kept on as vassal rulers. In that event Timur's usual policy was to destroy the city walls, fortresses and other defensive installations. Exception was made for rulers in certain key border areas which served as bastions against incursions. These march lords included Toktamish when he was first taken up by Timur, Taharten of Erzinjan, who guarded his borders against the Ottomans, and Ibrahim of Shirvan, who controlled Derbent and its famous "Iron Gate" and who blocked the expansion of the Golden Horde through the Caucasus into northern Persia.

Though Timur had ties with the sedentary population he placed prime reliance on his nomad followers as the mainstay of his power. Under Timur the Chagatais, as these Turco-Mongol nomad peoples were called, were a *Herrenvolk* or chosen people. They formed the skeletal structure of the army which was fleshed out by other units. And it was from the Chagatais that the senior officials, both civil and military, were recruited. Clavijo, who was able to observe one group at close hand, wrote that they were permitted to pasture their herds and to plant their crops wherever they wished. Paying no taxes, they were on permanent call as warriors. In war as in peace they moved together with their women and children and their herds.[8]

Like the Mongols, Timur allotted pasture lands called *yurts* to his nomadic followers. The summer lands were located at higher elevation and the winter ones in the plains. Separated by long distances, they required lengthy travel to get from one to the other.

Though Timur's nomadic followers, as they oscillated between one pasture and the other, caused much damage to cultivated lands, this did not mean that he neglected the latter. On the contrary, both Timur and his heirs were anxious to boost agricultural yields. So much harm had been done to agriculture during the Mongol invasion that full recovery had not been attained at the end of their rule. Timur did not allow land suitable for agriculture to go untilled. Not only were the old irrigation canals repaired and improved but new ones were introduced in areas where grain growing did not formerly exist. Damage to agriculture by the Mongol invasion was especially great in the Murghab river valley. Here, the historian Hafiz-i Abru tells us, Timur constructed twenty canals, erected buildings and planted crops. Even senior emirs and members of Timur's family were forced to take part in this work. Timur also introduced two new crops into Central Asia, the growing of flax and hemp. He forcibly chased back into Transoxiana the agricultural population that had, apparently, resided there prior to the Mongol period.

Possession or usufruct of cultivated land took on a variety of forms. As in Mongol times, a very substantial portion of the cultivated, arable land was owned and managed directly by the Treasury.

A second category was the soyurgal holding already discussed. As Timur's reign progressed, the tempo at which soyurgals were bestowed increased markedly. Often granted temporarily or for life, after Timur's death these acquired a fully hereditary character, passing from father to son.

A third category, characteristic of Muslim lands, was the *vakf* or religious endowment. Vakf income was set aside for the maintenance of the numerous mosques, medresehs and mausoleums that dotted the land. A vakf could involve a large area.

A fourth category was *mulk* or privately-owned land. Owners came from widely diverse backgrounds: the military-feudal elite, Ulema, merchants, officials and even some peasants.

The peasants, who constituted the overwhelming bulk of the rural population, lived in huts set higgledy-piggledy along a dirt road. Illiterate and downtrodden, they had little hope of improving their lot.

Those living on vakf land and also, apparently, those on mulk land worked as sharecroppers, remitting a certain percentage of the harvested crop. Contracts were short-term — three years was the maximum — so that the lot of the sharecroppers was precarious. They owned the hovels in which they lived but did not, it seems, have household plots or gardens.

Peasants were subject to a complicated system of taxes, imposts and duties, many of which carried over from the Mongol period of rule. These included a land tax, poll tax, levies for the support of various officials, including the tax collectors themselves, and extraordinary taxes collected to cover unforeseen contingencies, chiefly those relating to the military.

In addition, peasants were expected to furnish horses and carts for use in the postal system and to perform the *corvée*. The latter included work on roads, canals and bridges and on the construction of city walls and citadels, mosques, medresehs and palaces. Workers had to provide their own food and tools.

The revival of city life under Timur's rule saw a growth in commerce and in the produce of the artisans. The Mongol empire had, in its heyday, promoted trade and production. So too did Timur's huge state. The cities of Central Asia, and especially Samarkand, once more became way stations on the international trade routes linking China with the Mediterranean littoral and, to the south, with India.

Timur s last great campaign against the Golden Horde in 1395/1396 gravely weakened its economic underpinnings and helped remove any serious military threat from that quarter. It also shifted the international trade routes so that the profits from this trade now went into Timur's coffers. Thus the route which formerly went from southeast Europe to Sarai Urgench, Otrar, Taraz and Aulie-ata now originated at Trebizond and continued on to Sultaniya, Herat, Balkh, Samarkand and Taraz on eastward. From China came "silk cloth. . .especially satins, considered the best in the world" and porcelain. Wax, costly furs and hides came from Russia, the Volga region and Siberia. Iran furnished linen material and pearls. Aleppo offered glass, Circassia contributed its famous knives and Europe sent textiles and parchment. From the south caravans would arrive from India via Afghanistan loaded with spices, perfumes, indigo, fine white cloth and spears. "Enormous transactions were carried on there [Samarkand] in diamonds, and in precious stones, in musk and in rhubarb."[9]

Samarkand was itself a considerable center of production. Activity was greatest in textiles, pottery, metalworking and in the preparation of building materials (bricks, tiles, carved doors, chiseled stone) to sustain Timur's grandiose construction work. This was mostly performed by immigrants. While campaigning abroad, Timur carried off thousands of the most adept artisans, resettling them in Samarkand and in other parts of Transoxiana. Clavijo was struck by the polyglot nature of the capital's population. Turks, Arabs, Moors, Greeks, Armenian Catholics, Jacobites, Nestorians and Indians jostled one another in the streets. The number of peoples brought into Samarkand was so great that many had to be given temporary lodging in the suburbs and towns nearby.[10]

Stringent measures were taken to prevent anyone from leaving Transoxiana. Though Timur crossed the Amu Darya by bridge, he had this demolished after his passage. No pass was needed for anyone wishing to cross the Amu Darya into Transoxiana. A special authorization, however, was required for anyone wishing to leave. In traveling through Iran Clavijo often encountered officials scouring the country in search of orphans, vagrants or other flotsam, whom they then sent to Samarkand by force. By dint of such measures the population of greater Samarkand climbed to at least 100,000 people (elsewhere Clavijo raises this number to 150,00).

Travellers, especially merchants, were the beneficiaries of Timur's pacification measures. They had access to the postal roads which offered great security. A district in which a merchant was robbed had to indemnify him doubly for the losses he sustained and, moreover, to pay into Timur's treasury a fine five times as great as the loss.[11]

Timur and his heirs also fostered trade and the crafts by constructing special covered bazaars, streets and other commercial-artisan centers. We might, in this connection, describe Timur's actions in Samarkand. Despite the urban redevelopment undertaken in 1371/1372, the great volume of commerce was such that the city lacked proper facilities for the storage and display of wares. According to Clavijo, Timur therefore ordered the construction of a broad and wide street bisecting the entire city so that shops selling goods could be opened on both sides. The two emirs entrusted with this work were threatened with beheading if they dawdled. They thereupon began frantically to demolish all houses lying in the path of the new street. Relays of workmen succeeded one another "and the tumult was such day and night that it seemed all the devils of hell were at work here."[12] As a result of such febrile exertions the entire project was completed in but twenty days.

Timur's reign had a great fructifying influence on artisan production. Artisans were organized into guilds. As in medieval Europe, a clear division existed between the master of the shop and his apprentices and workmen, in token of which each had a different social and legal status. The crafts were narrowly specialized. The stepped-up demand not only increased the number of shops and workmen but brought greater work specialization and better quality and assortment of goods offered for sale. Those in such trades as metalworking, masonry and leatherworking customarily lived and worked in a certain street or quarter of the city. Timur's descendant Babur, in his remarkable *Memoirs,* states that in Samarkand every guild of artisans had a special bazaar or stalls. The artisans' status showed some improvement over Mongol times in that slaves no longer figured prominently in production. The artisan's life was, however, hedged about by various restrictions and his lot at times approached slavery. Clavijo, in describing the citadel in Samarkand, writes: "It is here that his Highness keeps his treasure, and none from the city without may enter save the governor of the Castle and his men. Within its walls however, Timur holds in durance and captivity upwards of a thousand workmen; these labour at making plate-armour and helms, with bows and arrows, and to this business they are kept at work throughout the whole of their time in the service of his Highness." [13] The many wars of Timur stimulated armaments production which was concentrated in Samarkand. Clavijo was well impressed with the plate armor shown him save that the plates were not thick enough "and they do not here know how properly to temper the steel." Armor destined for top military commanders was richly ornamented with jewels and covered with artistic designs. The armor and weaponry might even be covered with gold to match the magnificence of the clothing of Timur's magnates which was sewn with gold thread and decorated with pearls, rubies and other precious stones.

Food, apparently, was no problem in Samarkand. Clavijo, in his narrative, dwells upon the plenty, variety, cheapness and availability of food in the many shops in Samarkand. There were, he says, throughout the city open squares where cooked meat, roasted or in stews, could be purchased along with bread and excellent fruit "set out in a decent cleanly manner." These shops were open on a round-the-clock basis. A cheap and constant food supply must have been an important factor in allaying popular discontent with Timur's rule.

Like the peasants, the artisans were liable for a series of taxes and imposts. There was first the *tamga*, a tax on artisan production, which was continued from Mongol times. Other taxes included the poll and household taxes. The artisans and tradesmen also paid rent on their quarters. City real estate, especially market facilities, was regarded as a good investment vehicle by persons of wealth. Prices of goods were kept down by direct governmental action. Price-gougers were fined or even executed. Merchants, especially those engaged in long-distance trade, were not the only ones interested in keeping prices low. A considerable number of artisans produced goods for the court. This production was supervised by government officials. Guild elders were appointed by the government.

The craft guilds also participated prominently in the rich festivals organized by Timur on various pretexts. Their exhibits and floats formed an important part of the entertainment. And the craft guilds lent a hand in defending the city in time of war.

Under Timur, Samarkand became one of the greatest—if not the greatest—artisan and commercial centers of the Muslim world. This prosperity was somewhat artificial in that it was stimulated by the booty and tribute flowing in as well as by the city's position as the administrative center of a mighty empire.

Samarkand also became one of the great scientific and cultural centers of the Orient. Mathematicians, astronomers, theologians, poets, historians and musicians were, like the artists and artisans, brought to the city willy-nilly. Their presence not only satisfied Timur's vanity but also enhanced the international political significance of his capital.

It was as a builder, however, that Timur left his greatest imprint on the city, so much so that even today Samarkand is known as "the city of Tamerlane." The purpose of all this construction was to dazzle foreign envoys and visitors by its magnificence, by its great size and height, by its majestic portals and lofty domes.[14] As the inscription over Timur's palace of Ak Sarai in Kesh boastfully proclaims: "If you have doubts as to our power and munificence, look at our building." Timur's official biographer, Nizam ad-Din Shami, speaking of his construction activity, recalls the aphorism: "Buildings bear testimony to the greatness of the thoughts of the builder." Clavijo was astonished at the tempo and extent to which Timur carried on his building activities and he devotes many pages in his relation to their description. Ibn Arabshah records that Timur had several settlements constructed in the environs of the city which bore the names of Dimshih (Damascus), Baghdad, Misr (Cairo), Sultaniya and Shiraz. The first three were capitals of the greatest Muslim empires the world had seen: Damascus, the capital of the Umayyad caliphate, Baghdad, the capital of the Abbasid caliphate and Cairo of the Fatimid state. Sultaniya and Shiraz, the most important cities of northern and southern Iran, were among the foremost Muslim cities of the day. Yet in Timur's view they were but villages when compared with his capital.

Timur spent but little time while in Samarkand in his palace of Kok-Sarai in the citadel, preferring to take his repose during his infrequent sojourns in the city in the pleasure domes he built in the latter's bosky environs. Outside the circumference of the city's walls he created a ring of magnificent gardens, thirteen in number, bearing such mellifluous names as Paradise Garden, Heart's Repose Garden, etc., and dedicated either to one of his wives or to some other female family connection. These were laid out in an orderly, systematic way with a main axial avenue from which extended garden walks, the whole arrangement dividing the park into regular geometrical figures, triangular or hexagonal in shape. Decorative trees were alternated with fruit trees, shrubbery with lawn flowers. The types of flowers were so assorted that from early spring to late fall they alternated in blossoming. A system of irrigation canals covered the park; some parks also had fountains and cascades. The architectural ensemble was closely coordinated in planning with this verdant complex. The palace of the ruler rose in the center of the garden or formed the axis. On the borders of the geometrically shaped divisions of the park stood elegant kiosks, open shelters, pavilions or tents. During Timur's lengthy absences the suburban palace gardens were thrown open to the public, rich and poor, to stroll in and even pick the fruit. "The subjects of Timur were also to know how great was the might of their ruler."[15]

Timur's palaces contained many curiosities. Clavijo mentions a golden artificial tree as tall as a man whose fruit consisted of a prodigal number of precious gems and pearls. Birds made of gold enamel perched on the branches in various lifelike poses. Clavijo also mentions the beautiful carpets, basically red, which adorned Timur's tents and palaces.

The palaces and gardens of Timur disappeared in the course of the internal convulsions which followed his death. Only some archeological remains, depictions on miniatures and some eyewitness accounts allow us to form an approximate picture concerning their appearance.

Iranian artists, brought in large numbers by Timur to Central Asia, were Shiites, with the exuberant and permissive artistic traditions peculiar to that branch of Islam. They were, however, affected in their work by the experience, traditions and thematic requirements then ascendant in Central Asia where the population was predominantly Sunnite (orthodox) Muslim of the Hanafite branch. Indeed, the accomplishments of these craftsmen were much more in keeping with the style of Central Asia than of Iranian art, though containing in them some features of a purely Iranian origin.[16] Hanafite art in Central Asia was sober and stylized in emphasis, with arabesques playing an important decorative role. The depiction of birds, animals and men (except for wall paintings kept from the gaze of the rank and file) was eschewed, in keeping with Sunnite religious susceptibilities with regard to the depiction of life in human or animal form.

Soviet art historians have in recent years contended that the late 14th-early 15th centuries witnessed a new synthesis of the art of Central Asia and the Near East.[17] That art at this juncture took a new direction was realized by contemporaries, as when Ibn Arabshah explicitly states that Timur's garden palace complexes were constructed "in a new style." Polychrome decoration on buildings in particular attained a heretofore unexampled magnificence even for the Orient. What was begun under Timur in the arts was eagerly taken up by his heirs, the Timurids, with brilliant results.

CHAPTER XV
The Last Campaign

"Whenever I prepare for a journey I
prepare as though for death. Should
I never return, all is in order. This is
what life has taught me."
                    —Katharine Mansfield

In November 1404 Timur was now almost seventy. Despite a rock-hard constitution, a long lifetime of almost constant campaigning, the numerous wounds sustained in battle,[1] severe illnesses and the onset of old age had all taken their toll. Yet these infirmities did not slow down Timur appreciably. Clavijo, the Spanish envoy in Samarkand at this time, reported that the conqueror, though in his litter, was out most of the day superintending his mammoth building. At the feasts over which he presided he helped himself to heaping platters of roast horsemeat and drank wine often up to all hours of the night. Later Clavijo learned from supposedly reliable and knowledgeable sources that early in November Timur had suffered what may have been a stroke, that he "was in a very weak state, having lost all power of speech"[2] and that he might be on the very point of death according to his physicians' prognostications. His chamberlains (again according to Clavijo) were in fact so alarmed that they insisted that the envoys from Castile, Turkey and Mamluke Egypt leave for home the very next day in order to be spared embroilment in any disorders that might occur in the wake of Timur's demise. Clavijo and his party, despite vehement representations, were denied a final audience or message for their sovereign.

But was Timur in fact gravely ill? In Barthold's view he was in the midst of last minute preparations for his Chinese campaign and, anxious to maintain secrecy, found the presence of the envoys inconvenient.[3] The time factor certainly bears this out. Timur left Samarkand on his way to China not long after the envoys' departure, a very remarkable recovery for one who supposedly had only a slender contact with life shortly before. Moreover, according to Sharaf ad-Din, Timur "gave vests and belts to the ambassador of Egypt" and attached his own envoy to his party, bearing a long letter of reply concerning the case of Sultan Ahmed Jelair and Kara Yusuf. Castile was for Timur an inconsequential and distant state so that its envoys could be fobbed off with a story about grave illness. Mamluke Egypt, on the other hand, was very important in his scheme of things and hence merited quite different treatment.

If indeed he were ill, Timur recovered quickly. Bored with his palaces, pavilions and gardens, with his cosseted and luxurious sedentary existence, though he moved from one pleasure dome to another, Timur was determined, though he had returned to Samarkand only in late July 1404, to get on with what would have been his greatest campaign—the conquest of China. Neither his advanced age and infirmities nor the two thousand miles of harsh terrain he would have to traverse nor the formidable nature of his opponent nor the lack of any problems that could not have been resolved peacefully nor the absence of any clear and present danger from China would stay the conqueror.

Timur's reasons for invading China have been variously explicated. First, there was the equivocal nature of his relations with the Middle Kingdom. In 1368, or two years before his own advent to power, the Mongol or Yüan dynasty, founded by Chingis' grandson Kublai Khan, was overthrown and replaced by the Ming dynasty of native Chinese provenience. Hung-Wu (1368-98), the first Ming emperor, transferred the capital from Peking to Nanking. The Ming dynasty, in overthrowing the Yüan dynasty, in no way relinquished the latter's claim of suzerainty over all Mongol governments, including the Chagatai Ulus. In 1385 Hung-Wu sent envoys to Central Asia. In Mogolistan the Chagatai khan and the Dughlat emirs made no difficulty over recognizing the Ming emperor as their suzerain. When the envoys reached Samarkand, however, they were arrested and their release came only after protracted negotiations.[4] Contrariwise, this did not prevent Timur, in 1387, from dispatching an envoy to the Chinese emperor with a gift of fifteen horses and two camels. Horses and camels were sent every year thereafter, while in 1392 Timur also forwarded fabrics and weapons. In 1394 Timur sent an embassy with two hundred horses and a friendly letter thanking the emperor for his efforts in facilitating the considerable caravan trade between China and Central Asia and wishing him "happiness and long life."[5] For his part Hung-Wu in 1395 sent an embassy with a letter of thanks. Timur regarded his presents as free gifts. The

Ming emperor, both because of his claims to suzerainty over the Chagatai Ulus and the ancient Chinese imperial view that other states could
only have a client relationship to the Middle Kingdom, regarded these
as tribute and the visits of embassies as acts of homage.

As Timur's power waxed and his empire grew he began increasingly
to resent this subordinate status. Since China had once been part of the
old Chingisid empire, Timur may also have felt that as the restorer of
that empire he might turn the tables on the Ming emperor and subordinate China to Samarkand. In any event, in June 1404, just prior to
Clavijo's arrival in Samarkand, an embassy accompanied by a merchant
caravan of eight hundred camels arrived from the emperor Yung Lo
(1403-1424), brother and second successor to Hung-Wu. The object of
the embassy was to remind Timur that for seven years he had neglected
to send the annual tribute and to demand that Timur forward the latter
forthwith. Timur's sardonic reply was "that this was most true, and
that he was about to pay what was due: but that he would not burden
them, the ambassadors, to take it back to China on their return, for he
himself Timur would bring it."[6] That the Mings waited seven years to
make this demand was due to involvement in the broils of a succession
struggle. The embassy headed by An in 1395 and received by Timur in
the winter of 1397 while encamped near the Syr Darya, was not
allowed to return to China until after Timur's death, indicating that as
far back as 1397 Timur's attitude towards China had changed to one of
overt hostility.

Clavijo also indicates the sovereign contempt with which the Chinese
were regarded in Samarkand at this time. To give this attitude dramatic
effect, Timur publicly ordered that at state functions the Castilians be
seated ahead of the Chinese despite the fact that, according to Sharaf
ad-Din, Castile was known to be of paltry account. Indeed the latter, in
noting the Castilians' presence at one of these functions, remarks ". . .
for even the smallest of fishes have their place in the sea."

In Samarkand the Chinese emperor was mockingly referred to as the
"pig emperor." Clavijo even heard that Timur had ordered the beheading of the Chinese envoys. While it is doubtful that, if issued, such an
order was carried out, given Timur's views on diplomatic immunity,[7]
the rumor is indicative of the anti-Chinese feeling manifest at this time.

The prospect of a huge booty, beggaring what he had won in any
other of his wars, must have figured prominently in Timur's plans.

Timur's ostensible reason for invading China was to carry on the
holy war against the infidel, as enjoined by the Koran. Sharaf ad-Din, in

explicating Timur's motives, states that the latter, in bringing peace and tranquility to Asia, could not effect these laudable ends without "destruction, captivity, and plunder, which are the concomitants of victory." In these wars, Sharaf ad-Din continues, the blood of many Muslims had been spilled. Timur was now making war against China "hoping by that to obtain pardon of God for his former crimes." Timur's apologist avers that Timur wanted to die as a ghazi, a conqueror of infidels, so that he could reap the rewards in paradise promised by the Koran. Timur had, it should be noted, received overstated accounts of massacre and mistreatment of Muslims by the Mings in China, especially in Kansu province in the northwest.

That Timur could have conquered all China had he lived longer is extremely doubtful. Even the Mongols under Chingis Khan and his successors had taken seventy years (1207-1277), i.e., a period equivalent to Timur's entire lifetime. The Mongols, moreover, were faced by a China split into three feuding kingdoms, two of which were headed by "barbarian" rulers with only a slender lease on the loyalties of their Chinese subjects. Timur, at his advanced age, was a poor actuarial risk; besides, he would be facing a united China under a fresh and vigorous native dynasty whose emperor Yung Lo was a formidable military campaigner. Nonetheless, the threat to China was very grave. As Grousset points out, this time the Chinese would not be fighting a Kubilai Khan, deferential towards Buddhism and Confucianism, whose aspiration it was to become a true Son of Heaven. Rather, here was a Muslim fanatic "who in islamizing the country, would truly have destroyed Chinese civilization and debased Chinese society."[8] Henri Cordier, another French sinologist, declares in a similar vein that "It was the greatest danger from which the nascent Ming dynasty escaped."[9]

Timur's plan to invade China was no sudden improvisation or bolt from the blue; it had been simmering in his mind for some years. Logistics—ensuring that his enormous army received adequate supplies and provisions while under way—would be a mammoth problem. Consequently, as far back as 1397, he ordered the construction of a border stronghold on the Ashpara river in southern Kazakhstan. Several thousand families were resettled there. Their task was to develop agriculture and commerce and to lay up a large supply of victuals in the new fortress constructed still further out near Issyk-kul.[10] Sources indicate that Timur ordered a map prepared of the T'ien Shan range and western China several years before the invasion, and that this reached him while he was in Asia Minor campaigning against Bayazid.[11]

Timur also wanted to reconnoiter western Mongolia and the lands bordering on China and to build up a party or "fifth column" in Mongolia loyal to him. Several years prior to 1405 one of his commanders had successfully carried out a mission along these lines.[12]

Another source of intelligence was the trade caravan which accompanied the Chinese mission which Timur received upon his return from his western campaign in 1404. First, he ordered that the merchants and their goods be seized and that no one be allowed to return to China. Then he subjected some of the merchants and men accompanying the caravan to searching questions about the customs of the country, its wealth and population. Timur could have been under no misapprehension about the Leviathan foe he would face. One merchant, who had lived in Khanbalik [Peking], the old Chinese capital, for half a year told him that the latter was twenty times as large as Tabriz. Clavijo, who relates this information, expresses it as his opinion that that would make Khanbalik the largest city in the world "for Tabriz measures a great league and more across."[13] The merchant also declared that the military forces at the disposal of the Chinese emperor were so numerous that when he made war against a foreign country he could leave behind four hundred thousand cavalrymen as a security force in addition to numerous regiments of foot soldiers. The merchant revealed many other marvels about China to Timur and his intelligence officers.

By dint of these inquiries Timur had, according to Sharaf ad-Din, a detailed knowledge of the quality and state of the routes leading to China, the availability of water and fodder for each day's march and the nature of the steppes and mountains to be crossed. All this was recorded so that appropriate measures could be taken to ensure an unimpeded march.

Up to now only a few of Timur's men knew of his intentions. The next step was to whip up enthusiasm for the venture among his officers and then to issue the requisite marching orders. In the fall of 1404 a kurultai was convened to which the provincial governors, sharifs, generals and other notables were invited; it was held in the fair plains of Kan-i-gul near Samarkand, "whose air is more fragrant than musk and the water sweeter than sugar" (Ibn Arabshah). Ostensibly the kurultai was held to celebrate the marriages of five of Timur's grandsons, whose ages ran from nine to seventeen. The magnificence of the weddings is luxuriantly detailed by Sharaf ad-Din. In the case of Ulug Beg and Ibrahim-Sultan, sons of Shahrukh, it would be more accurate to speak of their formal engagements since they were still quite young.[14] Timur

provided for their future in other ways. To Ulug Beg he assigned Tashkent, Sauran, Yany (Jambul), Ashpara and Mogolistan while Ibrahim-
Sultan received Ferghana, Kashgar and Khotan. Their fiefs, in other
words, included areas still to be conquered, something which Timur
proposed to do with his huge army while en route to invade China.

For two months Kan-i-gul was the scene of entertainments and prodigious feasts at which incontinent quantities of food, wine and kumiss
were consumed; for if the marriage ceremonies were Muslim, the feasts
were *à la Mongole*. At the end of the festivities Timur convened an
assembly of his leaders, harangued them about the desirability of a
Jihad or Holy War against infidel China, and extracted the unanimous
approval of his auditors. Mobilization orders were then issued designat-
ing Tashkent as the staging area. Timur's plans for an invasion of China
had evolved very slowly but now in the month of December they were
put into execution with surpassing speed and dispatch.

Timur considered that an army of two hundred thousand picked
men, including both cavalry and foot, would suffice. This polyglot
force was drawn from present-day Soviet Central Asia, Iran, Afghanistan, from Turcomans in Anatolia and from the colonies brought into
Transoxiana from Iran, Azerbaijan and Iraq. As was his wont before
beginning a campaign, Timur distributed his treasure among his men.
The invasion force was divided into three groups: right wing, left wing
and center. Troops of the right wing were to camp at Tashkent, Shah-
rukhiya on the Syr river and Sairam; troops of the left wing were to
winter at Yassy and Sauran. Timur himself, with the center, proposed
to push on to Otrar, the city now in ruins which first saw the appearance of Chingis Khan's troops when he embarked on his fateful western
campaign which would ultimately take the Mongols into Eastern
Europe. Timur was determined to put his army into as good a striking
distance as possible that winter so as to catch the Son of Heaven off
guard later in 1405.

The difficulties of victualling and provisioning an army of this magnitude over such a vast and difficult terrain were formidable. To accom-
modate his men while in their staging area, Timur invited sutlers to
bring various goods. Timur himself purchased several thousand horses
which he distributed among his men, as well as weapons and other
necessities. He instructed his officers to check their men's equipment
very carefully and to collect as many supplies as possible lest anyone be
left behind for lack of equipment or provisions.

In addition, several thousand wagons full of seed grain were collected. These were to follow the army and, at suitable intervals, areas

would be planted so that the troops could harvest the grain on their way back. Finally, to meet unexpected contingencies, thousands of foal camels were to follow in the army's footsteps, whose milk could be drunk in case of need. Timur ordered the governor of his fortress on the Ashpara river to prepare "a thousand camel loads of the best meal." Ibn Arabshah takes delight in describing the desperate plight of the fortress governor in trying to comply with this order, since the mill wheels could not turn because of the ice in the streams. Timur, drawing upon his experience of several score years of campaigning in Asia, doubtless took other measures but the sources fail to tell us about them.

Timur managed to keep his invasion plans so secret that Clavijo and his party did not know of them. The Chinese, however, were not deceived. Though Yung Lo was ignorant of Timur's precise plans he knew that the latter was headed his way. Accordingly, he strengthened his garrisons in Kansu province, which Timur was expected to traverse, and instructed the governor there to make ready to repel Timur. Yung Lo also sent an embassy to the west whose mission would be "to enter into contact with India and other states, to surround the empire of Timur and in this manner to pin down his military force."[15]

On Christmas Day 1404 Timur left Aksulat with Otrar as his objective. Despite the good omens announced by his astrologers, heavy rains and then violent winds and snowfall hindered his way. Timur spent the nights in the steppes in reed cottages prepared beforehand. The cold increased daily; indeed, the winter of 1404/1405 was one of the severest on record for this region. When Timur crossed the Syr Darya he found that it was frozen to a great depth. Numerous horses and men perished along the way, while many a survivor had less than his normal allotment of fingers, toes, ears and nose. The snow and rain continued to fall. Timur's astrologers now descried bad omens.

On January 14, 1405 Timur arrived at Otrar where he lodged in the palace of the local governor. That same day one corner of the palace roof caught fire, which was interpreted as a bad sign. That night most of Timur's emirs had nightmares. Despite the cold, Timur was anxious to press on. The reports of the men sent ahead to reconnoiter were, however, anything but reassuring. One reported that the bridge ahead was impassable. Another advised that the snow in the mountains was two pikes high.

Undeterred, Timur refused to be weatherbound. Ordering his army to get ready to move out, he took leave of his wives and grandchildren who were to return to Samarkand. But fate decreed otherwise. In the middle of February Timur began to run a temperature. To shake off the bone-deep cold, he ordered a hot alcoholic drink prepared of *raki* and medicinal herbs. Again and again he emptied the beaker as he sought to shake off the chill. The result was a fever which gravely weakened him. The measures taken by his physicians, "who in that cold treated him by putting ice on his belly and chest," only aggravated his condition. "He coughed like a camel which is strangled, his colour was nigh quenched and his cheeks foamed like a camel dragged backwards with the rein."[16] Though his body was wracked with pain, his mind remained lucid to the end. He kept continually inquiring into the condition of the army.

Finally convinced of the hopelessness of his condition, Timur summoned his family and his emirs. He adjured them not to grieve and groan at his death but rather to pray to Allah on his behalf. He named his grandson Pir-Muhammad Jehangir his successor as supreme ruler in Samarkand and ordered those present to obey him. All, including the emirs, swore unfailing compliance with his wishes.[17] Pir-Muhammad had distinguished himself during the Indian campaign by his bravery and loyalty. Timur's last wish was to see Shahrukh again, but time ran out.

So that the conqueror should die in an aura of sanctity, all but the divines were banished from his presence. Outside his chamber several Koran readers and imams now began ululating the Arabic of the Koran, while another did the same at Timur's bedside. Timur himself uttered the profession of the faith — "There is no God but Allah and Muhammad is his Prophet" — several times. Sometime during the night of February 18, 1405 the angel of death Azrail appeared. Timur had ruled thirty-six years, leaving thirty-six living sons and grandsons.

Timur's body was washed and anointed with camphor, musk and rose water as ordained by Muslim funerary custom, and then encased in linen and laid in a coffin of ebony. He was buried in a temporary tomb in Samarkand in the Muslim manner: on his back with folded hands and outstretched legs, his head resting on his right cheek and his face turned toward Mecca.[18] Upon the completion of Muhammad-Sultan's mausoleum Timur's body was transferred there. In accord with his own wish, Timur was buried at the feet of Mir Sayyid Bereke so that he could in death make himself out as the latter's simple Muslim follower. The mausoleum now began to be called Gur-Mir, that is, "tomb of the Mir," i.e., Mir Sayyid Bereke. More commonly, though incorrectly, it is called Gur-Emir, "tomb of the Emir," that is, of Timur.[19]

The famed nineteenth century American traveller Eugene Schuyler called the Gur-Emir "the most interesting building in Samarkand." It is, in the opinion of the art specialist, David Talbot Rice, "one of the world's most perfect buildings." Modest in dimensions if compared with the Bibi Khanum mosque, it is priceless by virtue of its elegance and purity of architectural line. The outer walls are decorated rather austerely, the basic attention being focused on the massive drum and especially on its cupola. An impression of heaviness has been avoided by a skillful division of the cupola into sixty-four ribs which smoothly shade into the high cylindrical drum below. The turquoise glaze on the cupola gives it an especially smart appearance against the azure blue Samarkand sky. Inside the building one can see the nine cenotaphs of Timur and others which correspond to the actual tombs in the burial vault below. The handsome dark-green, nephritic jade cenotaph of Timur, unadorned save for some inscriptions, lies in the exact center of the building. Sarton calls it "the largest jade *object* in the world."[20] It weighs about 2,250 lbs. A narrow staircase communicates with the vault below where the sarcophagi lie exactly under the cenotaphs above. Of light marble, they are covered with intricate inscriptions. Timur rests in one of these. The Gur-Emir is today one of the main tourist attractions of Samarkand.

CHAPTER XVI
The Timurid Legacy

> "When the bull falls a
> thousand knives appear."
> —old Egyptian peasant saying

The steps taken by Timur to ensure a smooth and orderly transfer of power to Pir-Muhammad proved singularly unavailing. One problem was that when Timur died Pir-Muhammad was at Kandahar in southern Afghanistan, a considerable distance from Samarkand, the capital. Timur's emirs and chamberlains tried to keep his death a secret, wishing to gain time to take measures to secure the government in Samarkand until Pir-Muhammad arrived. But this proved difficult to do since Timur's men were accustomed to seeing him circulating among them. The situation was also confused because twice previously Timur had falsely put forth the news that he was dead "in order to probe who would then rebel against the provisions of his will for succession,"[1] and had then mercilessly crushed those who came out in rebellion.

Khalil-Sultan, aged twenty-two, ruler of Tashkent, "fair-skinned and fat like his father Miranshah, whom he resembled in face,"[2] acting on news he correctly considered to be reliable, assembled his men and fell upon the three privy chamberlains who had come to Samarkand to take over the treasury and government, killing one and forcing the others to flee to Shahrukh, Timur's youngest son, who ruled over Khurasan from his capital at Herat.

Though the emirs with Timur's army at Otrar tried at first to continue with the invasion of China, this proved to be impossible with the swift decline of central authority that followed Timur's death. Khalil-Sultan's usurpation of power touched off an armed struggle for the throne in which Timur's numerous descendants, basing themselves on their vast possessions or on this or that part of the army, took part. In the course of this struggle Pir-Muhammad, the heir designate, lost his life in 1406. The question of paramountcy in the eastern portions of

Timur's empire was settled only when Shahrukh succeeded in defeating his rivals, seizing Samarkand in 1409 and subjugating eastern Iran in 1413. This internecine strife was complicated by the mutinies of various commanders and revolts in certain cities. In the west the Timurid empire had an even harder time, since it was not only riven by rivalry among Timur's heir but was assailed by external enemies.

Timur's insistence on maintaining the succession to the imperial throne in the line of Jehangir, his oldest son, proved most unfortunate. This led to the passing over of Timur's youngest son Shahrukh. Historians generally have been well disposed towards the latter. Grousset, for example, states that not only did he have the best balanced temperament of any of Timur's progeny but he was the only one of them with political aptitude. Barthold declares that Timur's sons, except for Shahrukh, suffered from "psychic abnormality."[3] The German scholar Sarkisyanz refers to him as "perhaps one of the best rulers of Asia."[4] Timur possibly was annoyed with Shahrukh because he showed a preference for the Muslim Shariat over the Yasa of Chingis.

Shahrukh was only partially successful in restoring some show of unity to Timur's empire. One thing which might have helped him—the great wealth amassed by Timur in Samarkand—was squandered by Khalil-Sultan who, in his mad infatuation for his wife Shadi-Mulk, indulged her extravagant whims. More important were the decentralizing tendencies which grew apace after Timur's death. Shahrukh himself contributed to these by the prodigality with which he distributed soyurgals not only to his sons but to military commanders, especially during the first part of his reign when he sought to consolidate his position by winning them over. Soyurgal grants not only greatly increased in number but became hereditary. Another grave impediment to firm rule was the attitude of the appanage-holders, descendants of Timur, who increasingly looked upon themselves as vassals owing only perfunctory allegiance to their suzerain Shahrukh. In the words of Barthold: "Under Shahrukh the state still possessed sufficient force to be able in critical moments to deliver devastating blows but it was not in the position to establish firm order which would eliminate or prevent crises in the country."[5]

Shahrukh's remedy was to try to replace his nephews, whom he regarded as unreliable, with his own progeny as appanage rulers. He began a drive even against those nephews who had submitted to him voluntarily. By the early 1420s he had in large measure attained his objective. Ulug Beg, his oldest son, was installed as viceroy in Samarkand, Ibrahim-Sultan became appanage ruler of Shiraz, Suyurgatmish received Kabul, Ghazni and Kandahar while Baisonkor served as Shahrukh's vizier in his own capital as well as holding a large part of Khurasan as an appanage.

Shahrukh miscalculated, for his sons and grandsons proved no more reliable than his nephews and acted as quasi-independent rulers. Ulug Beg, for example, even minted money in his own name in Samarkand. But in theory the unity of the Timurid state was maintained in Transoxiana and Khurasan.

Though a gifted military leader, Shahrukh renounced Timur's wars of conquest. Good relations were resumed with China. Wars were waged but these were defensive in nature.

The greatest immediate threat to Timurid rule at this time occurred in the west. Western Iran, Azerbaijan and Iraq Arabi went to Miranshah and his sons Abu-Bakr and Omar-Mirza. The inexpiable enmity between the two sons of Miranshah, however, exploded into strife, allowing Ahmed Jelair to slip back into Baghdad and to reestablish himself there (1405) and Kara Yusuf, chief of the Black Sheep Turcomans, to return to Azerbaijan. An attempt by Miranshah and Abu-Bakr to oust Kara Yusuf ended disastrously, Miranshah being killed in battle. Kara Yusuf not only amputated more Timurid territory but, after a successful struggle against his old ally Ahmed Jelair, was able to add the Jelairid possessions to his own. The Black Sheep Turcoman state, now one of the largest in the Orient, stretched from Georgia in the north to Basra in the south.

Shahrukh, wishing to avenge Miranshah and descrying in the burgeoning Black Sheep Turcoman state a threat to his own position, led three expeditions into Azerbaijan against the Black Sheep, beginning with 1421, with but indeterminate results. In the end, in 1436, Shahrukh recognized Kara Yusuf's successor Jehan Shah as his viceroy. What this amounted to was the sanctioning of Black Sheep rule over Azerbaijan and the Jelairid realm. In 1458, in the confused period after Shahrukh's death, Jehan Shah annexed the Timurid possessions of Fars, Isfahan, Kerman and Iraq Adjemi. Nine years later (in 1467) Jehan Shah received his comeuppance, but not at the hands of the Timurids. Rather it was the rival White Sheep Turcoman confederation which supplanted the Black Sheep as masters of the former Timurid western possessions. This puissant state, with its capital at Tabriz, would last until the advent in 1501 of the Persian Safavid dynasty, which would reunite Persia.

In the east the death of Shahrukh in 1447 and of his son Ulug Beg in 1449 mark the watershed between the first and second periods of Timurid rule. Shahrukh could no more ensure a peaceful transition of power to his heir Ulug Beg than could Timur to his own heir. The death of Ulug Beg at the instigation of his own son Abdul Latif in 1449 and the assassination of the parricide six months later ushered in a second round of internecine strife even more devastating than the first. Even the nominal unity of the rump Timurid state in the east was now sundered; petty rulers struggled to maintain themselves in the shifting political kaleidoscope which brought the intervention of the Uzbeks, Mogols and others. The Timurids, who now ruled only over Transoxiana, Khurasan and present-day Afghanistan, were on bad terms with one another. At one point the energetic Abu-Said managed to reunite Transoxiana with Khurasan, but when in 1467 he invaded western Iran to force the White Sheep Turcomans to disgorge their gains he failed utterly and was taken captive and killed (1468). Abu-Said's career marks the last attempt to unify the Timurid possessions, though in truncated form.

Abu-Said's death touched off a new round of strife. Transoxiana and Khurasan went their separate ways. The throne in Herat was now occupied by Hussein Baikara (1469-1506) while in Samarkand the power went to Abu-Said's son Ahmed (ruling until 1494). Timurid rule in both areas was extinguished in the first years of the sixteenth century. While the Timurids admittedly faced formidable opponents in the now united Turkic Uzbek tribes of Central Asia and in the nascent power of the Shiite Safavids of Iran, internal factors alluded to earlier played a larger role in putting an end to Timur's political legacy.

Culturally, the Timurid period has been called by the French scholar Lucien Bouvat "one of the most brilliant periods of Muslim history. Its men of letters, its artists, its savants can be compared, without disadvantage, to those who made the times of the Umayyads and Abassids glorious."[6] Politically the Timurid period may be broadly divided into two periods with the death of Shahrukh (1447) marking the watershed. In the first period two large successor states emerge, one in the west under Miranshah and his sons, the other in the east under Shahrukh. The second period is marked by fragmentation into a number of petty states as each descendant of Timur sought to gain independent and unfettered control of an area, howbeit small, a development favoring the inroads of foreign invaders. Culturally the Timurid period is susceptible to no such division: the second half of the fifteenth century is as brilliant as the first. The same phenomenon of a time lag between political and cultural decline has been observed with regard to the Abassid Caliphate, during which Arabic power and civilization reached their meridians.* The Abbasid Caliphate, founded in 750 A.D., went into a swift and irremediable decline a century or so later. Yet the decay of political authority produced no immediate blighting effect on the rising Muslim science, art and scholarship; on the contrary, the latter were given a temporary fillip. The emergence of a dozen or so capitals from the Ebro to the Oxus after the pre-eminence of Baghdad had passed gave greater scope to artists and scholars who, if one patron proved to be unappreciative, could seek favor from another. Similarly, after Timur's death Herat (chiefly) and the other Timurid capitals rivalled Samarkand in attracting the choicest artists and intellectual spirits of the day.

Timur's interest in architecture and the other arts was subordinate only to that taken in martial exploits. His successors went one better as enthusiastic, passionate amateurs, as a few examples suffice to show. Ulug Beg, an outstanding astronomer as well as a poet and theologian; Hussein Baikara was an artist and poet. Babur, who went on to found the Mogul empire in India, produced his *Memoirs*, a book unsurpassed by any monarch which confounds the assertion that "Asia and Africa have no autobiographers."[7]

Though almost all the Timurid sovereigns were unstinting patrons of the arts and sciences, space allows us to allude briefly only to developments in the two main capitals, Samarkand and Herat, each with its own flavor and emphasis.

Samarkand's period of brilliance is inseparably linked with the name of Timur's beloved grandson Ulug Beg (1394-1449). In Barthold's words, "As a scholar on the throne, Ulug Beg remains completely unique in the history of the Muslim world; contemporaries could only compare him with the rule of the pupil of Aristotle [i.e., Alexander the Great]."[8] Despite the troubles of the succession struggle following Timur's death Ulug Beg received a handsome legacy. The city of Samarkand, with its gardens, buildings, parks and business quarters seething with commercial and artisan activity, remained intact. Nor had the scholars and the myriads of artists, architects and craftsmen whom

————————

*The same phenomenon repeats itself in the West — in Spain of the first and second halves of the sixteenth century.

Timur had regularly brought (through conquest) to his capital yet scattered to the four winds.

Ulug Beg knew Iranian literature well, even writing verses himself and surrounding himself with a number of poets. History was another interest. In painting he was the patron of the well-known artist Khodja Giyasaddin. His consuming passion, however, was for astronomy. To further this interest he constructed on the outskirts of Samarkand one of the most remarkable observatories in the world; in its equipment and in the significance of the work carried on there it was not to be equalled until a good deal later. In Barthold's view, the astronomical tables and catalogues of stars that were compiled represented "the last word of medieval astronomy and the highest plane astronomical science could achieve before the invention of the telescope."[9] As for architecture, some of the remarkable mosques, medresehs and palaces which he built in Samarkand, Bukhara and elsewhere may still be admired.

Herat, the northern Afghan city whose founding is ascribed to Alexander the Great, reached its greatest flowering in the fifteenth century under the Timurids when it became one of the great cultural, commercial and artisan centers of the Middle East. It maintained contacts with China, India, Muscovy and other states. Three Timurids in particular left their mark on this cultural and scientific endeavor: Shahrukh, Baisonkor, who was the most talented of Shahrukh's sons save for Ulug Beg, and finally, Hussein Baikara (c. 1469-1506) and his remarkable grand vizier Alisher Navoi, one of the great humanists of his day. In Babur's view: "There is not another city comparable to Herat in the entire world; its splendor and beauty in the time of Sultan Hussein, thanks to his rule and care, increased by ten or even twenty times." The poet Jami and the historians Mirkhond and Khondemir were merely the best known of the many men of letters living and working in Herat. The Herat school of miniaturists, led by the incomparable Bihzad, flourished at this time. Babur devotes many long pages to listing the astronomers, musicians, jurisconsults, physicians, theologians, calligraphers and other worthies who graced the court of Herat at this time. The artistic and scientific advances made in fifteenth century Herat have not been studied in all their amplitude to this day.

Timur has been explicated in terms of various historical figures. The most obvious parallel is Chingis Khan, and indeed Timur himself posed as the continuator and restorer of his empire. Their careers do offer striking parallels. Both were born into fairly humble though aristocratic families. Their early eareers were checkered with adversities and setbacks. Each broke with and ultimately eliminated his closest friend (and competitor), Timur with Hussein and Chingis with his blood brother or *anda* Jamuqa. In both cases their rise was painfully slow and their most difficult accomplishment was first to win out in the murderous elimination bouts with their rivals at home after which, having gained the afflatus of their art, their further conquests were comparatively swift and easy. In both cases their successes were facilitated by the disarray and division present in areas into which they extended their conquests, and both astutely promoted these discords to further their own ends. To state, however, that these areas were ripe for a Chingis or a Timur is not to say that any but this particular Chingis or Timur could have plucked the fruit.

Oddly enough the very success of Chingis and Timur has caused some writers to belittle their achievements as when Lynn Montross writes: "The phrase 'world's greatest conqueror' has been applied to Timur as well as to Jenghis Khan. Yet the similarity of Tartar and Mongol conquests leave room for scepticism." These "monotonously successful operations," he goes on to say, cause one to "wonder if the oppressed and fatalistic masses of the East were not more susceptible to invasion than Western peoples." In conclusion he gives it as his opinion that "In the end it would appear that an Asiatic conqueror of these centuries had only to gather some momentum to be assured of half-beaten opponents." Two points may be made here. First, the enemies of Chingis and Timur included some first-rate opponents. Second, the mistakes of omission or commission of their enemies did not automatically ensure victory to Chingis or Timur. As Louis Pasteur remarked in connection with another field of endeavor—scientific investigation: "In the field of experimentation, chance favors only the prepared mind."

Both Chingis and Timur were by nature prodigiously cruel and used this cruelty to strike terror and paralysis of will into the hearts of their opponents. They both employed terror to keep subjugated people in line once they were subdued. While both were illiterate, they appreciated and made use of the talents of cultured and educated outsiders. Both early showed a keen and vivid appreciation of the importance of trade in sustaining the prosperity of their states and in both merchants found a willing friend. Timur made war in the manner of Chingis and consequently has been disparaged as an imitator and plagiarist. Yet Chingis himself added little that was original to the art of war; rather, he improved and brought to the zenith of perfection the nomad form of warfare to which a number of earlier peoples such as the Hsiung-nu and

Huns had made their respective contributions.[10] Both made use of religion in effecting their conquests, but with a difference. Timur posed as the champion of Islam against heretics, Hindus and Christians. Chingis, on the other hand, preached religious toleration, thereby winning over to his side persecuted religious groups in states whose conquest he wished to compass.

Though illiterate, Timur was a man of some culture. His crimes in causing the destruction of so many centers of culture are more heinous and culpable than those of Chingis since he could appreciate the beauty of that which he destroyed. Timur interested himself in and knew the histories of the peoples he conquered. A complex and contradictory individual, his inner life was infinitely more intricate than that of Chingis, who to his death remained a brigand leader[11] and who retained his preference for Uighur culture even after making contact with the superior civilizations of China, Central Asia and Iran. Timur ruled over more civilized states than did Chingis, for it must be remembered that the definitive conquest of Iran and of China was the work of the latter's successors. While Timur posed as a Mongol and an upholder of the Yasa, the great law code of Chingis, the Shariat or Muslim law code was not displaced. It was Muslim divines who accompanied Timur and his troops, who fanaticized the latter and proclaimed Timur's victories. Although Timur's wars were usually against fellow Muslims, he sheathed them with the attributes of the *jihad* or Muslim holy war. Convenient pretexts were always found: the Mogols of Mogolistan, recent converts, were tepid in their profession of the faith; the Muslim Sultans of Delhi tolerated Hindus, though this was the only feasible policy in an area where Muslims were in a minority; or, where these arguments would not wash, Timur would label his opponents heretics. He would pose as a Sunnite in Shiite areas and as a Shiite in regions where Sunnites predominated. One recent study declares that "Timur was one of the worst enemies to whom Islamic civilization ever fell a victim."[12]

Christians in the path of Timur's armies were also slaughtered in great numbers. In Mesopotamia the Nestorians and Jacobite Christians have since that time been only pallid reflections of their former selves. Nor did Timur show any greater mercy to the Hindus and Zoroastrians he encountered in India and Iran.

Chingis has come down to us as the Mongol hero *par excellence*, the creator of a state which united all the Mongols for the first and only time in their history. Timur also survived in popular legend. The noted

German-Russian philologist Radloff (d. 1918) found songs about Timur among the Kirghiz and Tatars of Siberia. These tell of his piety, his misfortunes and his tenderness. One Kirghiz song calls him a poet and a bard. And in Anatolia, despite the imprecations of Ottoman historians, he survives in the facetiae of Nasir ad-Din Khodja as an often benign, amiable gentleman.[13]

Comparisons between Chingis and Timur have inevitably involved the character of the empires each founded. These have usually redounded to the favor of Chingis whose empire better withstood the rasure of time. The latter was Mongol in form with an authentic Chingisid as both its titular and factual head. Timur's empire, despite the Mongol influence, was Turkic. Militarily the Turkic Chagatais formed the bone and sinew of his military machine. Though Iranians, as well as others, were included in its ranks, Timur regarded the Chagatais as his most valiant warriors, as his own kith. He referred to the Iranians in terms of scarcely concealed contempt.

Despite this disparagement of the Iranians, he was in thrall to their culture. The great architectural and other artistic enterprises with which Timur sought to perpetuate his name were carried out by persons who were usually Iranian both in their culture and in their ethnic provenience.[14]

Surpassingly cruel and ruthless, Timur possessed other traits which softened these harsh lineaments somewhat. The affection and indulgence which he showed his sons and grandsons stands in marked contrast to the cruelties perpetrated by his opponents towards members of their own families, examples of which we have encountered in the course of our narrative. He forgave his son Miranshah whose follies in northwest Persia had almost led to the collapse of Timurid rule there. And there is the case of Timur's grandson Hussein who not only defected to the enemy during Timur's Syrian campaign but even fought in the ranks of the Syrians against his grandfather. Timur had him bastinadoed but then pardoned him and eventually even restored him to favor.

The cruelty which Timur showed on campaign is, on the whole, missing at home. The great *fêtes champêtres* which Timur organized outside Samarkand were, apart from a few public executions of corrupt officials, sedate affairs. One looks in vain for the refinement of sadism and perversion and the brutalization of spectators which, for example, speckles the pages of Roman history. We might note the gladiatorial contests in which men were pitted against wild animals or one another.[15] Emperors such as Domitian or Commodius used cripples as gladiators.

Trajan, in one record event lasting 117 days, used up 4,941 pairs of fighters. Constantine the Great, after his conversion to Christianity, threw pagan German prisoners to the lions in lieu of Christians.

Timur's treatment of foreign envoys was surprisingly mild and civilized. Though at times his own envoys were killed or imprisoned, he did not retaliate. Clavijo, who represented a relatively insignificant state, records the many marks of consideration and generosity shown him by Timur. These included a tour through Timur's private apartments in the tent city outside of Samarkand and through Ak Sarai, Timur's palace in Kesh.

Even Timur had his lighter moments, especially after he had imbibed much liquor—man's first tranquilizer. Clavijo, who was invited several times to attend the mammoth public festivities Timur organized in 1404, reports that on one occasion he saw Timur alone in his tent "where we found him in a state of much cheerfulness and contentment." Timur also enjoyed having his guests partake of alcohol. On another afternoon, Clavijo writes, he sent over some spirits "in order that when we should attend his presence we might be right merry." The next day "Timur appeared to be in excellent humor, drinking much wine and making all those of his guests present do the same." Timur, it should be mentioned, permitted himself and his warriors—the sack of Delhi being the notable exception—these drinking bouts only when not engaged in fighting. He would have approved of Chaucer's dictum that "a capitayne should live in sobreness."

Characteristically, after the celebrations marking the weddings of his grandsons in late 1404 just prior to his departure for the conquest of China, Timur issued an edict prohibiting thenceforward the drinking of wine in all parts of his realm. His reasons, Sharaf ad-Din informs us, were that wine took people away from their work and prompted unlawful and ill-intentioned deeds.[16] Practical considerations, not the prohibitions of the Koran and the Muslim law code (Shariat), motivated him, as was frequently the case.

Although Timur allowed himself numerous wives and concubines, his views on sex were, by Oriental standards, strait-laced. He was ill-disposed toward sodomy, nor were dishonest women admitted into his camp. Brothels, according to one account at least, were closed down in the principal cities of Timur's domain despite a great loss of revenue to the Treasury.[17]

Timur's empire broke up after his death, though it survived in truncated form for a century; Chingis Khan's empire, however, continued to prosper after an initial period of strife and turmoil. One authority notes that "On the whole the Timurid Empire remained poor in nomads by comparison with its neighbours in the west, which explains the inadequacy of its military enterprises."[18]

The Chingisids continued to make further gains of territory; indeed, much of the empire we associate with Chingis was acquired after his death. Timur's heirs, on the other hand, made no further conquests but, on the contrary, fought unprevailingly to keep their patrimony. Since both empires were economically geared to warfare, to a constantly replenished supply of booty and lands given as rewards for loyalty, the end of the period of conquest had an even greater impact than the closing of the frontier in American history. These wars at the same time kept the younger and more energetic part of the population away from the homeland, where they could cause trouble. This policy of continued conquest preserved the unity of Chingis' empire for three generations, though after Chingis' death this unity was admittedly precarious. The beginning of the decline of his empire coincided with the cessation of foreign conquests.[19]

Though Chingis, like Timur, assigned appanages to princes of the blood, his method of administering the agricultural lands inhabited by sedentary peoples dampened down separatist tendencies. These lands were ruled directly by governors appointed by and responsible to the great khan. Though the appanage princes received income from these lands, they did not themselves enjoy the right to collect taxes. The popular historian Harold Lamb alludes to the poor showing made by Timur's offspring. Yet in truth Timur, though survived by only two of his sons, had some descendants of above average abilities while many of Chingis' progeny proved to be merely mediocre. Grousset's explanation of the causes for the differing longevity of the two empires is more satisfying. Transoxiana, in his view, is a geographical center only in appearance. He discerns two types of domination in Asia. First there was that originating from the nomad inner heart of the continent (that of Chingis is a case in point) when "barbarians," animated by some primal, visceral urge such as hunger, spilled over into the peripheral areas (China, Iran, India, etc.), and imposed their writ over these sedentary nations. Then there were the great sedentary civilizations, themselves, superior to the nomad empires in that they always managed to assimilate their rude conquerors. Tranxosiana can be placed under neither of these two rubrics; it was composed of both elements. Timur's huge empire, having Transoxiana as its core, was an unstable creation that quickly fell apart once the conqueror's formidable, towering and extraordinary personality was removed from the scene.[20]

Timur could, of course, have translated his capital to a more central position in his domains. Shahrukh's transfer of his capital to Herat would seem to have been a move in this direction, though Herat was not located far enough to the southwest. There were precedents for such a more southerly center of empire in past history, empires which comprised much the same territories as that of Timur, but which lasted longer. This was true of the Persian Empire which also included Egypt. During the first two centuries of its widest extend (525-334 B.C.), Phoenician traders could range from the Indus river basin to the Atlantic seaboard of Europe, on the western extremity. The Seleucid state, the Persian Empire's successor, had, with the exception of Egypt and southern Syria, much the same Asian boundaries and economic structure as that of Timur. In both cases lower Iraq with its rich alluvial soil formed the economic mainstay.[21]

By Timur's time the irrigation system of southern Iraq was admittedly in a sad state of repair; perhaps this consideration bulked large in his thinking. Northwest Persia, where the Il-Khanids had maintained their capital, was a possible location for his capital city.

However, Timur showed only a perfunctory interest in his western possessions, which were assigned to a junior line of his house. His decision to base himself in Transoxiana may have been motivated not only by the natural feelings of a man for his homeland but also by his desire to use this area eventually for an invasion of China.

Timur regarded trade as the lifeblood and connective tissue of his empire. In the long term the prospects here were bleak. The voyage of Vasco da Gama in 1497 dealt a heavy blow to the ancient Asian land routes. Even though port cities such as Hormuz on the Persian Gulf now became intermediaries in this trade with Portugal, it was the latter that would reap the largest benefit from this new connection.

In summary, Timur not only failed to pick and strong and viable center for his empire — one associated with a historic mission of expansion — but he did not organize his realm to form an integrated whole. Nor was his empire animated by any religious or ideological mission. Timur's pose as the defender of the Muslim faith was regarded as the fraud it clearly was by the Muslim divines outside of Transoxiana. Ibn Arabshah was only one of a large number to consider Timur a bad Muslim; as we have seen, most of Timur's wars were against members of his own faith. Nor was his concept of the Chagatai as a *Herrenvolk* lording it over his other subjects, an attitude likely to endear him to other peoples. Timur's pose as the restorer and continuator of the empire of Chingis was hardly convincing either. Timur himself indicated its bankruptcy when in 1402, after the death of the khan Mahmud, the office was left unfilled despite Chingis' stipulation in his Yasa that no one could lawfully rule who was not of his seed.

Despite his failure to create a lasting empire, Timur's role in history was a most significant one. His activities imparted a new direction to the histories of Russia, the Ottoman Empire, and a host of other states. The importance of war as a vehicle of social, intellectual, economic and other societal changes is still in general insufficiently appreciated. Timur's wars profoundly changed the texture and quality of Central Asian and Middle Eastern life, and ushered in as well a brilliant new phase of Muslim civilization. The attention of historians has too often been riveted on the pyramids of skulls, the burning cities, the sieges and battles connected with Timur's name to the neglect of these underlying issues. Timur also deserves to be studied as one of the great captains of history, for his successes demand a fuller and deeper explanation than a mere modelling of his army after that of Chingis (so did some of his opponents) or the fissures and rifts dividing his enemies. Timur's career and proclaimed role are of interest in a world presently assailed by social perplexities so disturbing that some people, in their desire for security, peace of mind and good order would subscribe to Goethe's words: "I would rather commit an injustice than endure disorder." And Timur attracts attention by his personality *hors de pair,* a personality so striking that he has been the subject of innumerable plays, poems and other literary works of which Marlowe's *Tamburlaine* is only the most famous,[22] an interest which found its first expression among the literati of the Italian Renaissance.[23] And finally the history of Timur and his times deserves to be studied precisely because it is a part of history, of particular timeliness in a period in which mankind seeks William James' "moral equivalent of war." As the great biblical archeologist William Foxwell Albright once put it: "The lessons of man's past, as every archeologist discovers sooner or later, are humbling ones. They are also useful ones. For if anything is clear, it is that we cannot dismiss any part of our human story as irrelevant to the future of mankind."[24]

FOOTNOTES

CHAPTER I

1. Our information concerning this split is very obscure. Cf. B. Spuler, *The Muslim World: A Historical Survey.* Part II: *The Mongol Period,* Leiden, 1960, p. 45. The same author thinks the split occurred in 1346-47, other sources a little earlier.

CHAPTER II

1. Gonzales de Clavijo, *Embassy to Tamerlane, 1403-1406,* Translated from the Spanish by Guy Le Strange with an Introduction, New York and London, 1928, p. 206.

2. Walter J. Fischel, *Ibn Khaldun and Tamerlane. Their Historic Meeting in Damascus, 1401 A.D. (803 A.H.): A Study Based on Arabic Manuscripts of Ibn Khaldun's "Autobiography."* With a Translation into English and a Commentary, Berkeley and Los Angeles, 1952, pages 90, 120,n.

3. Léon Cahun, *Introduction à l'histoire de l'Asie. Turcs et Mongols des origines à 1405,* Paris, 1896, p. 445.

4. Fischel, , *Ibn Khaldun and Tamerlane,* pages 90, 120,n.

5. George Sarton, *Introduction to the History of Science,* vol. III, *Science and Learning in the Fourteenth Century,* in two parts, Baltimore, 1948, p. 1473.

6. Bernard Lewis, *The Arabs in History,* New York, 1960, p. 136. For other appreciations see Fischel, *Ibn Khaldun and Tamerlane,* pages 25, 34,n.

7. Fischel, *Ibn Khaldun and Tamerlane,* p. 46.

8. Ahmed ibn Arabshah, *Tamerlane or Timur the Great Amir,* Translated from the Arabic by J. H. Sanders, London, 1936, p. 295.

9. Clavijo, p. 220.

10. *Ibid.,* p. 221.

11. Fischel, *Ibn Khaldun and Tamerlane,* p. 38.

12. M. M. Gerasimov, *Portret Tamerlana (Oypt skul'pturnogo vos. na kran. osnove),* Kratkie soobshcheniya instituta istorii material'noi kultury imeni Ya. Marra, 1947, vyp. XVII, pages 14-21; M. M. Gerassimow [Gerasimov] , *Ich suchte Gesichter. Schädel erhalten ihr Antlitz zurück. Wissenschaft auf neuen Wegen,* Frankfurt-am-Main, 1968; M. M. Gerasimov, *The Face Finder,* Translated from the German by Alan Houghton Brodrick, London, 1971. For an illustration of the reconstructed skull see page 120. Also Hilda Hookham, *Tamburlaine the Conqueror,* London, 1962, p. 32.

13. Zoë Oldenbourg, *The Crusades*, New York, 1966, p. 23. Tsar Ivan the Terrible was also known for his insensate cruelty which may also, in part at least, have been prompted by physical suffering. Soviet experts, after removing his skeleton from his tomb in 1965 for study, concluded that "he must have suffered horribly for many years from osteophytes, which virtually fused his spine." See Michael Cherniavsky, "Ivan the Terrible as Renaissance Prince," *Slavic Review*, vol. XXVIII, No. 2, June, 1968, p. 195.

14. Ibn Arabshah, pages 310-311.

15. In 1383 Timur captured the chieftain who had inflicted these wounds and had him shot full of arrows.

16. Sharaf ad-Din Ali Yazdi, *The History of Timur-Bec, Known by the Name of Tamerlain the Great. Being a Historical Journal of His Conquests in Asia and Europe.* Translated into French by Petis de La Croix, 2 vols., London, 1723, vol. 1, p. 47.

17. *Ibid.*, vol. 1, p. 52.

18. *Ibid.*, vol. 1, p. 55.

19. See *Istoriya Samarkanda*, 2 vols., Tashkent, 1969, vol. 1, pp. 158ff.

20. E. G. Browne, *A Literary History of Persia*, vol. III, *The Tartar Dominion (1265-1502)*, Cambridge, Eng., 1951, p. 161.

21. V. V. Barthold, "Narodnoe dvizhenie v Samarkande v 1365 g.," *Sochineniya*, II (2), Moscow, 1964, p. 371.

22. Sharaf ad-Din, vol. 1, p. 64.

23. Another source (*Ocherki istorii SSSR: period feodalizma XI-XV vv.*, Moscow, 1953, p. 657) asserts that Maulana-zada was spared while in the shadow of the gallows because he was "wellborn" and "undoubtedly had ties with the Samarkand aristocracy."

24. Barthold, "Narodnoe dvizhenie," *Soch.*, II (2), p. 374.

25. Sharaf ad-Din, vol. 1, p. 68; See also L. G. Stroeva, *Vozniknovenie gosudarstva Timura*, Uchenye Zapiski LGU, Seriya Vostokovedcheskikh Nauk, vyp. 3, 1932, No. 128, pp. 73ff.

26. René Grousset, *L'Empire des Steppes*, Paris, 1960, p. 491.

27. Sharaf ad-Din, vol. 1, p. 122.

28. Quoted in Stroeva, p. 81.

29. Sharaf ad-Din, vol. 1, p. 126.

30. The parallel with Joseph Stalin is striking. The latter, while allied with Kamenev and Zinoviev in the struggle with Leon Trotsky in the mid-1920s, struck a moderate and conciliatory pose. Cf. John Lawrence, *A History of Russia*, New York, 1961, pages 293ff.

CHAPTER III

1. Sharaf ad-Din, vol. 1, p. 131.

2. *Ist. Samarkanda*, vol. 1, pp. 237-239. See also "Some Aspects of Fifteenth Century Samarkand," *Central Asian Review*, No. 5, 1957, pages 247-252.

3. *Ist. Samarkanda*, vol. 1, pages 167-168.

4. Barthold, *Sochineniya*, vol. II (1), p. 732.

5. The boundaries of this state corresponded to those of the modern Khanate

of Khiva, which was incorporated into the Tsarist Empire as a protectorate in the latter part of the nineteenth century.

6. Literally "daughter of a khan." The use of a title as if it were a name is commonplace in the annals of Central Asian history.

7. Paul Munier, *Trois grands empires de nomades d'Asie.* Conference prononcé le 28 janvier 1937 à l'Université indochinoise sous les auspices de la société de géographie de Hanoi, Hanoi, 1938, pages 20-21.

8. Sharaf ad-Din, vol. 1, p. 198.

9. *Ibid.,* pages 199-200.

10. V. G. Tizengauzen, *Materialy otnosyashchikhsya k istorii Zolotoi Ordy,* vol. II, Moscow and Leningrad, 1941, pages 251-252.

11. See the article on Toktamish in the *Encyclopaedia of Islam,* 1st Edition, vol. IV, Leiden-London, 1934, pages 807-809.

12. Quoted in M. G. Safargaliev, *Raspad Zolotoi Ordy,* Saransk, 1960, p. 139.

13. *Ibid.,* p. 142. The dating in this section follows the revisions of Safargaliev.

14. On the importance of these cities of Central Asia see *Kazakhstan v XV-XVIII vekakh (Voprosy sotsial'no-politicheskoi istorii),* Alma-Ata, 1969.

15. Russian historians, viewing the battle through the prism of history rather than through the eyes of a contemporary, have likened this to historically pivotal battles such as that of Tours in 451, when Attila and his Huns were stopped in their tracks and Western civilization was saved from (Eastern) barbarism. Cf. Michael Florinsky, *Russia: A History and an Interpretation,* 2 vols., New York, 1953, vol. 1, p. 66. Prince Dmitri Ivanovich, who received the cognomen "of the Don" (Donskoi) from the river near where the battle was fought, is regarded as one of the greatest of Russian heroes.

16. Most historians place the battle site near the Kalka river, which flows into the Sea of Azov. For the reasoning in favor of the change in venue, see Safargaliev, p. 143.

17. Casualty figures for the battle of Kulikovo show a very wide range. Russian chroniclers claim that as many as 200,000 combatants were killed. The Soviet military historian Col. Razin pares this down to 30,000 for the Russians and 150,000 for the Tatars. B. Ts. Urlanis, another Soviet authority, believes that the Russian losses are overstated "and that they were hardly over 10,000." Even the latter figure, which is much more credible, indicates losses of a considerable magnitude at a time when populations were much smaller than at present. Cf. M. S. Averbukh, *Voiny i narodonaselenie v dokapitalicheskikh obshchestrakh. Opyt istoriko-demograficheskogo issledovaniya,* Moscow, 1970, p. 122.

18. Tizengauzen, vol. II, pages 150-151.

CHAPTER IV

1. Sharaf ad-Din, vol. 1, p. 176.

2. *Ibid.,* p. 193.

3. Mirza, Arabic-Persian. Contraction of "emir-zade" or "emir's son." Title borne by princes descended from Timur. Cf. Tizengauzen, vol. II, p. 303.

4. Sharaf ad-Din, vol. 1, p. 205.

5. *Loc. cit.*

6. Ibn Arabshah, p. 22.

7. *Ibid.*, pages 22-23.

8. Ghiyath ad-Din [Ciyas ad-Din] Ali, *Dnevnik plkhoda Timura v Indiyu*, Moscow, 1958, p. 33.

9. Jean Aubin, "Comment Tamerlan prenait les villes," *Studia Islamica*, XIX, 1963, pages 119-120.

10. *Ibid.*, p. 120.

11. John Masson Smith, Jr., *The History of the Sarbadar Dynasty 1336-1381 A.D. and Its Sources*, The Hague and Paris, 1970, pages 80-81.

12. I. P. Petrushevsky, *Zemledelie i agrarnye otnoshenia v Irane XII-XIV vekov*, Moscow, 1960, pages 462-463.

13. Joseph von Hammer-Purgstall, *Geschichte des Osmanischen Reiches*, 10 vols., Graz, 1963, vol. 1, p. 267.

14. Sharaf ad-Din, vol. 1, p. 237.

15. *Ibid.*, p. 243.

16. *Ibid.*, p. 255.

17. *Istoriya Azerbaidzhana v trekh tomakh*, vol. 1, Baku, 1958, pages 198-199.

18. Sharaf ad-Din, vol. 1, pages 259-260. According to the latter, Toktamish pillaged Tabriz for six days after the city fell to his superior forces. He does not mention any use of trickery in gaining access to the city.

19. V. V. Barthold, *Four Studies on the History of Central Asia*, vol. II: *Ulugh-Beg*, Leiden, 1958, p. 28.

20. *Istoriya Azerbaidzhana*, vol. 1, pages 198-199.

21. W. E. D. Allen, *A History of the Georgian People. From the Beginning Down to the Russian Conquest in the Nineteenth Century*, London, 1932, p. 10.

22. *Istoriya Azerbaidzhana*, vol. 1, p. 197.

23. Aubin, "Comment Tamerlan," p. 114.

24. Ibn Arabshah, p. 45.

25. *Ibid.*, p. 46.

26. Arthur J. Arberry, *Shiraz. Persian City of Saints and Poets*, Norman, Okla., 1960, p. 51.

27. Laurence Lockhart, *Persian Cities*, London, 1960, p. 34.

28. Translation by A. J. Arberry, *Shiraz. Persian City of Saints and Poets*, p. 159.

29. That Hafiz was living in deep poverty at this time is, however, open to challenge. Carl Brockelmann, in his *History of the Islamic Peoples*, New York, 1947, pages 254-255, states that Hafiz was patronized by Shah Shuja who had him appointed professor of Islamic exegesis at the medreseh in Shiraz, a post which he held until his death in 1389.

30. Aubin, "Comment Tamerlan," p. 107.

CHAPTER V

1. Safargaliev, p. 137.

2. Grousset, p. 516.

3. Safargaliev, p. 137.

4. Sharaf ad-Din, vol. 1, p. 318.

5. *Ibid.*, p. 337.

6. *Ibid.*, p. 346.

7. Timur could have used two shorter routes: (a) via the elevated Ust-Urt plain between the Aral and Caspian Seas; (b) along the eastern shore of the Sea of Aral. The Russian general M. I. Ivanin, who knew the entire area at first hand and the special attributes of steppe warfare, indicates the fine calculation of factors which prompted Timur to select the third route: availability of water and pasturage, defense against sudden and deadly steppe fires, opportunities along part of the way to cloak his movements and to rest his men and animals and, in the event of defeat, the ability to beat an orderly retreat. Though the third route was the best, even this presented great difficulties and dangers which placed a premium on a commander's skill, resourcefulness and venturesomeness. Cf. M. I. Ivanin, *Ob voennom iskusstve i zavoevaniyakh mongolo-tatar i sredneaziatskikh narodov pri Chingiskhane i Tamerlane*, St. Petersburg, 1875, pages 191 ff.

8. Sharaf ad-Din, vol. 1, p. 363.

9. *Ibid.*, p. 153.

10. Ibn Arabshah, p. 14.

CHAPTER VI

1. Cf. H. L. Rabino, *Mazanderan and Astarabad*, London, 1928, pages 8-9. Mazanderan was formerly called Tabaristan.

2. Allen, pages 123-124.

3. A. Sanders, *Kaukasien, Nordkaukasien, Aserbaidschan, Armenien, Georgien. Geschichtlicher Umriss*, Munich, 1944, p. 185. According to the same authority, Bagrat did not win his freedom in 1387 but was kept as a hostage in Tabriz by Timur for some years. Some authors state that George VII succeeded his father Bagrat V as king in 1393, while others accept 1395.

4. Ghiyath ad-Din, p. 52.

5. Jean Aubin, "Tamerlan à Bagdad," *Arabica*, vol. 9, No. 3, 1962, p. 304.

6. *Ibid.*, p. 305.

7. Sharaf ad-Din, vol. 1, p. 441.

8. *Ibid.*, p. 442.

9. Hammer-Purgstall, vol. 1, p. 281.

10. According to Ibn Khaldun, Barkuk, after first treating the envoys well, became vexed with their attitudes and had them killed. See Walter J. Fischel, *Ibn Khaldun in Egypt. His Public Functions and His Historical Research (1382-1406). A Study in Islamic Historiography*, Berkeley and Los Angeles, 1967, pages 94-95.

11. Sir William Muir, *The Mameluke or Slave Dynasty of Egypt 1260-1517 A.D.*, London, 1896, p. 114. Hookham, p. 152, states that she was Ahmed's daughter.

12. Stanley Lane-Poole, *A History of Egypt*, vol. IV: *The Middle Ages*, New York, 1901, p. 333.

13. Ibn Sasra, *A Chronicle of Damascus, 1389-1397*, 2 vols., Berkeley, 1963, vol. 1, p. 198.

14. S. Zakhirov, *Diplomaticheskie otnosheniya Zolotoi Ordy s Egyptom (XIII-XIV vv.)*, Moscow, 1966. p. 96. See also Bertold Spuler, *Die Goldene Horde. Die Mongolen in Russland, 1223-1502*, Wiesbaden, 1965, pages 132 ff.

CHAPTER VII

1. Safargaliev, p. 137.

2. George Vernadsky, *The Mongols and Russia*, New Haven and London, 1953, p. 273.

3. Azerbaijan and the lands stretching to the north as far as Derbent had been under the rule of Miranshah, Timur's son, since 1392. Both Derbent and Shirvan were claimed by Toktamish who had coins minted there in his name (1388 and 1390). Cf. *Encyclopaedia of Islam*, 1st Ed., vol. IV, p. 809.

4. Grousset, p. 521.

5. Safargaliev, p. 162.

6. Sharaf ad-Din, vol. 1, pages 494-495.

7. Concerning this controversy see Safargaliev, pages 164 ff.

8. N. M. Karamzin, *Istoriya gosudarstva Rossiiskogo*, 5th ed., 3 vols., St. Petersburg, 1842, vol. 2, tom 5, gl. II, col. 86.

9. Aubin, "Comment Tamerlan," p. 88.

10. V. N. Sheviakov, *Podvig russkogo naroda v bor'be protiv tataro-mongol'-skikh zakhvatchikov v XIII-XV vekakh*, Moscow, 1961, p. 88.

11. P. A. Rappoport, *Ocherki po istorii voennogo zodchestva severo-zapadnei Rusi X-XV vv.*, Moscow and Leningrad, 1961, p. 132. Moscow has rarely been taken by force of arms.

12. L. V. Cherepnin, *Russkie feodal'nye arkhivy XIV-XV vekov, Chast pervaya*, Moscow and Leningrad 1948, p. 65.

13. ———— *Obrazovanie russkogo tsentralizonnago gosudarstva v XIV-XV vekakh*, Moscow, 1960, p. 676.

14. Cf. F. C. Hodgson, *Venice in the Thirteenth and Fourteenth Centuries. A Sketch of Venetian History from the Conquest of Constantinople to the Accession of Michele Steno. A.D. 1204-1400*, London, 1910, pp. 332-333; W. Heyd, *Histoire du Commerce du Levant au Moyen Age*, 2 vols., Amsterdam, 1959, vol. II, pp. 375-376.

15. Though these monks are specifically identified as Franciscans by our source, most of the monks at Timur's court were Dominicans.

16. Philippe Dollinger, *La Hanse (XIIe-XVIIe siècles)*, Paris, 1964, p. 286.

17. The amount of permanent economic damage which Timur did is exaggerated by most scholarly works. We know from the account of a merchant of Shiraz who visited New Sarai in 1438 that the city continued to occupy a considerable place in the commerce with Eastern Europe.

18. Ibn Arabshah, p. 88.

19. Josef Pfitzner, *Grossfürst Witold von Litauen als Staatsmann*, Brünn, 1930, pages 148-149.

CHAPTER VIII

1. Hookham, pages 187-188.

2. Sharaf ad-Din, vol. II, p. 46.

3. H. Desmond Martin, *The Rise of Chingis Khan and His Conquest of North China*, Baltimore, 1950, p. 46.

4. Sharaf ad-Din, vol. II, p. 7.

5. On the invasion routes used by Alexander the Great, Chingis Khan, Timur and other invaders of India see W. K. Fraser-Tytler, *Afghanistan. A Study of Political Developments in Central and Southern Asia,* London, 1953, pages 9-11.

6. The Safed-Posh or Black Robe Kafirs make up the main group of peoples inhabiting this area. For a discussion of the Kafirs see Eric Newby, *A Short Walk. A Preposterous Adventure,* New York, 1959, p. 86. See also H. C. Raverty, *Notes on Afghanistan and Part of Baluchistan,* London, 1888, pages 135ff.

7. Newby, p. 221.

8. In 1956 two English travelers in the area came across an inscription on an enormous rock a little to the northwest of where the above action is thought to have taken place. They were told by the local inhabitants that it was in the Kufic script and was made by Timur while on his way to India. Newby, p. 219.

9. V. D. Mahajan and Savitri Mahajan, *The Sultanate of Delhi,* Delhi, Bombay, Jullundur and Lucknow, 1963. On page 149 the authors state that "The necessity of giving help to his grandson was the immediate and real cause of Timur's invasion of India." The only difficulty with this interpretation is that Timur received a full report of his grandson's plight only upon arrival in India.

10. Kishari Saron Lal, *Twilight of the Sultanate. A Political and Cultural History of the Sultanate of Delhi from the Invasion of Timur to the Conquest of Babur, 1398-1526,* New York, 1963, p. 18.

11. Sharaf ad-Din, vol. II, p. 24. See also Ghiyath ad-Din, p. 99.

12. Sharaf ad-Din, vol. II, p. 24.

13. Lal, pages 319-320, Appendix A. Sharaf ad-Din, in magnifying the number killed, apparently thought that he was adding to the glory of the conqueror. The fact is that only males over fifteen were killed; Timur detailed one out of every ten of his men to stand guard over the women and children and the seized cattle.

14. Sharaf ad-Din, vol. II, p. 54.

15. *Ibid.,* p. 55.

16. *Cambridge History of India,* vol. III: *Turks and Afghans.* Edited by Lt. Col. Sir Wolseley Haig, New York and Cambridge, England, 1928, p. 198.

17. S. M. Ikram, *Muslim Civilization in India,* New York and London, 1964, p. 98.

18. Sharaf ad-Din, vol. II, p. 57.

19. Stanley Lane-Poole, *Mediaeval India under Mohammedan Rule (A.D. 712-1764),* London and New York, 1906, p. 157.

20. Sharaf ad-Din, vol. II, p. 58.

21. Mahomed Kasim Ferishta, *History of the Rise of the Mahomedan Power in India till the Year A.D. 1612.* Translated from the original Persian of Mahomed Kasim Ferishta by John Briggs, MRSS, Lt. Col. in the Madras Army, 2 vols., London, 1829, vol. 1, p. 492.

22. Ghiyath ad-Din, p. 117.

23. *Loc. cit.*

24. *Istoriya stran Azii i Afrkiki v Srednie Veka,* Moscow, 1963, p. 234.

25. Sharaf ad-Din, vol. II, p. 63.

26. Ferishta, vol. 1, p. 493..

27. Its renown, judging by the other buildings constructed by this sovereign,

must have been richly deserved. Unfortunately its destruction was so complete that even the location of the site is in doubt. Cf. Lal, p. 29.

28. Sharaf ad-Din, vol. II, p. 66.

29. *Ibid.*, p. 68.

30. *Cambridge History of India*, III, p. 200.

31. Even this is disputed by K. S. Lal (p. 42), who is sceptical as to how much booty Timur really took away. For him Timur's invasion was "an aimless visitation. . . . The victor had hardly gained much, but the vanquished had lost everything."

CHAPTER IX

1. Sharaf ad-Din, vol. II, p. 104.

2. For a reconstruction of the court see B. Stavisky, *V strane Roksany i Timura,* Moscow, 1970, p. 131; Dietrich Brandenburg, *Samarkand. Studien zur islamischen Baukunst in Uzbekistan (Zentralasien),* Berlin, 1972, pages 87-88.

3. V. V. Barthold, *Sochineniya,* vol. IV, Moscow, 1966, p. 116.

4. Some authors aver that Timur learned of Barkuk's death and his succession by his ten year old son Faraj—a very favorable development for Timur—towards the end of his Indian campaign. Barkuk, however, did not die until June 20, 1399 when Timur had already returned. Perhaps Timur, with his power of precognition, apprehended Barkuk's impending death earlier. Barkuk's health broke down irretrievably in the fall of 1398.

5. George Finlay, *A History of Greece. From its Conquest by the Romans to the Present Time. B. C. 146 to A.D. 1864,* vol. IV, Oxford, 1877, p. 390.

6. *Loc. cit.*

7. For a summary of this and other related correspondence contained in the Ottoman state archives, see Browne, vol. III, pages 203-206.

8. Ernst Werner, *Die Geburt einer Grossmacht—Die Osmanen (1300-1481). Ein Beitrag zur Genesis des türkischen Feodalismus,* Berlin, 1966, p. 174.

9. *Ibid.,* p. 175.

10. For the standard work on the Janissaries see Nahoum Weissmann, *Les Janissaires: Etude de l'organisation militaire des Ottomans,* Paris, 1964. See also G. Lewis, *Turkey,* London, 1957, pages 25 ff.

11. For a good discussion of the Ottoman army at this time see Harold W. V. Temperley, *History of Servia,* London, 1919, pages 106 ff.; "Harb, war," *Encyclopaedia of Islam,* New Ed., vol. III, pages 190-193; A. von Pawlikowski-Cholewa, *Die Heere des Morgenlandes. Militärische Beitrage zur Geschichte des nähen und fernen Orients,* Berlin, 1940, pages 269-293.

12. William Stearns Davis, *A Short History of the Middle East,* New York, 1922, p. 199. Two recent works which deal with the rise of the Ottoman state and its relationship to the Byzantine Empire are: Roderic H. Davison, *Turkey,* Englewood Cliffs, N.J., 1968, and Halil Inalcik, *The Ottoman Empire. The Classical Age, 1300-1600,* London, 1973.

13. This is called the Genoese colony of Pera in some works. Pera and Galata adjoin one another.

14. John W. Barker, *Manuel II Palaeologus (1391-1425): A Study in Late Byzantine Statesmanship*, New Brunswick, N.J., 1969, p. 215.

15. Clavijo, p. 135.

16. Barker, p. 505.

17. Hammer-Purgstall, vol. 1, p. 296.

18. Werner, p. 175.

19. *Ibid.*, pages 175-176.

20. *Ibid.*, p. 176.

CHAPTER X

1. Ibn Arabshah, p. 122.

2. Hammer-Purgstall, vol. 1, p. 297.

3. C. V. Barthold, *Sochineniya*, vol. VII, Moscow, 1971, p. 224.

4. Sharaf ad-Din, vol. II, p. 180. An adjacent quarry contains a stone weighing one thousand tons, the largest hewn rock in the world; this indicates the massive scale of the buildings at Baalbek.

5. For a photo-essay, see "Festival at Baalbek," *Aramco World Magazine*, May-June, 1972, pages 10-19.

6. "Harb," *Encyclopaedia of Islam*, New Ed., vol. III, p. 184.

7. H.A.R. Gibb (editor), *The Travels of Ibn Battuta, A.D. 1325-54*, 2 vols., Cambridge, 1958-62, vol. II, p. 160.

8. Sharaf ad-Din, vol. II, p. 188.

9. For a major Western source for Timur's takeover of Damascus see Walter J. Fischel, "A New Latin Source on Tamerlane's Conquest of Damascus (1400/1401) (B. De Mignanelli's 'Vita Tamerlani' 1416)," *Oriens*, vol. 9, No. 2, 1956, pages 201-232. This tallies in the main with the descriptions of Muslim historians. A summary of Ibn Taghri-Birdi's account is given in Nicola A. Ziadeh, *Damascus under the Mamluks*, Norman, Okla., 1964, pages 10-13.

10. Walter J. Fischel, in his two works, *Ibn Khaldun and Tamerlane* and *Ibn Khaldun in Egypt*, has made the deepest study of the contacts between the conqueror and the scholar. Prime reliance has been placed on these accounts.

11. Fischel, *Ibn Khaldun in Egypt*, p. 51.

12. David Ayalon, *Gunpowder and Firearms in the Mamluke Kingdom. A Challenge to a Mediaeval Society*, London, 1956, p. 11.

13. Jean Aubin believes that there was throughout these proceedings a persistent and perhaps voluntary misunderstanding on both sides as to the gold equivalent of the sums to be collected. The failure of the city's notables to deliver the amount expected, which they could have collected only via the use of extreme coercion, determined the fate of the city. Cf. Aubin, "Comment Tamerlan," pages 111-112.

14. According to H.A.R. Gibb, Umm Habiba died in Medina in 644 A.D. and "was almost certainly buried there." Gibb, vol. 1, p. 139.

15. Timur's fulminations were misdirected, for strict Muslim law forbids the raising of tombs and monuments over the graves of the faithful. Cf. Thomas Patrick Hughes, *A Dictionary of Islam*, Clifton, N.J., 1965, p. 635.

16. Fischel, "A New Latin Source," p. 225.

17. Heyd, vol. II, p. 469.

18. Edwin Pears, *The Destruction of the Greek Empire and the Story of the Capture of Constantinople by the Turks*, London, 1903, p. 140.

19. Sharaf ad-Din, vol. II, p. 214.

20. *Loc. cit.*

21. Aubin "Tamerlan à Bagdad," p. 308.

CHAPTER XI

1. Sharaf ad-Din, vol. II, p. 225.

2. "Bayazid I," *Encyclopaedia of Islam*, New Ed., vol. 1, p. 1119.

3. Sharaf ad-Din, vol. II, p. 232.

4. For a French translation of this letter see Marcel Brion, *Tamerlan*, Paris, 1963, pages 44-45. The year of the letter is incorrectly given as 1401.

5. There is no evidence that troops from Trebizond joined Timur's forces.

6. Hammer-Purgstall, vol. 1, p. 306.

7. Sharaf ad-Din, vol. II, p. 235.

8. *Loc. cit.*

9. Hammer-Purgstall, vol. 1, p. 307.

10. Sharaf ad-Din, vol. II, p. 244.

11. Though the sources concerning subsequent events, including the battle of Ankara, are copious, they have given rise to much muddle and absurdity in view of their mutually contradictory nature. The most judicious and percipient study to date, on which the present work makes large drafts, is G.Roloff, "Die Schlacht bei Angora (1402)," *Historische Zeitschrift*, 161, (1940), pages 244-262. M. M. Alexandrescu-Dersca's study, *La campagne de Timur en Anatolie (1402)*, Bucharest, 1942, while useful, must be used with caution since it is partly based on Timur's spurious "Autobiography." The same may be said of Ivanin's treatment, pages 218ff.

12. Sir Charles Oman, *A History of the Art of War in the Sixteenth Century*, London, 1936, p. 758. See pages 758-759 for a discussion of the limitations of Ottoman offensive capabilities.

13. *Ibid.*, p. 759.

14. Today trees are few on the Anatolian plain. Years of unrestricted grazing by goats and sheep have taken their toll.

15. Cf. Alexandrescu-Dersca, Appendix I: The Effectives of the Army of Timur, pages 112-113; Appendix II: The Effectives of the Army of Bayazid, pages 114-115.

16. In modern times even Frederick the Great and Napoleon, to magnify their achievements, were not above overstating the size of the enemy forces they encountered. Cf. Hans Delbrück, *Numbers in History*, London, 1913, p. 16.

17. Edouard Perroy, *Histoire générale des civilisations*, tome III, *Le Moyen Age*, Paris, 1955, p. 333.

18. Herbert Adams Gibbons, *The Foundation of the Ottoman Empire. A History of the Osmanlis up to the Death of Bayazid I (1300-1403)*, Oxford, 1916, p. 249.

19. Hammer-Purgstall, vol. 1, p. 310.

20. Sharaf ad-Din, vol. II, p. 251. The author's long account of the battle makes no further mention of the elephants.

21. "Germiyan," *Encyclopaedia of Islam,* New Ed., vol. II, p. 990.

22. See, for example, *The New York Times,* October 19. 1969. Excavations have revealed a far larger city than was previously thought to exist.

23. Barker, pages 507-508.

24. Constantin Jireček, *Geschichte der Serben,* 2 vols., Amsterdam, 1967, vol. 1, p. 140.

25. Clavijo, p. 136.

26. The city in Timur's time presented a somewhat different configuration than now. Since that time landfill has been used to extend the city's area into the bay. For a recent history of Smyrna (Izmir) see Yu. A. Petrosyan and A. R. Yusupov, *Izmir,* Moscow, 1973.

27. Aziz Suryal Atiya, *The Crusade in the Later Middle Ages,* London, 1938, p. 298; Hammer-Purgstall, vol. 1, p. 332.

28. Smyrna (Izmir) has a Mediterranean climate with all of the rain coming in the fall, winter and spring. This can be very heavy as the present author, who lived in the city for two years, can testify.

29. Muir, p. 124.

30. Lane-Poole, p. 334.

31. Gibbons, pages 258-259; Hammer-Purgstall, vol. 1, p. 334.

32. Hammer-Purgstall, vol. 1, pages 317 ff. For the view that Bayazid was indeed confined in an iron cage see N. Martinovich, "La cage du Sultan Bayazid," *Journal Asiatique,* vol. 211, 1927, pages 135-137. According to the same authority, Bayazid, in response to Timur's query as to what he would have done had he taken Timur captive, replied that he would have put Timur in an iron cage. The latter became so enraged that he applied this intended treatment to Bayazid. See also Gibbons, pages 255-256.

33. For a good summary of the various pertinent works and their respective views see Alexandrescu-Dersca, pages 94-95.

34. Cf. "Intihar, suicide," *Encyclopaedia of Islam,* New Ed., vol. II, p. 1246.

35. Sharaf ad-Din, vol. II, p. 326.

36. Owen Lattimore, *Nomads and Commissars. Mongolia Revisited,* New York, 1962, pages 11-12.

37. Sharaf ad-Din, vol. II, p. 318.

38. Abdul-Kerim Ali-zade, *Sotsial'no-ekonomicheskaya i politicheskaya istoriya Azerbaidzhana XIII-XIV vv.,* Baku, 1956, p. 393.

39. Sharaf ad-Din, vol. II, p. 319.

40. *Ibid.,* p. 320.

41. *Loc. cit.*

42. Aubin, "Comment Tamerlan," p. 93.

CHAPTER XII

1. For a map indicating the Castilian embassy's outward and return journey see Clavijo, p. 1 opposite.

2. Minorsky states that in Spain at the present time scholars are inclined to attribute the composition of the account to one of Clavijo's companions. Cf.

V. Minorsky, *La Perse au Moyen Age*. Convegno de Scienza Morali Storiche e Filoloiche—Oriente ed Occidente nel Medio Evo—Accademia Nazionale dei Lincei, Rome, 1957, p. 423. A more recent study, however, still accepts Clavijo as the author, adding that he may have been helped in working up his observations upon return to Spain by his old associate Alfonso de Páez. Cf. A. Y. Deymond, *A Literary History of Spain. The Middle Ages*, London and New York, 1971, p. 155.

3. *New Catholic Encyclopedia*, vol. 9, p. 934.

4. See, for example, V. Minorsky, "The Middle East in Western Politics in the 13th, 14th and 15th Centuries," *Journal of the Royal Central Asian Society*, vol. XXVII, 1940, pages 434 ff.

5. Heyd, vol. II, p. 266.

6. Silvestre de Sacy, "Mémoire sur une correspondence inédite de Tamerlan avec Charles VI," Académie des Inscriptions et Belles Lettres, *Mémoires*, tome 6, 1822, pages 470-522.

7. *Istoriya Samarkanda*, vol. 1, pages 181 ff.

8. H. Moranvillé, *Mémoire sur Tamerlan et sa cour par un Dominicain en 1403*, Bibliothèque de l'Ecole de Chartres, vol. 55, Paris, 1894.

9. de Sacy, p. 520.

10. *Istoriya Samarkanda*, vol. 1, p. 184; J. Delaville le Roulx, *La France en Orient au XIV siècle*, w vols., Paris, 1886, vol. 1, pages 389-390.

11. James Hamilton Wylie, *History of England under Henry the Fourth*, 4 vols., London, 1898; Reprint, New York, 1969, vol. IV, p. 316; *Original Letters Illustrative of English History*, Third Series, vol. 1, New York, 1970, pages 54 ff.

CHAPTER XIII

1. "Tamerlane—the greatest Mongol conqueror. Some military historians place him higher than Alexander of Macedonia and call him 'the Napoleon of Asia'." E. Razin, *Istoriya voennogo iskusstva s dreveishikh vremen do pervoi imperialisticheskoi voiny 1914-1918 gg.*, Moscow, 1940, p. 129.

2. FIL, "elephant," *Encyclopaedia of Islam*, New Ed., vol. II, p. 894.

3. Clavijo, p. 196.

4. Cf. *Narody srednei Azii i Kazakhstana*, Moscow, 1962, p. 171.

5. Sir Charles Oman, *The Art of War in the Middle Ages, A.D. 378-1515*, Rev. and Ed. by John H. Beeler, Ithaca, N.Y., 1953, p. 63.

6. Lyman D. Wilbur, "Surveying through Khoresm," *National Geographic*, June, 1932, p. 754.

7. Freytag-Loringhoven, Major-General Baron von, *The Power of Personality in War (Die Macht der Persoenlichkeit im Kriege)*, Harrisburg, Pa., 1955, p. 44. The author points out, by way of example, that lack of water greatly hobbled the movements of British forces during the Boer War.

8. Ayalon, p. 129.

9. *Histoire universelle des armées. Antiquité, Féodalité*, vol. 1, Paris, 1965, p. 235.

10. *Encyclopaedia of Islam*, New Ed., vol. III, p. 502.

11. Theodor Mommsen, *History of Rome*, 3 vols., 1854-56, quoted in Freytag-Loringhoven, p. 40.

12. Clavijo, p. 233.

13. Lattimore, p. 233.

14. Cf. "Harb," *Encyclopaedia of Islam,* vol. III, New Ed., pp. 180-181.

15. Sarton, p. 1469.

16. Slater Brown, *The World of the Desert,* Indianapolis and New York, 1963, p. 26.

17. *Narody Srednei Azii i Kazakhstana,* p. 205.

18. On Timur's army see also *Istoriya Uzbekskoi SSR,* 4 vols., Tashkent, 1967, vol. 1. pages 453-456; B. Zakhoder, "Imperiya Timura," *Istoricheskii Zhurnal,* No. 6, 1951, pages 84-86.

CHAPTER XIV

1. Islamic feudalism, it may be noted, differs from Western European varieties in that "The element of mutual obligation inherent in the nexus of feudal tenure in Western Europe is notably absent." Ann K. S. Lambton, *Landlord and Peasant in Persia: A Study of Land Tenure and Land Revenue Administration,* London, 1954, pages 53-54.

2. Ibrahim Muminov, *Rol' i mesto Amira Timura v istorii Srednei Azii v svete dannykh pis'mennykh istochnikov,* Tashkent, 1968, p. 22.

3. Clavijo, p. 248.

4. Sharaf ad-Din, vol. II, pages 321-323.

5. Aubin, "Comment Tamerlan," p. 93.

6. *Loc. cit.*

7. Sarton, p. 1468.

8. Clavijo pages 195-196.

9. Heyd, vol. II, p. 505.

10. Clavijo, p. 288.

11. Aubin, "Comment Tamerlan," p. 91.

12. Clavijo, p. 279.

13. *Ibid.,* pages 289-290.

14. For a large and sumptuous reproduction of these see *Istoricheskie Pamyatniki Islama v SSSR. Historical Monuments of Islam in the U.S.S.R. Les Monuments Historiques de l'Islam en U.R.S.S.,* Moslem Religious Board of Central Asia and Kazakhstan, Tashkent, ca. 1964.

15. N. I. Leonov, *Ulugbek — velikii astronom XV veka,* Moscow, 1950, p. 10.

16. A. Yu. Yakubovsky, *Mastera Iran v Srednei Azii pri Timure (Tablitsy CXIX-CXXIII),* Mezhdunarodny kongress Iranskom iskusstvo i arkheologii. Doklady, Leningrad, September, 1935, Moscow and Leningrad, 1935, p. 285.

CHAPTER XV

1. The wounds suffered in Sistan, which brought Timur the sobriquet "the lame," were only the most grievous of these.

2. Clavijo, p. 284.

3. Barthold, *Four Studies,* II, pages 47-48.

4. Grousset, p. 533.

5. E. Bretschneider, *Mediaeval Researches from Eastern Asiatic Sources,* 2 vols., New York, 1967, vol. 2 p. 260; Barthold, *Four Studies,* II, pages 48-50.

6. Clavijo, p. 290.

7. No such execution is mentioned in other sources. Even Clavijo relates it as hearsay.

8. Grousset, p. 534. Kubilai Khan's conquest of South China was, it should be noted, accompanied by much less destruction and loss of life than the earlier Mongol conquests in the north. Cf. L. A. Borokovka, *Vosstanie "krasnykh voisk" v Kitae,* Moscow, 1971, pages 5-6.

9. Henri Cordier, *Histoire générale de la Chine et ses relations avec les pays étrangers. Depuis les temps les plus anciens jusqu'à la chute de la dynastie Mandchoue,* 3 vols., Paris, 1920, vol. III, p. 3.

10. Barthold, *Four Studies, II,* p. 51.

11. Pawlikowski-Cholewa, p. 211.

12. Ivanin, pages 233-234.

13. Clavijo, p. 292.

14. T. N. Kary-Niyazov, *Astronomicheskaya shkola Ulugbeka,* Moscow and Leningrad, 1950, p. 28.

15. Shan Yue (editor), *Ocherki istorii Kitaya. S drevnosti de "opiumnykh" voin,* Moscow, 1959, p. 414.

16. Ibn Arabshah, p. 132.

17. Sharaf ad-Din, vol. II, pages 383-384.

18. The findings of Gerasimov, who helped open Timur's tomb in 1941. Gerasimov could find no substantiation of Ibn Arabshah's claim that Timur was buried in a steel coffin or Sharaf ad-Din's statement that Timur's face was turned towards the tomb of Sayyid Bereke. Gerassimow [Gerasimov], p. 156.

19. *Istoriya Samarkanda,* vol. 1, p. 243.

20. Sarton, p. 1471. Jade is really two stones. The cenotaph of Timur is made of nephrite, a silicate of magnesium. Jadeite or "imperial jade," a much newer discovery, is a silicate of aluminium. The most prized specimens in the collections of the Emperors of China consisted of jadeite.

CHAPTER XVI

1. Clavijo, p. 317.

2. *Ibid.,* p. 315.

3. V. V. Barthold, "Timur," *Entsiklopedicheskii slovar',* vol. 33, St. Petersburg, 1901, p. 197.

4. Emanuel Sarkisyanz, *Geschichte der orientalischen völker Russlands bis 1917,* Munich, 1961, p. 180.

5. Quoted in *Istoriya narodov Uzbekistana,* vol. 1, Tashkent, 1950, p. 369.

6. Lucien Bouvat, *L'Empire Mongole (2ème phase),* Paris, 1927, p. 201. For further details see the same author's "Essai sur la civilisation Timouride," *Journal Asiatique,* April-June, 1926, pages 193-299. Barthold, for his part, is much more impressed by the artistic than the intellectual side of Timurid civilization. He writes: "The period of creativity in the field of thought at this time had passed

for the entire Orient; in all branches of knowledge and literature the writers of the XVth century were only the imitators of their predecessors." Cf. V. V. Barthold, *Sochineniya,* vol. XIII, pages 74-75.

7. V. S. Pritchett, "Speaking of Books: Writing an Autobiography," *The New York Times Book Review,* Nov. 26, 1967, p. 2 states "And, in fact, the 'I' is a relatively new invention. To start with, it is exclusively European in origin. Asia and Africa have no biographers."

8. Barthold, *Sochineniya,* vol. IV, p. 196.

9. *Loc. cit.*

10. Interestingly enough, Napoleon himself effected no fundamental innovations in tactics, strategy or weaponry, but confined himself to changes in detail.

11. Barthold, *Four Studies on the History of Central Asia,* vol. II, *Ulugh-Beg,* p. 38.

12. P. M. Holt, Ann K. S. Lambton and Bernard Lewis (Eds.), *The Cambridge History of Islam,* 2 vols., Cambridge, England, 1970, p. 170, vol. 1.

13. Cahun, pages 458-460.

14. Barthold, *Histoire de l'Asie Centrale,* Paris, 1945, p. 178.

15. See Michael Grant, *Gladiators,* London, 1968, for an extended treatment of this "sport." He characterizes (p. 104) the pleasure Romans took in this activity as "horrifyingly brutal and perverted."

16. Muminov, p. 12.

17. Aubin, "Comment Tamerlan prenait les villes," p. 455.

18. *Encyclopaedia of Islam,* New Edition, vol. 1, pages 147-148.

19. Cf. *Tataro-mongoly v Azii i Evrope. Sbornik statei,* Moscow, 1970, pages 112-113.

20. Grousset, p. 495.

21. "On the Frontier" — review article of Freya Stark's *Rome on the Euphrates: The Story of a Frontier,* in *The Times (London) Literary Supplement,* Nov. 24, 1966, pages 1057-1058.

22. For a study in depth of these literary works see Ottokar Intze, *Tamerlane und Bajazet in den Literaturen des Abendlandes,* Erlangen, 1912.

23. The earliest evidence of this scholarly interest in Timur dates from the time of the renowned Italian Renaissance scholar Poggio Bracciolini (1380-1459) who, from 1453 was the historiographer of the city of Florence. This touched off a flurry of interest. A standardized *Vita Tamerlani* was evolved by the scholar-pope Aeneas Silvio de Piccolomini (1405-1464), Pius II from 1458, which was followed with embellishments by other Renaissance scholars. And although Asia remained beyond the ken of Machiavelli in his historical writings and musings, the image of Timur as elaborated by Machiavelli's predecessors is considered to have been an important formative element in his concept of *The Prince,* his best-known and most influential work. See Eric Voegelin, "Machiavelli's Prince: Background and Formation," *Review of Politics,* April, 1951, p. 162.

24. *The Johns Hopkins Magazine,* March, 1964, p. 16.

BIBLIOGRAPHICAL ESSAY

Though many of the primary sources bearing on the life of Timur have been irretrievably lost, enough remains to reconstruct the great conqueror's life and deeds with a fair degree of accuracy. These sources are of two forms: annals, and material remains (inscriptions, coins, *objets d'art,* buildings, etc.) of his age. The written sources are preeminently of two kinds. (1) works composed at the behest of Timur himself or his heirs, of a semi-official character and bearing the bias inherent in such sponsorship: (2) works written by persons who lived during Timur's time or not long after who had no official connection with his court or those of his heirs. The latter could and do take a more impartial stance and are especially valuable when they describe the same events as the semi-official Timurid historians, allowing us to check the one against the other.

Timur took great pains to ensure that his name and deeds were perpetuated for posterity. To that end he kept with him, when on campaign or in court, personal secretaries and "educated persons of his time" of Uighur or Persian provenance. These were ordered to write down all that was said or done. Timur himself would at frequent intervals check these accounts to ensure their accuracy. If doubts arose or points needed clarification, eyewitnesses were interrogated and, if necessary, written enquiries were sent out or embassies despatched to secure the desired information. This systematic recording of the activities of Timur begins only around 1369 or 1370, i.e., beginning with his proclamation as ruler of Transoxiana, as only then was he in the position to keep secretaries. Earlier events could be reconstructed only according to the recollection of Timur himself or of other eyewitnesses whose names, unfortunately, are not recorded.

Eminent men of letters were charged with rewriting these notes in an elegant but simple style. One or several writers were assigned to draw up an account of a particular campaign, for example. Regrettably, only Ghiyas (or Ghiyath) ad-Din's journal of the Indian campaign has come down to us. A Russian translation of the Persian original has been published (Ghiyas ad-Din Ali, *Dnevnik pokhoda Timura v Indiyu,* ed. L. Zimin, 1915; Moscow, 1958. The author prefaces his detailed account of the campaign with a short sketch of Timur's previous wars. It is written in an ornate, overwrought style rather than in simple, easily understood language and hence did not satisfy Timur. It is not known if the author personally accompanied Timur on his Indian campaign or simply reworked the accounts of others. Internal evidence indicates that the work was written some time before March 1403.

Timur also commissioned two biographies. Only the second, that of Nizam ad-Din Shami, is extant. It is entitled *Zafar-nama* or "Book of Victories," a title suggested by Timur himself. The author, a native of Shams in the environs of Tabriz, first met Timur in 1393 during his conquest of Baghdad. In the winter of 1401/1402 he entered Timur's service and accompanied him on his campaigns. Timur asked him to write his biography since a previous effort by an unknown hand was unsatisfying. Nizam ad-Din drew upon this work and on the accounts of individual campaigns mentioned above. He also tapped oral as well as written testimony not used by the first biographer. Nizam ad-Din's work differs from that of Ghiyas ad-Din in two particulars: it is simpler in style and, unlike the latter, covers the entire scope of Timur's career down to 1404, just before Timur's death, when it stops. It also contains a preface describing conditions in Central Asia around 1360 when Timur first looms on the historical scene. His account of Timur's Indian campaign is an abridgment of the work of Ghiyas ad-Din. Though apologetic in tone, the *Zafar-nama* is of exceptional importance as a source for the study of Timur and his time. In 1937 Félix Tauer published a critical edition of the Persian text in Prague: Félix Tauer, (ed.), *Histoire des conquêtes de Tamerlan intitulée Zafarnama par Nizamuddin Sami,* 2 vols., Prague, 1937 and 1956).

The *Zafar-nama* of Nizam ad-Din was supplanted in 1425 by a work bearing the same title written by a fellow countryman, Sharaf ad-Din al-Yezdi, a native of Yezd in southwestern Persia. Sharaf ad-Din wrote his work at the behest of Ibrahim-Sultan, son of Shahrukh. Sharad ad-Din states that Ibrahim-Sultan, with the aid of secretaries, wrote the original which he himself then reworked. The role of Timur's grandson in composing this work is, however, probably much exaggerated. Sharaf ad-Din makes unstinting use of Nizam ad-Din's biography, incorporating entire sections "even down to citations" (Lucien Bouvat). There is also much new material. Not only did Sharaf ad-Din quarry additional material from the same sources used by Nizam ad-Din but he also tapped other sources as well, notably the chronicle "Tarikh-i Khani" written in poetical form by Timur's Uighur secretaries, which has not been preserved. He also includes eyewitness testimony not found elsewhere. It is the fullest account of Timur's life, covering not only his death but the period thereafter. It contains a voluminous introduction describing political events in that part of the world from the time of Chingis Khan down to Timur, based largely on the work of the famous Persian historian Rashid ad-Din. Curiously enough, the oldest manuscripts of the *Zafar-nama* do not contain this introduction; perhaps it was the work of another hand.

Sharaf ad-Din's account is written in a surpassingly magniloquent and flowery style. He is even more apologetic with regard to Timur's actions than is Nizam ad-Din. As the scholar Fèlix Nève puts it: "He described with equal complacency all the acts of his [Timur's] life, and reported with enthusiasm not only his victories but also his most reprehensible acts with a tranquility of mind tantamount to tacit approval; he never found, as it were, a word of sympathy or excuse for his adversaries, not a word of pity for the vanquished or the victim." Sharaf ad-Din converts Timur's infrequent military setbacks into victories. The biased and tendentious nature of his work can, however, be easily seen through and proper allowances made. The work was translated into French by François Pétis de la Croix (1652-1712), secretary-interpreter for oriental languages to King Louis XIV of France, under the cumbrous title *Histoire du Timur bec, connu sous le nom de grand Tamerlan, empereur des Mongoles et Tartares.* It was published posthumously in 1722 by Pétis de la Croix's son. In 1723 it was translated from the French into English by J. Darby. Both translations enjoyed a great vogue and served as the chief sources for European writings about Timur in the eighteenth and nineteenth centuries. Pétis de la Croix omitted the long introduction noted above. He also realized that the French reader "could never digest the figurative and frequent poetical expressions of the Persian style" and therefore sought to give the substance and thoughts of the author rather than to make a word-for-word transposition of the original into French. Nonetheless much of the bloated wordiness of the original remains, though some of the passages are admittedly beautiful. Present-day scholars consider the version of Pétis de la Croix to be out of date and a freshly annotated translation is needed. Sharaf ad-Din's *Zafar-nama* was published under the editorship of Malawi Muhammad Ilahdad, *Bibliotheca Indica,* 2 vols., Calcutta, 1887-1888, but it is not annotated.

Another valuable source is the *Anonymous Iskender.* In 1927 the Russian orientalist V. V. Barthold published a study identifying the unknown author as a certain Mu'in ad-Din Natanzi. The latter was in the service of Timur's grandson Iskender, governor of Fars and Isfahan. Natanzi composed his work at the latter's behest in 1413-1414. The work is mainly based on primary sources in the Turkic language which are not extant. Since the account includes facts not encountered elsewhere, it is of extraordinary importance as a supplementary source. It exists in three manuscript copies—in Leningrad, London and Paris. It has not been published.

Other important fifteenth century Timurid court historians included the life of Timur in their works. These were Muhammad Fazlal Allakha Musevi, Abd-ar Razzak Samarkandi, Hafiz-i Abru, Mirkhond and Khondemir. The first of these, Musevi, wrote in Fars for Timur's grandson Iskender-Sultan. Though his work, *Asakhkh at-tabarikh* ("The Truest of Chronicles"), is based on Nizam ad-Din's *Zafar-nama*, it contains many stories not found elsewhere. Judging by internal evidence, the Uighur chronicle is the basis of certain of these. Abd-ar Razzak Samarkandi's work was drawn up in 1470-1471 and is in two parts: the first deals with Timur, the second with his youngest son Shahrukh (Abd-al Razzak, *Matlaal-sadayn*, ed. by M. Shafi, Lahore, 1941 and 1949).

Hafiz-i Abru, who was in the service first of Timur and then of his successors, was present during the conqueror's capture of Aleppo and Damascus. He is best remembered for his *Zobdetot-Tevarikh* ("Cream of the Chronicles"), an immense compilation made at the request of Timur's descendant Baisonkor. The chapters on Timur are of great value. Though using the same sources as Mu'in ad-Din's history, Hafiz-i Abru was able to extract much information not found in the latter work.

Though the best known of the fifteenth century Persian historians is Mirkhond (d. 1498), his universal history entitled *Roozatos-Safa* ("Garden of Purity"), which contains a section on Timur, is overrated (Bouvat). Much more valuable is the *Habibos-Siyer* ("Friend of Biographers") of his grandson and disciple Khondemir (or better, Khwandamir). An excerpt from the latter has been published under the title *Timur, Great Khan of the Mongols,* Bombay, 1900.

The most important of the authors hostile to Timur is Ahmed ibn Arabshah whose book in rhymed Arabic prose, *Adraib al Makdur fi Nawaib Timur* ("Marvels of Destiny in the Life of Timur"), pulses with hatred of the conqueror. ("Impostor," "bastard," "evil one" are some of the epithets used). A Damascene by origin, born in 1388, the twelve year old lad was brought to Samarkand in Timur's train after the latter's taking of Damascus in 1400. He received a good education, mastering several languages and later, after having travelled a good deal in Timur's realm, served as secretary to the Ottoman sultan at Adrianople. Though Arabshah's work on Timur is too ornate in style for Western tastes, it has been acknowledged as a literary masterpiece by scholars of Arabic literature such as Claude Huart. None of Arabshah's other works achieved the same renown, suggesting that animus might be one of the principal mainsprings of literary inspiration. Despite his patent bias, Arabshah does not deny Timur his high intellect, organizational talent or military genius. The work is based not only on the author's personal recollections but on the tales of eyewitnesses and participants in Timur's campaigns. Arabshah's account often contradicts Sharaf ad-Din and other official historians and is very valuable as a check on the latter. It appeared in various European versions, first (Leyden, 1576) in Egyptian, of which P. Vattier made a very defective French translation published in Paris in 1658. Samuel Manger published a Latin translation with Arabic text in 1767-1772, but this has many errors. The best edition of the Arabic text appeared in Calcutta in 1818. The English translation by J. H. Sanders under the title *Tamerlane, or Timur the Great Amir*, London, 1936, has drawn the fire of such scholars as Yakubovsky and Zeki Velidi Togan. A fresh English translation is needed.

The hostile work of another contemporary, Thomas de Medzoph, an Armenian monk, is worthy of mention, though it is inferior to Arabshah's work both as to scope, intrinsic historical value and literary merit. Medzoph's *An Abridged History of the Sovereigns of the Orient, of the Impious and Cruel Monster Langthamour [Timur] and of Others* is a history of Armenia from the beginnings of Timur's military career to the subjugation of the Turkmen by Timur's son Shahrukh. Medzoph, in his youth, personally witnessed some of the calamities which befell his people and was able to interrogate eyewitnesses as to others. He wrote his work about 1425 when he was approximately fifty years old. Though arid in appearance, his relation contains valuable details concerning the horrors attending Timur's passages through Armenia. Though Medzoph's chronicle still remains unedited, it forms the basis of the work of Félix Nève, *Exposé des guerres de Tamerlan et de Schah-Rokh dans l'Asie occidentale, d'après la chronique Arménienne inédite de Thomas de Medzoph*, Bussels, 1870.

Other unfriendly sources including the Ottoman chroniclers Saeddin and Ashik-pasha-zade, are important for an account of the hostilities between Timur and Bayazid. The substance of these and the Byzantine historians (Ducas, Chalcondylas, etc.) who provide a useful control on the former, is contained in J. von Hammer-Purgstall, *Geschichte des osmanischen Reiches,* vol. 1, Graz, 1963, pages 306ff.

The historian Ibn Khaldun's eyewitness account of his meetings with Timur in early 1401, described in the text, and of the Syrian campaign of 1400/1401, is a most precious source. It is written in a lean, fair-minded, matter-of-fact style. For an English translation see Walter J. Fischel, *Ibn Khaldun and Tamerlane: Their Historic Meeting in Damascus, 1401 A.D. (803 A.H.: A Study Based on Arabic Manuscripts of Ibn Khaldun's "Autobiography,"* with a translation into English and a commentary, Berkeley and Los Angeles, 1952. See also the same author's *Ibn Khaldun in Egypt. His Public Functions and His Historic Research (1382-1406). A Study in Islamic Historiography,* Berkeley and Los Angeles, 1967, for a summation of this material and further research findings. Fischel cites the various Mamluke sources bearing on the life of Timur.

By far the most valuable Western travel account is that by Ruy González de Clavijo, Castilian envoy to Timur's court, who arrived in 1404 and spent several months there. Though his notions of China and the routes thereto are muddled, his accounts of Timur and his progeny, his court and campaigns, are those of a cool, intelligent and detached observer and are an indispensable supplement to the works of oriental historians. Leaving Samarkand at the end of 1404, he progressed homeward so slowly that he received information en route concerning Timur's death and the intestinal strife which broke out among his heirs. His work was first published in the original Spanish in Seville in 1582 and republished in Madrid in 1782. In 1881 the original text with annotations and translation into Russian was published in St. Petersburg by I. I. Sreznevsky, *Dnevnik puteshestviya ko dvoru Timura v Samarkand v 1403-1406 gg.* The two English versions are Clement R. Markham's *Narration of the Embassy of Ruy Gonzales de Clavijo to the Court of Timour at Samarkand, A.D. 1403-6,* Hakluyt Society Series, XXVI, London, 1859 and an improved version by Guy Le Strange, *Embassy to Tamerlane, 1403-1406,* London, 1926. The latest account is Francisco López Estrada, *Embajada a Támorlan – Estudio y edición de un manuscrito del siglo XV,* Madrid, 1943. This contains a careful philological investigation of the oldest text of the journal. The editor also furnishes detailed historical information concerning the embassy.

Another famous Western travel account is that of the Bavarian soldier Johannes Schiltberger. Taken prisoner at Nicopolis in 1396, he served as a soldier first with Bayazid and then with Timur. Then, after further adventures, he returned home in 1427. His account was published in German: K. Fr. Neumann, *Reisen des Johannes Schiltberger*, Munich, 1859. Later an annotated English translation appeared: J. B. Telfer, *The Bondage and Travels of Johann Schiltberger, a Native of Bavaria, in Europe, Asia and Africa, 1396-1427*, Hakluyt Society Series I, LVII, London, 1879). Schiltberger's information, owing to his lack of education, is much less varied and precise than that of Clavijo and is almost without value as a source for the political events of his sojourn. The chief merit of the Bavarian soldier's work lies in his descriptions of the battles and episodes in which he participated and of the places he visited.

Two other contemporaneous Western accounts should be mentioned. The first is that of Archbishop John of Sultaniya who spent some time at Timur's court. It is entitled *Mémoire sur Tamerlan et sa cour par un Dominicain en 1403*, edited by H. Moranvillé, in the *Bibliothèque de l'Ecole des Chartes*, t. LV, 1894, pages 433-464. The second account, that of the Italian merchant Mignanelli, has been translated by W. J. Fischel under the title "A New Latin Source on Tamerlane's Conquest of Damascus (1400/1401)," *Oriens*, vol. 9, No. 2, 1956, pages 201-231.

For Timur's correspondence with Charles VI of France see Silvestre de Sacy, *Mémoire sur une correspondence inédite de Tamerlan avec Charles VI (1403)*, in *Mémoire de l'Académie des Inscriptions et Belles Lettres*, t. VI, Paris, 1822, pages 470-522. Russian chronicle writing of the fifteenth-sixteenth centuries is of importance with regard to the early life of Timur, emphasizing his humble origins and beginnings in life as a robber and thief, as well as for his invasion of Russia in 1395. This information is summarized in L. V. Cherepnin, *Obrazovanie russkogo tsentralizonnago gosudarstva v XIV-XV vekakh*, Moscow, 1960, pages 673 ff.

Mention must also be made of the Memoirs (*Malfuzat*) and Institutes (*Tuzukat-i-Timuri*), a treatise on the art of war, both works being attributed to Timur himself and collectively known as his "autobiography." The authenticity of this work is still a very vexed question. It is not mentioned by any of the official Timurid court historians though, as has been noted, Timur and his successors took an active interest in the chronicling of their reigns. Moreover, the circumstances surrounding the "discovery" of this account in the seventeenth century arouse suspicion. Abu Talib, a Persian who allegedly found a Persian manuscript

translation of this work, never produced the original. Nonetheless the
translation was brought to Europe and published. In 1783 the text and
English translation of the Institutes were published in London by Major
Davy and Joseph White. This was followed in 1787 by a French translation by Professor Langlès. In 1830 Major Charles Stewart brought out
the Memoirs in London. The "autobiography," which enjoyed a great
vogue in Europe, was considered genuine by most scholars until the end
of the 19th century when C. P. Rieu made an incisive indictment of this
work in his *Catalogue of Persian MSS in the British Museum,* vol. 1,
London, 1879-83. Since that time the prevailing opinion among scholars is that the work is spurious, though a few still remain unconvinced.
The noted French medievalist Ferdinand Lot, for example, argued ve-
hemently in the book's favor in his *L'art militaire et les armées au
Moyen Age en Europe et dans le proche Orient,* vol. II, Paris, 1946,
pages 354-355. Sir John Malcolm, in his *History of Persia,* London,
1815 and 1829, p. 285, note c, not only accepted the work as authentic
but declared that it "contained all the wisdom of Solomon." British
and indigenous historians of the history of India have been and still are
prone to accept the work as a canonical source, possibly because there
is such a dearth of other material for this period of Indian history. So
are a number of 20th century French scholars. Soviet historians, on the
other hand, generally tend to reject the book. Other authors attempt to
straddle the fence. Sir Percy Sykes, in his *History of Persia,* London,
1930, vol. II, p.121, conceded that the "autobiography" was a questionable source but went on to use it since it was "of considerable value
and of great interest as showing his [Timur's] ideals and personality."
Si non e vero e ben trovato! Harold Lamb, in his popular biography
Tamerlane, New York, 1928, rejects Timur as the author of these works
but thinks that the real author worked with authentic materials; hence
he accepts "some of the incidents.. . .as apparently authentic." The
author of the present work considers the "autobiography" a forgery
but has utilized some important secondary accounts accepting it as a
source, taking care, however, not to incorporate material based on these
apocrypha.

Space limitations preclude more than a cursory glance at the vast
modern literature dealing with Timur and his period. Readers are directed for more information to the critical bibliography in Denis Sinor, *Introduction à l'étude de l'Eurasie Centrale,* Wiesbaden, 1963, pages 327-
329, which cites other critical bibliographies, and to Marcel Brion, *Tamerlan,* Paris, 1963, pages 369-378. See also J. D. Pearson, compiler,

Index Islamicus, 1905-1955, Cambridge, Eng., 1958; *Index Islamicus Supplement, 1956-1960,* Cambridge, Eng., 1962; *Index Islamicus, Second Supplement, 1961-1965,* Cambridge, Eng., 1967. The Soviets have published the *Sochineniya* or works of the great Russian orientalist V. V. Barthold in eight volumes. These contain valuable bibliographies of Soviet and other relevant works which have appeared since his death in 1930.

The following military historians must be used with caution since they all use Timur's "Autobiography" as one of their main sources: M. I. Ivanin, *Ob voennom isskustve i zavoevaniyakh mongolo-tatar i sredneaziastkikh narodov pri Chingiskhane i Tamerlane,* St. Petersburg, 1875; François-Bernard, *Expédition de Timour-i-Lènk (Tamerlan) contre Toqtamiche, Khan de l'Oulous de Djoutchy en 793 H./1391 de J. C. Textes arabes, persans et turks, publiés et traduits, avec des notes et éclaircissements,* Amsterdan, 1975. Reprint of St. Petersburg edition, 1835; Alfred von Pawlikowski-Cholewa, *Die Heere des Morgenlandes. Militärische Beiträge zur Geschichte des nähen und fernen Orients,* Berlin, 1940; A. Razin, *Istoriya voennogo iskusstva,* Moscow, 1940, 2 vols.; also the work of Ferdinand Lot mentioned above. Hans Delbrück's doughty and venerable *Geschichte der Kriegskunst,* 4 vols., Berlin, 1900-36, unfortunately does not include either Chingis Khan or Timur in its ambit. Sir Charles Oman, in his *History of the Art of War in the Middle Ages,* 2 vols., London, 1924; 2nd, rev. ed., N.Y., 1969, has an unsatisfactory chapter on Tatar warfare in an otherwise admirable work. The same may be said of Lynn Montross' *War through the Ages,* New York, 1940, which in dealing with the Middle Ages is based largely on Oman's work. What is needed is a specialized study of Timur's art of war which does not use the "Autobiography" as one of its sources. A good beginning is Jean Aubin's "Comment Tamerlan prenait les villes," *Studia Islamica,* XIX, 1963.

†††††

In addition to the written sources Timur's life and times are well served by the remains of material culture. Primacy of place goes here to the architecture (mosques, mausoleums, palaces, medresehs, kiosks, etc.) of the Timurids, a number of which have survived in whole or in part despite the rasure of time, long periods of neglect and the many earthquakes occurring in this region. Most of these are in Samarkand and Kesh (Shahrisyabz). Much can be learned from them about the building techniques of the time, the modes of artistic expression (carving, painting, faience and mosaics) and the motifs and themes of this ornamentation. This work sheds much light on the cultural ties of Transoxiana with neighboring countries and on the impact and influence of the artisans and craftsmen resettled by Timur. Much can also learned from inscriptions on palaces, tombs and other structures as to when they were built, by whom, the significance attached to their construction and Timur's titularity and genealogy. The inscription on the famous jade cenotaph of Timur in the Gur-Emir must, however, be viewed with caution. According to this, Timur and Chingis Khan shared a common ancestor and hence were related. This claim, advanced after Timur's death, is one which even encomiasts such as Nizam ad-Din Shami and Sharaf ad-Din Yezdi did not put forth in their works.

Other material remains include artistic objects often associated with architecture such as carved wooden doors, stone Koran stands (there is a well preserved one in the Bibi Khanum mosque), bronze candle holders and pottery, all of which provide important insights into the Timurid period. And finally there is the Timurid money which, though disappointing from an esthetic standpoint, sheds much light on economic and political life by such factors as where the coins were struck, by whom and in what quantity, where found, the content of gold, silver or baser metals, the inscriptions stamped on them, etc. All these seemingly mute remains are indispensable as a check on the written sources and as a supplement to the latter. Archeological excavations currently being carried out in Transoxiana and elsewhere continue to bring more information to light.

INDEX

Abd-ar-Razzak Samarkandi, 42, 196
Abu-Bakr (b. (Miranshah), 136, 179, 184
Abu Muslim, 69
Abu-Said, 66, 230
Afrasiyab, 51
Ahmed Jelair ibn Oweis (Persian sultan), 71, 72, 99, 134, 145, 147, 162, 166, 182, 184, 218
Aida Kutshapa, 78
Aintab (Gaziantep), 148
Airdi Birdi, 85
Ak-Buga, 61
Ak Koyunlu (Whit Sheep Turkomans), 75, 177
Ak Orda, 54-55
Ak Sarai, 55, 213, 236
Akbulak, 97
Akkerman, 112
Aktai, 110-111
Albright, William Foxwell, 239
Aleppo, 149-152
Alexander the Great, 9, 33, 65, 121, 132, 200, 201, 213
Algu Khan, 20
Ali Bek, 36, 61, 88
Ali Muayyid, 69
Ali Pasha, 173
Alinjak, 73, 161
Alisher Navoi, 232
Amid (Diyarbekir), 103
Anatolia, 184
Andkhui, 66
Ankara, 173-174
Antisthenes, 33

Araxes, 168-169
Armenia, 75
Armenians, 76, 144
Asanbuga, 152
Assassins, 95, 153
Astarabad, 71
Astrakhan, 114-115
Atilmish, 147-148, 153, 182
"autobiography" of Timur, 195
Azov (Tana), 113-114

Baalbek, 152
Babur, 132, 211, 231
Bacon, Francis, 32
Baghdad, 99-100, 162-163, 184
Bagrat V (K. of Georgia), 95
Bailakan, 187
Balkh, 45
Baltychka, 57
Barkuk (Mamluke sultan), 100, 104, 111, 172
Barlas (clan), 20-21
Barthold, V. V., 217, 228, 231, 232
Batu, 16, 18, 52
Bayan Selduz, 35
Bayazid Jelair, 24, 34, 35
Bayazid I Yildirim (Ottoman sultan), 59, 104, 108, 135, 139-140, 147,
    167, 170, 172, 173-174, 189
Behisni, 148
Bek-Bulat, 91, 107
Belenitsky, A. M., 199
Bhatnir, 123
Bib Khanum mosque, 133-134
Bihzad, 232
Bikidgek, 35, 37, 186
Black Death, 191
Black Prince, 203
Borak Khan, 20
Börte, 16
Boucicault, 142
Bouvat, Lucien, 230

Burhan ad-Din Ahmed (Cadi), 104
Bursa (Brusa), 173, 178
Bustan Sarai, 51
Byzantines, 179

Caffa (Feodosiya), 60, 112
Castile, 189-190
Central Asia, 15
Chagatai Ulus, 17
Chagatais, 23, 159, 169, 197, 208, 235, 238
Charles VI Valois (K. of France), 190-193
Chateaumorand, 142
Chaucer, 236
China, 119, 183, 217, 219-220
Chingis Khan, 9, 19, 65, 119, 122, 132, 203, 233, 239
Chios, 182
Clausewitz, 195, 201
Clavijo, Ruy Gonzales de, 27, 142, 178, 187, 189, 190, 197, 199, 208,
    210, 211, 213, 219, 223, 236
Cleitus, 33
Constantinople, 141-142, 172
Cordier, H., 220
Croesus, 179

Damascus, 153 ff.
Daryal Pass, 109
Davud, Emir, 50
Delhi, 122-, 125-130
Delhi Sultanate, 119-120, 132
Deopalpur, 123
De Mignanelli, 160-161
de Mine, William, 180
Derbent, 108-109
dervishes, 140
Dilshad-agha, 62
Dizful, 96
Dmitri Ivanovich (Donskoi), (grand prince of Muscovy), 59-60, 113

Eastern Turkistan, 15
Edessa, 102, 161

Edigei, 57, 61, 84, 91, 116, 122, 167
Edward III (K. of England), 203
Egypt, 108
Ephesus, 180, 182
Erzerum, 76
Eugene of Savoy, 201

Faraj (gov. of Baghdad), 162-163
Faraj (Mamluke sultan), 147, 155, 182
Ferghana, 51
Ferishta, 127
Firoz Shah Tuglak, 120
Firuzkuh, 188
Five Years War, 93 ff.
Francis (Dominican friar), 143, 168
Fushanj, 67

Galata, 142
Genoese, 60, 142, 179, 182
George VII (K. of Georgia), 95, 137, 165
Georgia, 104, 108, 136-138, 161, 185-187
Georgian Military Highway, 74, 109
Georgians, 73
Ghiyas ad-Din Pir Ali, 66-67
Ghiyath ad-Din, 98, 128
Gilan, 93
Goethe, 239
Golden Horde, 16
Great Umayyad mosque, 160
Grousset, R., 45, 237
Gur-Emir, 224
Guyuk, 18

Hadji Barlas, 24, 34, 35
Hafiz, 80
Hama, 161
hazaras, 50
Henry IV (K. of England), 193-194
Henry VIII (K. of England), 177
Herat, 67, 231-232

Hilman river, 70
Hindu Kush, 120-121
Hulagu Khan (founder of Hulagid or Il-Khanid state), 18, 95, 183
Hung Wu (Ming emperor), 219
Hussein, Emir, 35 ff., 46-48
Hussein Baikara, 231-232
Hussein Sufi (ruler of Khorezm), 52-53

Ibn Arabshah, 28, 90, 91, 116, 158, 215
Ibn Battuta, 78
Ibn Khaldun, 32, 157-158
Ibn Muflih, 156
Ibn Shahana, 150
Ibrahim Shirvanshah, 74, 136, 185, 187
Ibrahim-Sultan, 221
ikta, 205
Il-Khanids, 190-191
Ilichmich Aglen, 85
Ilyas Khodja, 35, 37, 62
India, 119-132
"Institutes" of Timur, 195
Iron Gate (Derbend), 73
Isa, 178
Isfahan, 77

Jadwiga, 107
Jahannuma, 125
James, William, 239
Jami, 232
Jammu, 131
Jamuqa, 233
Janibeg, 60
Janissaries, 175-178
Jats, 23
Jehan Shah, 229
Jehangir, 53, 63, 65
Jelairs, 20
jihad, 234
John Greenlaw (Archbishop of Sultaniya), 191
John (Regent of Byzantium), 142, 168

Kabul, 122

Kafirs (Siah-Posh or Black-Robed Kafirs), 121-122

Kan-i-gul, 221

Kandahar, 70

Kara Koyunlu (Black Sheep Turkomans), 75, 104, 177

Kara Mehmed, 76

Kara (Black) Tatars, 183

Kara Yusuf, 104, 145, 168, 182, 184, 218, 229

Karabagh, 74, 165, 169, 172, 187, 207

Karakorum, 17

Karshi, 21

Kart state, 66-68

Kazagan, 23

Kazan Khan, 22

Kazancha, 61

Kebek Khan, 21-22

Keikosrau, 44, 47, 53

Keikubad, 44

Kemakh, 170

Kerbela, 100, 163

Kesh (Shahrisyabz), 24, 27, 55, 213, 236

Khalil-Sultan, 228

Khan-zada, 53

Khanbalik (Peking), 221

Khawaf, 67

Khawak Pass, 120

Khinduvan, 45

Khizr Khodja, 86, 131-132

Khorezm, 9, 52, 58, 84

Khurasan, 25, 67,

Kipchak steppe, 16, 87

Kiprian (metropolitan), 112

Knights of Rhodes, 180

Koiradzhak, 111, 114

Kok Sarai (Blue Palace), 51, 213

Kosovo (battle of), 141

Kubilai Khan (Chinese emperor), 18, 20, 220

Küchük dagh, 88

Kuli-oglan, 21, 91

Kulikovo (battle of), 60, 83, 113

Kunche-oglan, 84, 107
Kunduzcha (battle of), 89-91
Kurds, 75-76, 99, 166
Kutahya, 179

Lal, K. S., 126-127
Lamb, Harold, 237
Lattimore, O., 203
Lesbos, 182
Lithuanian Grand Principality, 56, 60
Lurs, 72

Mahanasar, 94
Mahmud Khan, 84, 163, 178
Mahmud Shah, 120
Malatiya, 144, 172
Malek Hussein Kart, 69
Mallu Iqbal Khan, 120, 127
Mamai, 56, 61
Mamlukes, 107, 111, 119, 172, 182
Mangu-Timur, 55
Manuel II (E. of Byzantium), 140
Manuel III (E. of Trebizond), 139, 168
Mardin, 102-103, 161
Marlowe, Christopher, 239
Maulana Nasir ad-Din Umar, 125
Maulana-zada, 39-42
Maverannahr (see Transoxiana)
Mazanderan, 93, 95
Mehmed II Fatih (Ottoman sultan), 142
Mehmed (Ottoman prince), 178
"Memoirs" of Timur, 195
Meshed, 188
Mir Bayazid, 35
Miranshah, 66, 68-69, 75, 100, 102, 131, 193, 229, 230
Mirza Iskender, 166
Mogolistan, 20
Mogols, 20, 23, 40, 86
Mommsen, 202
Moscow, 61, 108, 112

Mosul, 102
Mtzkhet, 95
Mubarak Shah, 20
Muhammad-Sultan Jehangir, 63, 135, 166, 171, 183
Muiad, Emir, 47
Muizz ad-Din, 66
mulk, 209
Multan, 120, 123
Munke, 18
Murad I (Ottoman sultan), 141
Muscovy, 83
Muzaffarid dynasty, 98

Napoleon, 29, 202
Nasir ad-Din khodja, 235
Nestorian Christians, 234
New Sarai, 56, 60, 111, 115
Nikopolis, crusade of, 141-142

Oadak-Khatun, 28
Oman, Sir Charles, 172
Omar-shaykh, 80, 85, 89, 98, 103
Orda, 55
Osman Abbas (Emir), 81
Otrar, 223-224

Panizati, Bufillo, 180
Pasteur, Louis, 233
Pir-Muhammad Jehangir, 63, 120, 123, 224, 227
post roads, 18, 210

Qamar ad-Din, 62

Radloff, 235
Rai Dul Chand, 122
Rashid ad-Din, 134
Riazan, 112, 113
Roloff, G., 175
Romans, 235, 236
Roustem, 134

Saadi, 72
Sacy, Silvestre de, 192-193
Safavid dynasty, 229
Saheb Caran (title), 49
Sali-sarai, 41, 43
Samarkand, 37, 39-42, 50-51, 92, 110, 133-134, 167, 169, 187, 205,
    210-215, 218, 225, 228-229, 235
Sarai-Mulk-Khanum, 47, 134
Sardis, 179
Sari, 94
Sarton, George, 225
Sasy-Buka, 55
Sayf al-Din, Barlas, 65, 66, 165
Sayyid Bereke, 46, 49, 90, 224
Schuyler, Eugene, 224
Sebzevar, 39, 69
Seljuk empire, 140
Semirechie, 20
Serbedars, 39-40, 66, 69
Serbs, 141, 177
Seven Years War, 135-188
Shadi Beg, 117, 167
Shah Mansur, 79, 98
Shams al-Din Almalik, 109-110
Sharaf ad-Din, 36, 47, 63, 79, 94, 95, 98, 101, 119, 127, 160, 219,
    220, 221
Shariat, 236
Shahrukh, 30, 165, 227-229, 238
Sharif Ali of Sheki, 134-135
Shihabuddin Mubarak Tamin, 122
Shiraz, 79
Shustar, 96
Sistan, 36, 70
Sivas, 143-144, 171, 202, 217, 219-221
Smyrna (Izmir), 180-182
soyurgal, 205, 209, 228
Stephen Lazarevich, 177
Sudun, 149
Suleiman (Ottoman prince), 143, 177
Sultan-Hussein, 154-155

Sultaniya, 71
Suyurghatmish Oglan Khan, 46, 84
Suvorov, A., 202
Sveti Tzkhoveli, 95
Sygnakh, 56

Tadjiks, 21
Taharten, 77, 137, 143, 165, 168, 170, 185, 208
Tahir (son of Sultan Ahmed Jelair), 135, 138
Takrit, 101-102
Tamarshirin, 22
Tamerlane (see Timur)
tamga, 212
Tana (Azov), 113-114
Taragai, 27
tarkhan, 206
tavachis, 85, 93, 196
Terek (battle of), 110-111
Tiflis, 187
Timur (Timur-i-lenk, Tamerlane): ancestors, 27-28, education, 28-29,
    wives, 28, 236, appearance, 30-33, titles, 48-49, death, 223-224
Timur-Kutluk, 84, 91, 116, 117, 122
Timur-Malik-Oglan, 58
Timur-Shah-Oglan, 24
Timurtash, 148, 153
Tire, 180
Tobol river, 88
Tokat, 174-175
Tokhta-Kiya, 58
Toktamish Khan, 56, 61, 71, 75, 80, 83-84, 89-91, 104, 107-108, 117,
    208
Transoxiana, 17, 20
Trebizond, empire of, 138-139
Tugluk-Timur, 24, 34
Tulamba, 122-123
Tuli-Khodja, 56
Tului Khan, 17
tuman, 22, 50
Turkistan, 59
Tus, 69, 81
Tver, 61

Ugedai Khan, 17
Uldja-Turkan-Agha, 36
Uldjaitu, 71
Ulug Beg, 221-222, 228, 231
ulus, 16
Ulus of Juchi, 16, 55
Union of Krewo, 107
Urgench, 15, 53, 58, 84
Ural (Yaik) river, 89
Urus Khan, 56, 58
Uzbek Khan, 60

vakf, 209
Van (lake), 104
Van (castle), 77
Vasco da Gama, 238
Vasilii I (Grand Prince of Muscovy), 113
Vauban, 200
Venetians, 179
Virgin of Vladimir (icon), 112
Vitovt, 107, 116
Volga Bulgar state, 16, 59, 111
Vorskla (battle of), 116, 167

Wali (Emir), 70

Yagailo, 91, 107
Yasa (Yasak), 19, 239
Yelets, 112
Yeni Shehir, 178
Yulduz valley, 86
Yung Lo (Ming emperor), 219, 220)
Yazzadar, 156
yurt, 208
Yusuf Sufi, 54

Zarandj, 70
Zayn al-Din Abu Bakr, 67, 77, 79
Zeki Velidi Togan, 27
Zindger-sarai, 23, 71
Zoroastrians, 99, 234